0

THE American Constitution FOR AND AGAINST

THE American Constitution FOR AND AGAINST

THE FEDERALIST and Anti-Federalist Papers

Selected and edited, with an Introduction, by

J. R. POLE

HILL AND WANG / NEW YORK

A division of Farrar, Straus and Giroux

Printed in the United States of America
Published simultaneously by Collins Publishers, Toronto
First edition, 1987
Designed by Helen Barrow

Library of Congress Cataloging-in-Publication Data
The American Constitution.
Bibliography: p.
1. United States—Constitutional history—Sources.
I. Pole, J. R. (Jack Richon) II. Title: Federalist.
III. Title: Anti-Federalist.
KF4515.A44 1987 342.73′029 86-31795
347.30229

Preface

The debates of the Constitutional Convention in Philadelphia were only the beginning of a long series of public arguments which raged up and down the continent and died down with the final adoption of the Constitution in the summer of 1788. Of all the numerous publications of the period, the most famous is The Federalist, *written by Alexander Hamilton, James Madison, and, to a much lesser extent, John Jay, under the collective Roman pseudonym Publius.*

There have been several editions of the collected essays, beginning almost immediately after the first run in the New York newspapers, and people have been inclined to feel that the Federalist Papers must have said all there was to be said in favor of the Constitution. In fact, however, many other able publicists entered the debate. But the Federalist Papers are the most comprehensive and intellectually powerful of the pro-Constitutional arguments; they have often been viewed as authoritative; they are and will remain the most prominent; and they have always formed an appropriate set for a single volume—a fact immediately recognized by the authors.

Anti-Federalist tracts, on the other hand, are far more widely scattered, and they have had to be collected from a much greater range of sources. They reflect the views of different regions and different social and economic interests. Yet the two sets of arguments, for and against the Constitution, are closely related—at times the debaters seem to be in the same room. The purpose of the present collection is to make both sets of arguments readily available to students and teachers.

This aim means that some material must be sacrificed to the exigencies of space. A fully comprehensive collection would defeat its own purpose by running to several volumes. But many of the Anti-Federalist arguments are repetitive and can be discarded without much intellectual loss. The Federalist Papers are more compact; but many pages are given to the explanation of institutional details, and whole essays delve into remote historical examples whose bearing on the Constitution is not immediate. For the reader looking for the essential principles of The Federalist, *the present selection contains all the more important arguments, indicates whose interests were at stake, whose ox was being gored and by whom, and what the Constitution was expected to achieve.*

Behind this volume lies the work of earlier editors. For the Anti-Federalists I have relied mainly on The Anti-Federalist *(Chicago, 1985), edited by Murray Dry from the late Herbert J. Storing's* The Complete Anti-Federalist *(Chicago, 1981). The editorial notes provide much the fullest and best guidance I have found, and I acknowledge them with a gratitude that must be shared by all scholars. I need hardly add that Dry's volume should be used by students who wish to pursue these matters in greater detail. I have also relied on Cecelia M. Kenyon's* The Antifederalists *(Indianapolis, 1966), whose introduction is expanded from her famous article "Men of Little Faith," published in* The William and Mary Quarterly *XII, 1 (January 1955). I have also used the ratification debates of Massachusetts and New York. The text of* The Federalist *used here is adapted from Jacob E. Cooke (Middletown, Conn., 1961). His scholarly references have also proved valuable.*

My own introduction is intended to suggest the connections between the recent history of continental and state government, the political ideas of the age, and the actual structure of the new Constitution—all of which provide the immediate context of the debate. I want to thank Mark Kaplanoff and Jack P. Greene for reading and commenting on the introduction. They are in no way responsible for the opinions I have expressed, or for the editorial choices that form the bulk of this book. My aim has been to give students a grip on essentials and to excite their interest in further study of this classical episode in modern history.

J.R.P.
ST. CATHERINE'S COLLEGE
OXFORD
August 5, 1986

Contents

THE

American Constitution

FOR AND AGAINST

INTRODUCTION
The Struggle for the Constitution

THERE WERE two fundamental reasons for calling the Constitutional Convention. The first was that the system of government by which the states had leagued themselves under the existing Articles of Confederation appeared to be cracking up. In the opinion of some of the best-informed persons in various parts of the country, unless something was done to strengthen the system the new nation known as the United States of America would soon cease to exist. This collapse would have been succeeded by new groupings—which was one possibility, and it might have been allowed to happen. The second reason, which arises directly from the first, was that these best-informed people represented a cluster of powerful interests—military, political, commercial, manufacturing, agricultural, and legal—which had much to lose by the collapse of the Union, and saw that they had much to gain by forming a stronger and more centralized nation.

The rapidly developing crisis, as these men perceived it, had its roots in the origins of the Continental Congress. We cannot appreciate the situation that existed in 1786, immediately before the call to the Convention, without going back at least to 1774, before the colonies had any collective body of their own to speak or act for them. Every one of these colonies had its own separate history, its own domestic form of government, and its own lines of connection to the British Crown. Britain, through Crown and Parliament, ultimately ruled them all, but it ruled them separately, not in any collective capacity; the only collective government known to the American colonies was the British government itself. Many links existed among the individual colonies and more were developing all the time. There were numerous trade links both overland, along the rivers, and up and down the coast; there were religious movements, beginning in the Great Awakening of the early 1740s and continued in many later revivals, which spilled across colony boundaries and united people in feelings that transcended local political allegiances. There were also movements of population and settlement which took no notice of boundaries, for the frontiers between colonies imposed no controls over personal movements. All free Americans alike were subject to the Crown and all alike claimed the benefits of traditional British liberties.

By the summer of 1774, after twelve years of controversy with British authorities, leading men in all the colonies had come to the reluctant conclusion that these British liberties were very seriously threatened in the colonies and that the only way to get the British government to listen to them was by collective action. The First Continental Congress, which met in Philadelphia in September 1774, was composed of delegations appointed by the provincial conventions which had taken over from the former assemblies (only Georgia was not yet represented). This Congress adopted a series of petitions accompanied by economic measures—non-importation and eventually non-exportation agreements—as a means of bringing pressure on British opinion, on the British economy, and, through them, on Parliament.

These efforts failed, and in the spring of 1775 a Second Continental Congress found itself confronted with the more forbidding tasks of raising an army and opening negotiations with European nations from which it needed financial help, military supplies, and eventual diplomatic recognition. The main aim of most of the leaders was to force Britain into making concessions that would enable the colonies to remain within the Empire: not many Americans fancied their chances outside the largest empire in the Western world. But when in August 1775 King George III declared a state of rebellion in his American colonies, and in December Parliament stopped all trade with the colonies, the Americans were propelled toward the ultimate choice: surrender or independence.

All this time, the Congress, in which each colony voted as a single unit, increasingly assumed the powers and attributes of an American government. It raised an army and appointed Colonel George Washington of Virginia as its general and commander-in-chief. It appointed army officers and quartermasters. It appointed from among its own members two committees to raise supplies and to negotiate with foreign powers—one of these eventually becoming a foreign affairs committee. No government can function without the ability to finance its own operations, and the Congress had the disadvantage of not being able to tax individuals—since it consisted only of delegations from colonial legislatures. This problem was met by imposing requisitions on the colonies based on assessments of their resources and populations. The Congress also tried to finance itself by raising loans both at home and abroad. And taking on itself one of the most significant powers of a sovereign state, it issued money on its own authority. The rapid and incessant depreciation of this Continental currency and the resulting inflation were among the most chronic difficulties that the Congress had to contend with during the War of Independence.

In June 1776, after all hopes of conciliation seemed to have been exhausted, and faced with the urgent need to convince the French court that the Americans were serious and would stick by their agreements, the Congress recommended the individual colonies to form independent governments, which they rapidly did. Then, on July 2, the Congress formally resolved on American independence, which it declared on the fourth.

The Congress was acting without any established constitutional basis; its authority sprang from the undoubted fact that, by its very existence, it had a mandate from the colonial legislatures. Considering the Congress as a form of government exercising the powers of government, it is worth noting that all the powers it exercised were brought into existence by the necessities of the situation, in which only the Congress could act in the interests of the new states. If it had not been able to raise, pay, and supply an army, it would not have been able to fight the war; if it had not been able to raise finance, it would not have been able to do anything else; if it had not been able to negotiate with foreign powers, it would have had no hope of success against Britain. And we may add that if it had not assumed to itself the authority to declare American independence the individual colonies would not have done so—or would not have been able to make it effective—and there would have been no United States. The Congress also had to try to intervene to settle disputes between states, such as Pennsylvania and Connecticut, over rival claims to territory, which threatened serious disruption. But none of these powers in any way exceeded the most obvious needs of the situation which had called the Congress into being and which justified its continued existence. The Congress reached into the states only by its authority to communicate with state Committees of Correspondence and with state legislatures; it had no authority over individuals, and its powers could not directly threaten individual civil liberties. The most serious problems arose not from an excess of congressional power but from the frequently renewed discovery that its powers were not extensive enough for its responsibilities.

The war was nearly over before a formal constitutional basis was agreed to. The Articles of Confederation—America's first attempt at a constitution—were eventually signed in March 1781. Under the Articles, however, the United States, despite its name, resembled a league of sovereign states rather than a sovereign state in itself. The position was in many ways ambiguous. But the Congress had no power of coercion either on states or on individuals.

Ten years forward from the Declaration of Independence, in the summer of 1786, all the deficiencies of the Confederation had been fully exposed, and the motives that had called it into existence had lost much of their original force. The War of Independence had been won, after a struggle lasting nearly eight years, and against odds that seemed at times too heavy for so frail a power to surmount. As Thomas Jefferson had foreseen, victory removed the Americans' strongest motive for unity. It removed the urgency of supporting the Confederation, and this in particular meant that the states were much less willing to raise money from their own citizens to meet the requisitions imposed by the Congress.

During the war, the Congress made loans which came back in the form of public debts. The heaviest weight of these congressional debts was owed in the middle and northeastern states; when the war was over, short of raising new requisitions, it was looking more and more unlikely that the Congress would be able to pay its domestic creditors. It was not in anyone's interest that the whole structure should be allowed to collapse, but, on the other hand, each state legislature was responsible in the first instance to its own people, on whose votes its members depended. The postwar years brought new and extremely severe hardships to many areas of the Union. After eight years of war, Americans were suddenly able to buy the cheap but seemingly luxurious British manufactures that now flooded the markets, and most of them could not resist the temptation. One consequence was that hard money drained out of the country, and soft, or paper, money had to be issued by several state legislatures. These new issues did not generally depreciate anything like as rapidly as the old Continental currency had done, but the movement reawakened the fears of creditors and men of property. Many of them made money out of money by lending at interest, and any legislation that threatened the value of money itself seemed an attack on their livelihood.

One of the most ominous developments from the point of view of the Congress occurred when state legislatures began to take over the responsibility for paying the congressional debt where it was owed to their own citizens. Even before the end of the war, in 1782, Maryland provided that its citizens could exchange their national debt holdings for securities issued by the state. Several states acted to take up the responsibility for paying the interest on various military certificates issued by the Congress or under its authority. In 1784 Pennsylvania, whose citizens held $2,500,000 worth of loan-office certificates and over $3 million in other forms, began the biggest of the state initiatives toward assumption of the national debt, which it followed with a further act in 1785. This process lightened the burden on Congress but it also appreciably diminished its authority over the states. From the immediate point of view of creditors who were looking to Congress for repayment, it even seemed to have lost its principal reason for existing.

States were also quarreling among themselves. New Jersey and New York had an ungainly dispute about the maintenance of the lighthouse at Sandy Hook, in Jersey territory but essential to the navigation of New York Harbor. More serious were bitter disputes over internal tariff barriers. The prices of goods imported into the small states of New Jersey and Connecticut, which had no significant harbors, were largely at the mercy of tariffs imposed by their rich and powerful neighbors Pennsylvania and New York. It should therefore come as no surprise, when we look ahead to the Constitution, that all these powers were taken from the states and put exclusively into the hands of the Congress; and that New Jersey and Connecticut were among the earliest states to ratify, and by overwhelming majorities.

One of the most potentially serious of Congress's problems arose from its responsibility for foreign affairs. The Congress had appointed its delegation to negotiate the Peace of Paris and had ratified the treaty which ended the war. That treaty had certain very specific consequences for citizens of the United States. Many Americans, especially in the Chesapeake states, owed pre-war debts to British merchants, but they were none too ready to pay them after the peace had been signed. But although Congress had the accepted authority to make war and peace in the name of the states, it had no power to enforce the terms of the treaty within state boundaries. Within those boundaries each state was sovereign, and the only courts were those of its own judiciary. But these courts were very much inclined to see disputes involving their own citizens from the state's point of view rather than that of the international obligations of the United States.

Men at the center of events were better placed to observe the implications than those who never looked beyond state borders. A new nation, with everything to prove about itself, could ill afford to begin by admitting to other nations that it was incompetent to enforce its own treaty obligations. The British took advantage of America's failures as an excuse for refusing to evacuate certain forts on the northern borders which were within American territory. These things may have been only pinpricks at the time, but they damaged America's reputation as concerned both its good faith and its ability to defend itself. National credit was even more deeply implicated in the repayment of foreign debts to the Netherlands and France, which Congress managed to service in the mid-eighties only with the greatest difficulty. These were just the sort of issues which men at the center could see more clearly and which armed them with a sense of the urgency of correcting the political structure of the Union.

The financial weakness of the Confederation was compounded by its constitutional form. Any amendment to the Articles required the unanimous consent of the contracting states. Two different plans were put forward in 1781 and 1783, aimed at giving the Congress more finance through control of customs revenues, but both failed for want of unanimous support. Members of Congress were comparing the Confederation to the diet of Poland, in which every nobleman had a vote, and one vote could veto all the rest. And Poland was in the process of being partitioned among its more powerful neighbors.

The United States had more time than Poland since it had three thousand miles of water between itself and Europe and no powerful neighbors on its own continent. But this benign situation could not be expected to last forever. Britain still ruled Canada;

Spain ruled Florida and Louisiana (ceded to France in 1800); and Indian tribes and nations on the frontiers were often capable of matching the Americans in local strength. Renewed alliances between Indian (or Native American) nations and European powers would open up once again the question of American autonomy on the American continent; such combinations might determine the limits of American settlement. The possibility that Europe's interest in North America would revive with demonstrations of America's weakness could not be ignored by prudent men.

By the summer of 1786, moves were afoot in Congress to strengthen the powers of Congress under the Articles. But in September of that year, commissioners from five states—New York, New Jersey, Pennsylvania, Delaware, and Virginia—met in Annapolis on Virginia's call to discuss ways "To Remedy Defects of the Federal Government." This meeting, so thinly attended, did no more than propose a general convention to meet in Philadelphia the following spring, and urged Congress to authorize that convention.

During the late summer and autumn months, disturbing news came from Massachusetts. The constitution of that state had been ratified in 1780 by a convention representing every incorporated town; it seemed to be a model of the principle of government by consent. Yet discontent with the legislature's fiscal policies had reached such a pitch, and currency was in such short supply, that western farmers were forming armed bands to close the courts—thus preventing them from enforcing foreclosures in settlement of debts. The farmers could pay neither their taxes nor their creditors. They did not want another revolution, but they desperately needed time and they needed currency. The movement, known as Shays's Rebellion, had spread far beyond its western sources before it was put down in January 1787, by a military force raised by the state and paid for in part by alarmed Bostonians. It may not have been a very formidable revolt. But it sent a shiver of alarm through the nerves of men of substantial property in other parts of the Union. They had no other recourse than representative government and the laws of property to protect them. Now they began to look to the prospect of a strong central government, more directly responsive to their needs, and shielded against the direct influence of such local insurgencies. The rather lethargic interest of Congress in promoting the proposed convention in Philadelphia was notably stimulated into action by the news from Massachusetts, and state legislatures stepped up their participation by nominating delegations to go to Philadelphia. The angry and anxious farmers of Massachusetts had played a larger part in American history than they could ever have expected.

Shays's Rebellion had a particular resonance for educated Americans which was not lost on the men who assembled, gradually and often tardily, in Philadelphia during April and May. Their education was largely a shared education in ancient history, with varied measures of instruction in the histories of Britain and Europe. Some, naturally, had read much more widely, and had reflected more deeply, than others (though two of the best of these, John Adams of Massachusetts and Thomas Jefferson of Virginia, were serving their country on European missions and could take no part in the deliberations). A large corpus of writings on jurisprudence, the law of nations, on contracts and the origins of society, and on political science and morality formed another part of the educated man's stock of knowledge, which many of the delegates brought into action at Philadelphia.

One important truth, inculcated by a knowledge of history and particularly of ancient history, was that republics had a very poor record of survival. They had an inherent tendency to become unstable, not only because of the threat of external enemies but because of defects in their political and economic structure. History taught, or seemed to teach, that political societies passed through a cyclical lifespan which ended in decline and dissolution, a process to which republics were believed to be particularly vulnerable. Unless a republic possessed great internal political strength, it was liable to degenerate into a mere democracy, which was not far from mob rule; out of disorder, insecurity of property and person, and disrespect for law, a dictator would emerge to restore order, but at the price of republican liberty. Was it possible, then, that a republic could be ruled in a manner that provided for personal safety only by a form of government that was too strong for individual liberty? It was a serious question. No one could be at all sure that an answer had been found.

The reason why Shays's little rebellion was more important than the angry farmers could have imagined, and why its reverberations went far beyond the boundaries of Massachusetts, was precisely that it fed these fears. It seemed to men who had spent days and nights studying the history of the ancient world in order to instruct themselves in the art of politics that this was just the sort of episode they had heard of before. It was fresh evidence of the well-known truth that republics were liable to instability, and what was worse, it proved what many men who had been through the war already suspected, that Americans were in no way morally superior to the operation of these laws of behavior.

The men of Philadelphia were, without exception, men of property. As representatives of the leadership of their several states, they were accustomed to the deference of ordinary people—the yeomanry and tenants of the country, the tradesmen, mechanics, and laborers of the towns. The experiences of war and internal commotion had done much to disrupt the old colonial order and to change the leaders. But a basic respect for the recognized qualities of leadership, represented in visible forms of social, economic, educational superiority, and often in the advantage of a distinguished family name, survived these disruptions. The leadership had its own interest in stabilizing the social order which established its own position.

In many respects the members of the Constitutional Convention, whom Jefferson referred to as "an assembly of demi-gods," were rather typical provincial representatives of the Enlightenment. They were men who had plenty of experience in the world of affairs. They managed their own estates and businesses, conducted their own accounts, supervised their own servants or slaves, and mixed all this with such judicial or political responsibility as fell to men of their social position. There were very few specialists in those days. A plantation owner might well practice a little law and handle his own legal affairs. One would not expect a merchant to know much about soils and seeds, but he might well own some land and interest himself in these things too. Such men were also well known among their neighbors. If the esteem in which they were held was in a traditional sense "due" to their social position, it was in most cases a position they had earned. With some of the great men of New England and New York and with more of the Southern grandees, a strong element of inheritance went into the basis of this position, but that hardly diminished the holder's need to make his own exertions to maintain it in his lifetime.

In Europe, the Enlightenment allied speculative thought with its many problem-solving activities. In America, it was a practical Enlightenment that predominated. Improvements in agriculture were a widespread and typical interest. The oldest and most venerated member of the Convention, Dr. Benjamin Franklin of Philadelphia, a Fellow of the Royal Society of London, had invented useful things as various as the lightning rod and a stove for heating houses. It was characteristic of the prevailing mood that the American Philosophical Society, of which Franklin was a principal founder, had "the promotion of useful knowledge" as part of its full title.

Political ideas were of somewhat similar stuff. They were tools for the construction and management of society. Americans of that age were very little interested in abstract thought; many of them had private time to read philosophers and theologians, and exchanged ideas in their correspondence, but their public time was consumed in the pursuit of practical and public ends. When John Dickinson of Delaware said in the Convention, "Reason may mislead us; experience must be our guide," he meant that they should apply reason to experience, but by experience he did not refer only to their own generation's memories. History was the experience of mankind; but abstract reason, not grounded in such knowledge, could not be trusted as a practical guide to human needs.

The political reason of Americans was directed to the problems of republican government. Americans were understandably disenchanted with monarchy, and in any case there was no appropriate social base for royalty anywhere in the new nation. A republic was what they had, and their greatest need was to devise ways of making republican government work.

Many of the references to history, jurisprudence, and political thought in the texts that follow are concerned in one way or another with this problem. The French *philosophe*, the Baron de Montesquieu, whose great book, *The Spirit of the Laws*, was published in 1748, was prominent in these debates because so much of his work seemed to apply very closely to the American condition. For Montesquieu, each distinct form of government, monarchy, aristocracy, and the republican or democratic, had its own appropriate spirit; that of democracy was virtue. Virtue has meant different things to different people at different times; it is a concept more to be distinguished than generalized. For the age of Enlightenment, it had lost the more opportunistic connotations that it had had for Machiavelli and some of his Renaissance followers or contemporaries. Its most valued element was the idea of what we would now call "public spirit," a disposition to do things and make sacrifices for the good of the community of which one is a member, and not to set one's own narrow notion of private interest before everything else.

Montesquieu was important for another reason. Like most French *philosophes*, he was a warm admirer of the British Constitution. Many Continentals believed that England uniquely had discovered the principle of balancing order with individual liberty. One of the most important elements was supposed to be the separation of the different branches of government in such a way that none of them could swallow up the others. Actually, Montesquieu's reading of British constitutional arrangements was not very accurate, but for present purposes what matters is that Americans believed, with some justice, that the British system had become corrupt: the crown, or executive, had gained too much control in the legislature. So Americans tended to prefer some arrangement that would establish a formal separation. Still more important was the fundamental English principle that the law of the land must be free from arbitrary interference by the executive. A judiciary independent of either of the other branches became a keystone of British and American liberties.

There was nothing inevitable about the Constitution that emerged from the deliberations at Philadelphia. As one reads the debates, it is not difficult to imagine that a majority might have favored a different arrangement. Although there was general approval of the principle of separation of the branches or "powers" of government, no one could have foreseen the precise forms this would take. The framers of the Virginia Plan, which, for want of any alternative, constituted the agenda at the beginning of the Convention, did not intend to produce the rigid separation between executive and legislature that eventually emerged in the Constitution, which was more rigorous than any other known system of government. Each branch of government is separately described, without any suggestion of priority or even of their relationship to each other, beyond what can be inferred from their several duties. None of the delegates went to Philadelphia expecting to sign a constitution that would take the general principle of separation to such meticulous precision. (Most, indeed, only expected to help strengthen the Articles, without changing their fundamental character.) If the Virginia Plan had prevailed, it is probable that presidents would almost always have been drawn from the membership of Congress and would have remained closer, perhaps more accountable, to it. But the precision has in fact proved impracticable, and immense amounts of time and resources have been and are spent in crisscrossing and circumventing the separate responsibilities of Congress and the executive.

Each of the states had a "republican" form of government, yet they differed from each other in important respects, and they differed still more in the social arrangements over which state constitutions presided. Notwithstanding all these reservations, it remains true that, whatever form of constitution emerged from Philadelphia, it would have embodied the main republican principles to which all subscribed in one form or another. In this sense, the men of Philadelphia enjoyed the advantage of a pervasive consensus of principles. There was no one to argue for the advantages of monarchy, or inherited privileges (except those inherited by whites over blacks and by men over women, the latter of which were taken for granted); no one advocated that the rule of law should be set aside at the arbitrary will of the executive.

The consensus extended to principles of representative government which had been made familiar by generations of colonial experience and, behind that, by the British parliamentary system. Everybody respected the British system in its pure form; but everyone agreed that it had become corrupted by an excess of executive—monarchical—power. The dangers that threaten republics, and the republican element in a mixed monarchy like the British, were familiar to all; and men of that generation had learned both from history and from practice the Whig maxim that power always tends to aggrandize itself. The debates that follow in this collection are infused with this understanding of human nature. Both sides are alert to the need for effective safeguards against the ever-recurring threat of the abuse of power.

The new American states, in their new sovereign capacities, formed their own constitutions. (Two, Connecticut and Rhode Island, retained their old charters.) These precedents accustomed Americans to the idea that independent governments should be based on—and legitimized by—written constitutions. Most of them embodied some statement of the principle of the separation of powers, but gave effective power to the legislature—including the power to make executive and judicial appointments. Many of these constitutions were preceded by declarations of individual rights, intended as restraints on government interference with liberty of person and property and (within limits) of conscience. When these new governments were set in motion, legislative power, rather than separation, quickly emerged as the dominant theme. As we have seen, some state legislatures had pursued fiscal and economic policies that frightened the interests of property; some had also shown extreme severity toward those who had remained loyal to the crown—the Loyalists or Tories—and had confiscated their estates and driven them into exile. Many men of substance felt some residual sympathy with the Loyalists, whose difficulties in the Revolution they could understand; and they felt more keenly the alarming implications of these attacks on property. These issues were deeply divisive. So, also, was the question of the legitimacy of the Bank of North America, established by the Congress and sponsored by Pennsylvania in 1783. The turbulent politics of Pennsylvania focused largely on this issue.

So the leading men, in many respects the representative men, of this generation had learned another and rather ominous lesson about power, and they had learned it not only from history and theory but from their own experience. This lesson was that a popular government is as liable to abuse its power as an aristocratic or monarchical one. The complex machinery of the Constitution, with its familiar checks and balances, was designed just as much to absorb the shocks of excessive power in the democratic branches of the government as to safeguard against abuse from the top. Understanding this theme will help to explain many of the arguments that follow in the texts.

The Convention had two essential tasks. The first was to devise a form of republican government which would remain stable, retaining its essentially republican character, while overcoming the historic tendency to cyclical decline. The second was no less fundamental. It was to build a constitution out of existing materials. Americans would not be attracted by some completely new and theoretical scheme. They knew and liked their old and tried institutions. Where they had been found defective, they might be corrected; where new needs came to light, they could be attended to by methods which had already been tested by experience. Nothing comes through more clearly from the debates, in the Constitutional Convention, in the state ratifying conventions, and in the published tracts for and against, than this element of underlying experience in the ways of self-government. This was what distinguished the Americans from many Europeans of their own time. The makers of the French revolutionary constitutions only a year or two later did not have this background of experience in government and were much more susceptible to visionary theory.

Some of the most earnestly discussed issues of the time have lost their significance. The problem of how to exercise power over a territory too large for face-to-face politics had not been resolved by political science; and American territory, already very extensive, was served by a worse road system than the Romans had built to rule Europe eighteen hundred years earlier. Montesquieu had laid it down that republican government could not be maintained over an extended territory. Anti-Federalists threw this argument again and again at the new Constitution, charging that it would lead directly to aristocracy or tyranny. One of the more effective Federalist replies was that several of the larger states, including Massachusetts and Virginia, were already too large by Montesquieu's principles! And yet no one had suggested that they be broken down into smaller units.

The structure of the new government provided another reply. Representative government had been invented in Europe, but as Madison pointed out, Americans had found a way of applying it to an extended territory; and the elaborate system of representation contained in the Constitution would do the two essential tasks. It would prevent the central government from grasping excessive power, because representatives were always to be responsible to their electors; and it would, in turn, screen the central government from the elemental force of popular passions.

But in all this elaborate debate about political machinery, what had become of the *essence* of republican government, its spirit, the quality of virtue? The Federalists might well be satisfied with the answer, for the system of representation was fully expected to select the best men in each community. And the best men were those who were known for their worth—their wealth, their education, their practical wisdom and experience, and above and including all these, for their willingness to turn these qualities to the service of the commonwealth as a whole rather than to their own partisan or private interests. That was the true meaning of virtue to the people of the time. It was also a long-received and prevailing belief that virtue was possible only among those who were freed from too many practical, day-to-day pressures and had the leisure for study and reflection and a disposition to take long views. Ownership of property liberated a man from being dependent on the will of another; ownership of landed property, or of substantial commercial assets, had the additional value of giving him an interest in the permanent stability of the society. Thus interest and virtue were united. However, although this view was quite sincerely held by men who had read widely in history and philosophy and had reflected on what they had read, it did not pass unquestioned by men who claimed to speak for the humbler and more vulnerable classes of society. One of these, Melancton Smith of New York, denounced the Constitution, writing under the pseudonym of "Plebeian," a very unusual claim to make about one's social status when addressing the public! (And, incidentally, not true; he was a substantial merchant.)

The Anti-Federalists began by sharing much of the philosophical background that produced these views. Although distinct traces of class interest, expressed in terms of opposition to "aristocracy" and of fears about the motives of "the great," are to be found in much of their language, it would be wrong to think of them as seeking a different social order. Allowing for considerable variations among them, one can see in their writings a general preference for preserving the existing order. What they feared was that the new Constitution would be made use of as an instrument of political power to the advantage of a new elite, great merchants, aggrandizing landowners, moneyed men who made wealth out of transactions rather than out of production, assisted always by skillful lawyers. They deeply suspected the motives of the group of men who were trying to shift the locus of political power from the states, with their thirteen different political centers, to a single consolidated government. This word "consolidated" comes up again and again in their writings. Anti-Federalists differed in a number of ways, just as they lived in widely disparate areas, but they had very much in common this desire to prevent a consolidation of power over the states.

For this reason, they continued to insist on the concept of "sovereignty" in the states—a concept that could not effectively survive the adoption, by the states' own voluntary act, of a Constitution which acted directly on individuals as citizens of the United States. (The Anti-Federalist tracts have a shattering effect on the Southern states-rights arguments of the 1850s: but they went unread in the crisis of disunion.)

More than anything else, however, the Anti-Federalists demanded the addition of a bill of rights. They were unconvinced by the rather lame Federalist arguments that individual rights were protected by the state constitutions, that the new government could never impinge on the liberties of the individual, or that a bill of rights might actually weaken the federal government and thus impair the very protections which it had the power to bestow. The deliberate omission of a bill of rights seemed to many Anti-Federalists to represent a damaging admission of the ulterior motives of their opponents. There can be little doubt that if a bill of rights had been included in the original draft, the Constitution would have encountered much less opposition.

The reasons given for the omission were not wholly convincing. While the Federalist–nationalists may well have believed that there could be no serious threat to personal liberties under the new government, they were more anxious to avoid hobbling it by any restrictions that might be turned against their favored concept of "energy." That, for them, was the more serious question. And in view of the damaging unpopularity of this omission, it is interesting to reflect how it came about.

The Convention agreed to keep its deliberations secret. This decision was later attacked by the Anti-Federalists, but it was not out of step with American legislative precedent, and there is no evidence of opposition to it in the Convention. It had the advantage of freeing members to speak openly and to change their minds without being accused of inconsistency by political enemies outside. It also had an adverse effect, however, which has not generally been noted. As the summer wore on, the members got more and more used to each other's company, often locked in argument, but in a sort of political vacuum: they could not refer back to their constituents or even their friends for comment, and they did, gradually, lose touch with public sentiment. There is no doubt that the omission of a bill of rights was a grave mistake and that the Constitution could not have been adopted without substantial assurances that the appropriate amendments were forthcoming. The mistake might have been avoided if the members had not, temporarily, lost their sense of being themselves members of the constituent community they served.

The point is often made that the focus of American political thought had shifted from the preoccupation with rights in the period of independence to a more mundane concern for the protection of interests by the time of the Constitution. In a formal sense this is true; Madison's famous *Federalist Ten* constructs differences of property out of the free exercise of differences in human faculties, and makes it the principal duty and object of government to protect resultant inequalities. But in a more fundamental sense the comment is superficial. The importance of individual rights was not really in question; it may be said that rights had been absorbed into interests. Every individual had an interest in his rights, and it became the obligation of government to ensure that individuals were free to exercise their interests without impairing the interests of others.

By concentrating on the states, and insisting that all the needs of the moment—and of the future—would be served by conforming to the original purpose of devising ways to stiffen the Articles of Confederation, the Anti-Federalists left the door open for a dialectical coup by their enemies. The Federalists were able to speak in the name of a new political entity, the people of the United States as a whole; and it was the Federalists who could present themselves as the truly democratic standard-bearers of the newly found principle of majority rule. The majority, of course, was now to be the majority of the whole Union, not of individual states.

This principle was weakened by two elements in the Constitution. One was the compromise by which each state was to retain equal representation in the Senate. There was no way to defend this on the principles that Hamilton and Madison genuinely believed in. The nationalists had fought it strenuously in the Convention; but Madison made the best of it by stressing the attractiveness of this aspect to the very people who felt that the states were threatened.

The other issue was slavery and the slave trade. Bitter criticisms of these violations of the most basic of republican, and Christian, principles had been voiced in the Convention—some of them from such slaveholders as George Mason of Virginia. But the issue was not one that united the Anti-Federalists *as* Anti-Federalists. Whatever some Southern Anti-Federalists may have thought, few of them were prepared to stand out and denounce their region's social foundations; moreover, voting against the compromise would have been futile, for the defeat of the Constitution would not have been a blow against slavery; a new confederation of the Southern states, which was regarded as one possible outcome, would certainly have been a slavery confederation. Similarly, a continuation of the existing Confederation would leave slavery intact in the states where it existed.

Nevertheless, the compromise by which the Southern states were permitted to import slaves from Africa for another twenty years was subjected to devastating criticism in some, at least, of the Anti-Federalist papers. More serious still was the violation of the principle of individual representation contained in the Federal Ratio—the arrangement by which three-fifths of the slave population were to count as persons for purposes of computing representation, an obvious violation of the majority principle. How many individuals were influenced to oppose ratification because of these arguments, it is impossible to say. The compromise was the price of union, and failure to ratify would not make slaves any better off.

Anti-Federalists remained unconvinced by one of the most serious Federalist causes of concern about this very question of the survival of the Union itself. In the year or so before the Convention met, nationally minded men such as James Madison and James Wilson were so convinced that the present regime could not long survive that they regarded a much more centralized system as the minimum price of any form of American union. The alternative seemed to be a breakup of the states into various possible confederations. At first there would probably have been three—one uniting the New England states (with or without New York); another uniting the middle states, and leaving the Southern states to find some form of association for themselves. But New York, with its magnificent harbor and its confident self-sufficiency, might have remained an independent state.

The dangers of conflict among these groups, which had already been demonstrated, would be very much compounded as settlement spread into the West. The fact that the old Congress had proved strong enough to pass an ordinance to govern the settlement of new territories and their gradual admission as states—one of its last acts in 1787—gave no grounds for future confidence. If the Confederation broke up, there would be no general government, no mediator, no authority over whatever groups the states might form. The concern of the Federalists, which their opponents thought to be fanciful, were directed to very real dangers. The Federalists were more apprehensive than the Anti-Federalists, and at the same time more realistic and more ambitious.

The dangers of disruption enter prominently into the arguments of the first nine numbers of *The Federalist*, accompanied by some very shrewd and closely observed remarks about human nature and about the behavior of nations, whether in the form of monarchies or republics. Federalists were people who had much to hope for from a stronger union, as well as much to fear from a dissolution. They knew that the materials they had to build with were republican materials, and they believed that the Constitution which they commended to the people provided the government with the necessary energy to give assurance of economic progress and military defense, and was provided with sufficient internal safeguards against the human propensity to abuse power. One of the most crucial statements is Madison's in *Federalist Ten* that the Constitution provides "a Republican remedy for the diseases most incident to Republican Government."

Federalists have sometimes been depicted as people preoccupied with fears of human nature, as historical pessimists. Certainly, they felt that they had seen the dangers of unlicensed liberty and popular rule. But this fails to do justice to the other side of the picture. For Federalists were more confident of the prospects of expansion than their opponents. They were numerous in the great states like Massachusetts, Pennsylvania, and Virginia, which in any case would wield vast influence by their numbers—a significant consequence of the majority system in national politics; but they were also powerful in small or thinly peopled and geographically exposed states, ranging from New Jersey and Connecticut to South Carolina and Georgia, which were well aware of the need for more powerful protection than they could provide for themselves.

Anti-Federalists collected some of their voting strength from areas that were more economically marginal and did not depend on the international or even the regional market for their livelihood. Farmers in these areas felt threatened by the power they feared would pass into the hands of the rich. Apprehensions of this sort seem to have been more prevalent in the country than in the towns, where the prospects of economic growth would carry the artisan along with his employers. But Anti-Federalism was also strong in states, including Massachusetts, Pennsylvania, and Virginia as well as New York, which were already doing comfortably well under the Confederation. In the New York ratifying convention, Robert Lansing, a leading Anti-Federalist, went as far as to say that, although a dissolution of the Union would grieve him, it would not threaten any particular damage to New York, with its natural resources and close ties to New England.

There were many people in these states, not by any means confined to the economically more vulnerable classes, who did not sense the urgency pressed by the Federalists. They agreed that the Articles needed strengthening but were well satisfied with the performance of their states under the existing regime; in the draft Constitution, rather than in the Articles of Confederation, they sensed a threat to the order of things, under which they had managed to survive and some of them were beginning to prosper. The highly articulate arguments presented in many of the passages in this collection are not the outpourings of the ill-educated or the unprivileged; but they do in some cases—see Melancton Smith of New York—express the fears of the poor with more sympathy and understanding than come from the Federalists.

The Convention's rule of secrecy was pretty closely observed. Only after the draft Constitution had been circulated to the states could the people at large begin to form an opinion. Criticism then began to appear, mainly in the form of essays contributed to newspapers. When the state ratifying conventions began to meet, these adverse opinions were expressed in a large number of speeches, several of which are reprinted here. The debate went on through the whole period of ratification, lasting into the summer of 1788.

The original decision to write a defense of the Constitution was made by Alexander Hamilton, who was alarmed by the virulence of the criticism in the New York newspapers. He soon secured the agreement of John Jay, also of New York, and James Madison of Virginia to collaborate with him, the latter joining the team in November, with *Federalist Ten* as his first contribution. Jay dropped out because of illness, but the other two continued to correspond. They were in New York City in the autumn and winter of 1787–88 and probably conferred frequently. (Such informal meetings do not leave records.) During the period of publication, arguments and counter-arguments flew back and forth. In this edition, it seemed appropriate to let the Anti-Federalists speak first, and to give their spokesmen a clear run, rather than to intersperse contributions for and against. The dates of publication will give readers the opportunity to place the essays in the course of the debate. *The Federalist* essays follow, abbreviated by necessary cuts and omissions.

The Federalist, often alternatively known as *The Federalist Papers*, has exerted tremendous influence and is quite correctly regarded as a classic of eighteenth-century political writing. Thomas Jefferson once declared it "the best commentary on the principles of government, which was ever written." In saying so, he distinguished it from works of a more theoretical nature, and it is important for readers to realize its limitations. The authors were not trying to write political theory; they were engaged in evoking in their readers the applications of ideas which were already known and very generally believed by Americans. In the best sense of the word, *The Federalist* is a work of propaganda, not of theory, and should be regarded as such. The strength of these essays lies in the extraordinary skill with which they explain the provisions of the Constitution in terms of republican principles as understood in America. Hamilton—who appears to have written fifty-one of the eighty-five essays—would have preferred a much stronger government, and Madison regarded state representation in the Senate as a disastrous error. They would both have preferred to find themselves writing in support of a more centralized instrument. But they had to make the best of the one they had, in which cause they wrote with remarkable clarity and conviction.

As propagandists, the authors, writing as though they were a single person, played on the fears of their readers and appealed deliberately to their interests. They argued that the Constitution would be good for commerce, fishing, and agriculture; they argued that it was the least that was necessary to save the new nation from disintegration; they answered specific Anti-Federalist criticisms as they went along, week by week. They also systematically examined the structure of the new Constitution in terms of its provisions for legislature, judiciary, and executive departments; its treatment of federal-state relations; its effects on the individual; and many other considerations. Though directed to the people of New York, the essays were reprinted and must have formed opinions in other states. They have been forming opinions ever since.

This functional character of *The Federalist* makes it necessary to conclude with a word of caution about its authority as an interpretation of the intent of the Constitution. Historians, political scientists, and, not least, federal judges have been tempted to cite these essays as authority for the true meaning of the framers of the Constitution; after all, Hamilton and Madison were members of the Convention and now, as its principal proponents, could be regarded as authorities on its meaning, wherever doubts might arise. But Hamilton and Madison were in profound disagreement with each other on these questions in the years that followed. The fact is that the Constitution as urged and pleaded for by Publius was the Constitution which the authors hoped and believed Americans would agree to adopt as their own, at the particular time in American history when these debates took place. Under different conditions, they might well have used other arguments and stressed somewhat different interpretations. *The Federalist* is a historical document of the highest importance; but it is not the ultimate authority on the true intent and meaning of the Constitution of the United States, even at the time of signing. Still less has it had that authority in later times.

A NOTE ON PSEUDONYMS

Eighteenth-century pamphleteers commonly adopted pseudonyms. These not only protected the privacy of individuals engaged in heated controversy but were used to suggest a wider public interest than that of the individual writer. Classical education may have been the preserve of the few, but certain heroic names were common knowledge. Publius Valerius, whose name was invoked by the authors of *The Federalist*, was celebrated for having established republican government in Rome after the overthrow of Tarquin.

Ever since John Dickinson had styled himself "A Farmer in Pennsylvania" in 1767, however, the invocation of virtuous rusticity had an appeal which could be used effectively against the sophistication of power and privilege. It is noteworthy that although several Anti-Federalists assumed the name and mantle of ancient heroes of liberty, more of them liked to call themselves just plain farmers. It was neighbor speaking to neighbor, rather than an educated aristocracy talking down to the plain people. As has been noted, Melancton Smith took this tactic to the length of calling himself "Plebeian."

THE ANTI-FEDERALISTS

The Federal Farmer

Observations Leading to a Fair Examination of the system of Government Proposed by the Late Convention; And to several Essential and Necessary Alterations in It. In a Number of Letters from the Federal Farmer to the Republican.

Note. The Letters of the Federal Farmer were long attributed to Richard Henry Lee. This attribution has been questioned, first by William W. Crosskey in *Politics and the Constitution* (Chicago, 1953) II, 1299–1300, and later by Gordon S. Wood in "The Authorship of the Letters from the Federal Farmer," *William and Mary Quarterly*, April 1974. No satisfactory alternative having been suggested, the question remains open. The *Letters* began to appear in October 1787 and were widely read in pamphlet form.

FROM
I
October 8, 1787

. . . The first principal question that occurs, is, Whether, considering our situation, we ought to precipitate the adoption of the proposed constitution? If we remain cool and temperate, we are in no immediate danger of any commotions; we are in a state of perfect peace, and in no danger of invasions; the state governments are in the full exercise of their powers; and our governments answer all present exigencies, except the regulation of trade, securing credit, in some cases, and providing for the interest, in some instances, of the public debts; and whether we adopt a change, three or nine months hence, can make but little odds with the private circumstances of individuals; their happiness and prosperity, after all, depend principally upon their own exertions. We are hardly recovered from a long and distressing war: The farmers, fishmen, &c. have not yet fully repaired the waste made by it. Industry and frugality are again assuming their proper station. Private debts are lessened, and public debts incurred by the war have been, by various ways, diminished; and the public lands have now become a productive source for diminishing them much more. I know uneasy men, who wish very much to precipitate, do not admit all these facts; but they are facts well known to all men who are thoroughly informed in the affairs of this country. It must, however, be admitted, that our federal system is defective, and that some of the state governments are not well administered; but, then, we impute to the defects in our governments many evils and embarrassments which are most clearly the result of the late war. We must allow men to conduct on the present occasion, as on all similar ones. They will urge a thousand pretences to answer their purposes on both sides. When we want a man to change his condition, we describe it as miserable, wretched, and despised; and draw a pleasing picture of that which we would have him assume. And when we wish the contrary, we reverse our descriptions. Whenever a clamor is raised, and idle men get to work, it is highly necessary to examine facts carefully, and without unreasonably suspecting men of falshood, to examine, and enquire attentively, under what impressions they act. It is too often the case in political concerns, that men state facts not as they are, but as they wish them to be; and almost every man, by calling to mind past scenes, will find this to be true.

Nothing but the passions of ambitious, impatient, or disorderly men, I conceive, will plunge us into commotions, if time should be taken fully to examine and consider the system proposed. Men who feel easy in their circumstances, and such as are not sanguine in their expectations relative to the consequences of the proposed change, will remain quiet under the existing governments. Many commercial and monied men, who are uneasy, not without just cause, ought to be respected; and, by no means, unreasonably disappointed in their expectations and hopes; but as to those who expect employments under the new constitution; as to those weak and ardent men who always expect to be gainers by revolutions, and whose lot it generally is to get out of one difficulty into another, they are very little to be regarded: and as to those who designedly avail themselves of this weakness and ardor, they are to be despised. It is natural for men, who wish to hasten the adoption of a measure, to tell us, now is the crisis—now is the critical moment which must be seized, or all will be lost: and to shut the door against free enquiry, whenever conscious the thing presented has defects in it, which time and investigation will probably discover. This has been the custom of tyrants and their dependents in all ages. If it is true, what has been so often said, that the people of this country cannot change their condition for the worse, I presume it still behoves them to endeavour deliberately to change it for the better. The fickle and ardent, in any community, are the proper tools for establishing despotic government. But it is deliberate and thinking men, who must establish and secure governments on free principles. Before they decide on the plan proposed, they will enquire whether it will probably be a blessing or a curse to this people.

The present moment discovers a new face in our affairs. Our object has been all along, to reform our federal system, and to strengthen our governments—to establish peace, order and justice in the community—but a new object now presents. The plan of government now proposed is evidently calculated totally to change, in time, our condition as a people. Instead of being thirteen republics, under a federal head, it is clearly designed to make us one consolidated government. Of this, I think, I shall fully convince you, in my following letters on this subject. This consolidation of the states has been the object of several men in this country for some time past. Whether such a change can ever be effected in any manner; whether it can be effected without convulsions and civil wars; whether such a change will not totally destroy the liberties of this country—time only can determine.

To have a just idea of the government before us, and to shew that a consolidated one is the object in view, it is necessary not only to examine the plan, but also its history, and the politics of its particular friends.

The confederation was formed when great confidence was placed in the voluntary exertions of individuals, and of the respective states; and the framers of it, to guard against usurpation, so limited and checked the powers, that, in many respects, they are inadequate to the exigencies of the union. We find, therefore, members of congress urging alterations in the federal system almost as soon as it was adopted. It was early proposed to vest congress with powers to levy an impost, to regulate trade, etc. but such was known to be the caution of the states in parting with power, that the vestment, even of these, was proposed to be under several checks and limitations. During the war, the general confusion, and the introduction of paper money, infused in the minds of people vague ideas respecting government and credit. We expected too much from the return of peace, and of course we have been disappointed. Our governments have been new and unsettled; and several legislatures, by making tender, suspension, and paper money laws, have given just cause of uneasiness to creditors. By these and other causes, several orders of men in the community have been prepared, by degrees, for a change of government; and this very abuse of power in the legislatures, which, in some cases, has been charged upon the democratic part of the community, has furnished aristocratical men with those very weapons, and those very means, with which, in great measure, they are rapidly effecting their favourite object. And should an oppressive government be the consequence of the proposed change, posterity may reproach not only a few overbearing unprincipled men, but those parties in the states which have misused their powers. . . .

FROM
IV
October 12, 1787

. . . In the year 1788* the people of the United States make a federal constitution, which is a fundamental compact between them and their federal rulers; these rulers, in the nature of things, cannot be bound to take notice of any other compact. It would be absurd for them, in making laws, to look over thirteen, fifteen, or twenty state constitutions, to see what rights are established as fundamental, and must not be infringed upon, in making laws in the society. It is true, they would be bound to do it if the people, in their federal compact, should refer to the state constitutions, recognize all parts not inconsistent with the federal constitution, and direct their federal rulers to take notice of them accordingly; but this is not the case, as the plan stands proposed at present; and it is absurd, to suppose so unnatural an idea is intended or implied.

* Evidently a misprint, either for 1778, when the Articles of Confederation were drafted, or for 1781, when they were adopted. (Editor)

I think my opinion is not only founded in reason, but I think it is supported by the report of the convention itself. If there are a number of rights established by the state constitutions, and which will remain sacred, and the general government is bound to take notice of them—it must take notice of one as well as another; and if unnecessary to recognize or establish one by the federal constitution, it would be unnecessary to recognize or establish another by it. If the federal constitution is to be construed so far in connection with the state constitutions, as to leave the trial by jury in civil causes, for instance, secured; on the same principles it would have left the trial by jury in criminal causes, the benefits of the writ of habeas corpus, etc. secured; they all stand on the same footing; they are the common rights of Americans, and have been recognized by the state constitutions: But the convention found it necessary to recognize or re-establish the benefits of that writ, and the jury trial in criminal cases. As to *expost facto* laws, the convention has done the same in one case, and gone further in another. It is part of the compact between the people of each state and their rulers, that no *expost facto* laws shall be made. But the convention, by Art. I Sect. 10 have put a sanction upon this part even of the state compacts. In fact, the 9th and 10th Sections in Art. I. in the proposed constitution, are no more nor less, than a partial bill of rights; they establish certain principles as part of the compact upon which the federal legislators and officers can never infringe. It is here wisely stipulated, that the federal legislature shall never pass a bill of attainder, or *expost facto* law; that no tax shall be laid on articles exported, etc. The establishing of one right implies the necessity of establishing another and similar one.

On the whole, the position appears to me to be undeniable, that this bill of rights ought to be carried farther, and some other principles established, as a part of this fundamental compact between the people of the United States and their federal rulers.

It is true, we are not disposed to differ much, at present, about religion; but when we are making a constitution, it is to be hoped, for ages and millions yet unborn, why not establish the free exercise of religion, as a part of the national compact. There are other essential rights, which we have justly understood to be the rights of freemen; as freedom from hasty and unreasonable search warrants, warrants not founded on oath, and not issued with due caution, for searching and seizing men's papers, property, and persons. The trials by jury in civil causes, it is said, varies so much in the several states, that no words could be found for the uniform establishment of it. If so, the federal legislation will not be able to establish it by any general laws. I confess I am of opinion it may be established, but not in that beneficial manner in which we may enjoy it, for the reasons beforementioned. When I speak of the jury trial of the vicinage, or the trial of the fact in the neighbourhood,—I do not lay so much stress upon the circumstance of our being tried by our neighbours; in this enlightened country men may be probably impartially tried by those who do not live very near them; but the trial of facts in the neighbourhood is of great importance in other respects. Nothing can be more essential than the cross examining witnesses, and generally before the triers of the facts in question. The common people can establish facts with much more ease with oral than written evidence; when trials of facts are removed to a distance from the homes of the parties and witnesses, oral evidence becomes intolerably expensive, and the parties must depend on written evidence, which to the common people is expensive and almost useless; it must be frequently taken ex parte, and but very seldom leads to the proper discovery of the truth.

The trial by jury is very important in another point of view. It is essential in every free country, that common people should have a part and share of influence, in the judicial as well as in the legislative department. To hold open to them the offices of senators, judges, and offices to fill which an expensive education is required, cannot answer any valuable purposes for them; they are not in a situation to be brought forward and to fill those offices; these, and most other offices of any considerable importance, will be occupied by the few. The few, the well born, etc. as Mr. Adams calls them, in judicial decisions as well as in legislation, are generally disposed, and very naturally too, to favour those of their own description.

The trial by jury in the judicial department, and the collection of the people by their representatives in the legislature, are those fortunate inventions which have procured for them, in this country, their true proportion of influence, and the wisest and most fit means of protecting themselves in the community. Their situation, as jurors and representatives, enables them to acquire information and knowledge in the affairs and government of the society; and to come forward, in turn, as the centinels and guardians of each other. I am very sorry that even a few of our countrymen should consider jurors and representatives in a different point of view, as ignorant troublesome bodies, which ought not to have any share in the concerns of government.

I confess I do not see in what cases the congress can, with any pretence of right, make a law to suppress the freedom of the press; though I am not clear, that congress is restrained from laying any duties whatever on printing, and from laying duties particularly heavy on certain pieces printed, and perhaps congress may require large bonds for the payment of these duties. Should the printer say, the freedom of the press was secured by the constitution of the state in which he lived, congress might, and perhaps, with great propriety, answer, that the federal constitution is the only compact existing between them and the people; in this compact the people have named no others, and therefore congress, in exercising the powers assigned them, and in making laws to carry them into execution, are restrained by nothing beside the federal constitution, any more than a state legislature is restrained by a compact between the magistrates and people of a county, city, or town of which the people, in forming the state constitution, have taken no notice.

It is not my object to enumerate rights of inconsiderable importance; but there are others, no doubt, which ought to be established as a fundamental part of the national system.

It is worthy observation, that all treaties are made by foreign nations with a confederacy of thirteen states—that the western country is attached to thirteen states—thirteen states have jointly and severally engaged to pay the public debts.—Should a new government be formed of nine, ten, eleven, or twelve states, those treaties could not be considered as binding on the foreign nations who made them. However, I believe the probability to be, that if nine states adopt the constitution, the others will.

It may also be worthy our examination, how far the provision for amending this plan, when it shall be adopted, is of any importance. No measures can be taken towards amendments, unless two-thirds of the congress, or two-thirds of the legislatures of the several states shall agree.—While power is in the hands of the people, or democratic part of the community, more especially as at present, it is easy, according to the general course of human affairs, for the few influential men in the community, to obtain conventions, alterations in government, and to persuade the common people they may change for the better, and to get from them a part of the power: But when power is once transferred from the many to the few, all changes become extremely difficult; the government, in this case, being beneficial to the few, they will be exceedingly artful and adroit in preventing any measures which may lead to a change; and nothing will produce it, but great exertions and severe struggles on the part of the common people. Every man of reflection must see, that the change now proposed, is a transfer of power from the the many to the few, and the probability is, the artful and ever active aristocracy, will prevent all peaceable measures for changes, unless when they shall discover some favourable moment to increase their own influence. I am sensible, thousands of men in the United States, are disposed to adopt the proposed constitution, though they perceive it to be essentially defective, under an idea that amendments of it, may be obtained when necessary. This is a pernicious idea, it argues a servility of character totally unfit for the support of free government; it is very repugnant to that perpetual jealousy respecting liberty, so absolutely necessary in all free states, spoken of by Mr. Dickinson.—However, if our countrymen are so soon changed, and the language of 1774, is become odious to them, it will be in vain to use the language of freedom, or to attempt to rouse them to free enquiries: But I shall never believe this is the case with them, whatever present appearances may be, till I shall have very strong evidence indeed of it.

Yours, &c.
The Federal Farmer.

FROM
VII
October 12, 1787

. . . Efforts among parties are not merely confined to property; they contend for rank and distinctions; all their passions in turn are enlisted in political controversies—Men, elevated in society, are often disgusted with the changeableness of the democracy, and the latter are often agitated with the passions of jealousy and envy: the yeomanry possess a large share of property and strength, are nervous and firm in their opinions and habits—the mechanics of towns are ardent and changeable, honest and credulous, they are inconsiderable for numbers, weight and strength, not always sufficiently stable for the supporting free governments: the fishing interest partakes partly of the strength and stability of the landed, and partly of the changeableness of the mechanic interest. As to merchants and traders, they are our agents in almost all money transactions; give activity to government, and possess a considerable share of influence in it. It has been observed by an able writer, that frugal industrious merchants are generally advocates for liberty. It is an observation, I believe, well founded, that the schools produce but few advocates for republican forms of government; gentlemen of the law, divinity, physic, &c. probably form about a fourth part of the people; yet their political influence, perhaps, is equal to that of all the other descriptions of men; if we may judge from the appointments to Congress, the legal characters will often, in a small representation, be the majority; but the more the representatives are encreased, the more of the farmers, merchants, &c. will be found to be brought into the government.

These general observations will enable you to discern what I intend by different classes, and the general scope of my ideas, when I contend for uniting and balancing their interests, feelings, opinions, and views in the legislature; we may not only so unite and balance these as to prevent a change in the government by the gradual exaltation of one part to the depression of others, but we may derive many other advantages from the combination and full representation; a small representation can never be well informed as to the circumstances of the people, the members of it must be too far removed from the people, in general, to sympathize with them, and too few to communicate with them: a representation must be extremely imperfect where the representatives are not circumstanced to make the proper communications to their constituents, and where the constituents in turn cannot, with tolerable convenience, make known their wants, circumstances, and opinions, to their representatives; where there is but one representative to 30,000 to 40,000 inhabitants, it appears to me, he can only mix, and be acquainted with a few respectable characters among his constituents, even double the federal representation, and then there must be a very great distance between the representatives and the people in general represented. On the proposed plan, the state of Delaware, the city of Philadelphia, the state of Rhode Island, the province of Main, the county of Suffolk in

Massachusetts will have one representative each; there can be but little personal knowledge, or but few communications, between him and the people at large of either of those districts. It has been observed, that mixing only with the respectable men, he will get the best information and ideas from them; he will also receive impressions favourable to their purposes particularly. Many plausible shifts have been made to divert the mind from dwelling on this defective representation, these I shall consider in another place. . . .

Brutus

The Essays of Brutus, which were published in *The New York Journal* between October 1787 and April 1788, may well have influenced Hamilton's decision to embark on a comprehensive defense of the Constitution.

Brutus has generally been considered to be Robert Yates of New York, but the attribution is inconclusive.

The pseudonym is presumably intended to recall Marcus Brutus, one of the leaders of the conspiracy which assassinated Julius Caesar to prevent him from making himself king. Shakespeare's *Julius Caesar* and Plutarch's *Lives* were sources with which all educated people would be familiar at that time.

II
November 1, 1787

To the Citizens of the State of New-York.
I flatter myself that my last address established this position, that to reduce the Thirteen States into one government, would prove the destruction of your liberties.

But lest this truth should be doubted by some, I will now proceed to consider its merits.

Though it should be admitted, that the argument[s] against reducing all the states into one consolidated government, are not sufficient fully to establish this point; yet they will, at least, justify this conclusion, that in forming a constitution for such a country, great care should be taken to limit and definite its powers, adjust its parts, and guard against an abuse of authority. How far attention has been paid to these objects, shall be the subject of future enquiry. When a building is to be erected which is intended to stand for ages, the foundation should be firmly laid. The constitution proposed to your acceptance, is designed not for yourselves alone, but for generations yet unborn. The principles, therefore, upon which the social compact is founded, ought to have been clearly and precisely stated, and the most express and full declaration of rights to have been made—But on this subject there is almost an entire silence.

If we may collect the sentiments of the people of America, from their own most solemn declarations, they hold this truth as self evident, that all men are by nature free. No one man, therefore, or any class of men, have a right, by the law of nature, or of God, to assume or exercise authority over their fellows. The origin of society then is to be sought, not in any natural right which one man has to exercise authority over another, but in the united consent of those who associate. The mutual wants of men, at first dictated the propriety of forming societies; and when they were established, protection and defence pointed out the necessity of instituting government. In a state of nature every individual pursues his own interest; in this pursuit it frequently happened, that the possessions or enjoyments of one were sacrificed to the views and designs of another; thus the weak were a prey to the strong, the simple and unwary were subject to impositions from those who were more crafty and designing. In this state of things, every individual was insecure; common interest therefore directed, that government should be established, in which the force of the whole community should be collected, and under such directions, as to protect and defend every one who composed it. The common good, therefore, is the end of civil government, and common consent, the foundation on which it is established. To effect this end, it was necessary that a certain portion of natural liberty should be surrendered, in order, that what remained should be preserved: how great a proportion of natural freedom is necessary to be yielded by individuals, when they submit to government, I shall not now enquire. So much, however, must be given up, as will be sufficient to enable those, to whom the administration of the government is committed, to establish laws for the promoting the happiness of the community, and to carry those laws into effect. But it is not necessary, for this purpose, that individuals should relinquish all their natural rights. Some are of such a nature that they cannot be surrendered. Of this kind are the rights of conscience, the right of enjoying and defending life, etc. Others are not necessary to be resigned, in order to attain the end for which government is instituted, these therefore ought not to be given up. To surrender them, would counteract the very end of government, to wit, the common good. From these observations it appears, that in forming a government on its true principles, the foundation should be laid in the manner I before stated, by expressly reserving to the people such of their essential natural rights, as are not necessary to be parted with. The same reasons which at first induced mankind to associate and institute government, will operate to influence them to observe this precaution. If they had been disposed to conform themselves to the rule of immutable righteousness, government would not have been requisite. It was because one part exercised fraud, oppression, and violence on the other, that men came together, and agreed that certain rules should be formed, to regulate the conduct of all, and the power of the whole community lodged in the hands of rulers to enforce an obedience to them. But rulers have the same propensities as other men; they are as likely to use the power with which they are vested for private purposes, and to the injury and oppression of those over whom they are placed, as individuals in a state of nature are to injure and oppress one another. It is therefore as proper that bounds should be set to their authority, as that government should have at first been instituted to restrain private injuries.

This principle, which seems so evidently founded in the reason and nature of things, is confirmed by universal experience. Those who have governed, have been found in all ages ever active to enlarge their powers and abridge the public liberty. This has induced the people in all countries, where any sense of freedom remained, to fix barriers against the encroachments of their rulers. The country from which we have derived our origin, is an eminent example of this. Their magna charta and bill of rights have long been the boast, as well as the security, of that nation. I need say no more, I presume, to an American, than, that this principle is a fundamental one, in all the constitutions of our own states; there is not one of them but what is either founded on a declaration or bill of rights, or has certain express reservation of rights interwoven in the body of them. From this it appears, that at a time when the pulse of liberty beat high and when an appeal was made to the people to form constitutions for the government of themselves, it was their universal sense, that such declarations should make a part of their frames of government. It is therefore the more astonishing, that this grand security, to the rights of the people, is not to be found in this constitution.

It has been said, in answer to this objection, that such declaration[s] of rights, however requisite they might be in the constitutions of the states, are not necessary in the general constitution, because, "in the former case, every thing which is not reserved is given, but in the latter the reverse of the proposition prevails, and every thing which is not given is reserved." It requires but little attention to discover, that this mode of reasoning is rather specious than solid. The powers, rights, and authority, granted to the general government by this constitution, are as complete, with respect to every object to which they extend, as that of any state government—It reaches to every thing which concerns human happiness—Life, liberty, and property, are under its controul. There is the same reason, therefore, that the exercise of power, in this case, should be restrained within proper limits, as in that of the state governments. To set this matter in a clear light, permit me to instance some of the articles of the bills of rights of the individual states, and apply them to the case in question.

For the security of life, in criminal prosecutions, the bills of rights of most of the states have declared, that no man shall be held to answer for a crime until he is made fully acquainted with the charge brought against him; he shall not be compelled to accuse, or furnish evidence against himself—The witnesses against him shall be brought face to face, and he shall be fully heard by himself or counsel. That it is essential to the security of life and liberty, that trial of facts be in the vicinity where they happen. Are not provisions of this kind as necessary in the general government, as in that of a particular state? The powers vested in the new Congress extend in many cases to life; they are authorised to provide for the punishment of a variety of capital crimes, and no restraint is laid upon them in its exercise, save only, that "the trial of all crimes, except in cases of impeachment, shall be by jury; and such trial shall be in the state where the said crimes shall have been committed." No man is secure of a trial in the county where he is charged to have committed a crime; he may be brought from Niagara to New-York, or carried from Kentucky to Richmond for trial for an offence, supposed to be committed. What security is there, that a man shall be furnished with a full and plain description of the charges against him? That he shall be allowed to produce all proof he can in his favor? That he shall see the witnesses against him face to face, or that he shall be fully heard in his own defence by himself or counsel?

For the security of liberty it has been declared, "that excessive bail should not be required, nor excessive fines imposed, nor cruel or unusual punishments inflicted—That all warrants, without oath or affirmation, to search suspected places, or seize any person, his papers or property, are grievous and oppressive."

These provisions are as necessary under the general government as under that of the individual states; for the power of the former is as complete to the purpose of requiring bail, imposing fines, inflicting punishments, granting search warrants, and seizing persons, papers, or property, in certain cases, as the other.

For the purpose of securing the property of the citizens, it is declared by all the states, "that in all controversies at law, respecting property, the ancient mode of trial by jury is one of the best securities of the rights of the people, and ought to remain sacred and inviolable."

Does not the same necessity exist of reserving this right, under this national compact, as in that of these states? Yet nothing is said respecting it. In the bills of rights of the states it is declared, that a well regulated militia is the proper and natural defence of a free government—That as standing armies in time of peace are dangerous, they are not to be kept up, and that the military should be kept under strict subordination to, and controuled by the civil power.

The same security is as necessary in this constitution, and much more so; for the general government will have the sole power to raise and to pay armies, and are under no controul in the exercise of it; yet nothing of this is to be found in this new system.

I might proceed to instance a number of other rights, which were as necessary to be reserved, such as, that elections should be free, that the liberty of the press should be held sacred; but the instances adduced, are sufficient to prove, that this argument is without foundation.—Besides, it is evident, that the reason here assigned was not the true one, why the framers of this constitution omitted a bill of rights; if it had been, they would not have made certain reservations, while they totally omitted others of more importance. We find they have, in the 9th section of the 1st article, declared, that the writ of habeas corpus shall not be suspended, unless in cases of rebellion—that no bill of attainder, or expost facto law, shall be passed—that no title of nobility shall be granted by the United States, &c. If every thing which is not given is reserved, what propriety is there in these exceptions? Does this constitution any where grant the power of suspending the habeas corpus, to make expost facto laws, pass bills of attainder, or grant titles of nobility? It certainly does not in express terms. The only answer that can be given is, that these are implied in the general powers granted. With equal truth it may be said, that all the powers, which the bills of right, guard against the abuse of, are contained or implied in the general ones granted by this constitution.

So far it is from being true, that a bill of rights is less necessary in the general constitution than in those of the states, the contrary is evidently the fact.—This system, if it is possible for the people of America to accede to it, will be an original compact; and being the last, will, in the nature of things, vacate every former agreement inconsistent with it. For it being a plan of government received and ratified by the whole people, all other forms, which are in existence at the time of its adoption, must yield to it. This is expressed in positive and unequivocal terms, in the 6th article, "That this constitution and the laws of the United States, which shall be made in pursuance thereof, and all treaties made, or which shall be made, under the authority of the United States, shall be the supreme law of the land; and the judges in every state shall be bound thereby, any thing in the *constitution*, or laws of any state, *to the contrary* notwithstanding.

"The senators and representatives before-mentioned, and the members of the several state legislatures, and all executive and judicial officers, both of the United States, and of the several states, shall be bound, by oath or affirmation, to support this constitution."

It is therefore not only necessarily implied thereby, but positively expressed, that the different state constitutions are repealed and entirely done away, so far as they are inconsistent with this, with the laws which shall be made in pursuance thereof, or with treaties made, or which shall be made, under the authority of the United States; of what avail will the constitutions of the respective states be to preserve the rights of its citizens? should they be plead, the answer would be, the constitution of the United States, and the laws made in pursuance thereof, is the supreme law, and all legislatures and judicial officers, whether of the general or state governments, are bound by oath to support it. No priviledge, reserved by the bills of rights, or secured by the state government, can limit the power granted by this, or restrain any laws made in pursuance of it. It stands therefore on its own bottom, and must receive a construction by itself without any reference to any other—And hence it was of the highest importance, that the most precise and express declarations and reservations of rights should have been made.

This will appear the more necessary, when it is considered, that not only the constitution and laws made in pursuance thereof, but all treaties made, or which shall be made, under the authority of the United States, are the supreme law of the land, and supersede the constitutions of all the states. The power to make treaties, is vested in the president, by and with the advice and consent of two thirds of the senate. I do not find any limitation, or restriction, to the exercise of this power. The most important article in any constitution may therefore be repealed, even without a legislative act. Ought not a government, vested with such extensive and indefinite authority, to have been restricted by a declaration of rights? It certainly ought.

So clear a point is this, that I cannot help suspecting, that persons who attempt to persuade people, that such reservations were less necessary under this constitution than under those of the states, are wilfully endeavouring to deceive, and to lead you into an absolute state of vassalage.

Brutus.

FROM
III
November 15, 1787

. . . The first important object that presents itself in the organization of this government, is the legislature. This is to be composed of two branches; the first to be called the general assembly, and is to be chosen by the people of the respective states, in proportion to the number of their inhabitants, and is to consist of sixty five members, with powers in the legislature to encrease the number, not to exceed one for every thirty thousand inhabitants. The second branch is to be called the senate, and is to consist of twenty-six members, two of which are to be chosen by the legislatures of each of the states.

In the former of these there is an appearance of justice, in the appointment of its members—but if the clause, which provides for this branch, be stripped of its ambiguity, it will be found that there is really no equality of representation, even in this house.

The words are "representatives and direct taxes, shall be apportioned among the several states, which may be included in this union, according to their respective numbers, which shall be determined by adding to the whole number of free persons, including those bound to service for a term of years, and excluding Indians not taxed, three fifths of all other persons."—What a strange and unnecessary accumulation of words are here used to conceal from the public eye, what might have been expressed in the following concise manner. Representatives are to be proportioned among the states respectively, according to the number of freemen and slaves inhabiting them, counting five slaves for three free men.

"In a free state," says the celebrated Montesquieu, "every man, who is supposed to be a free agent, ought to be concerned in his own government, therefore the legislature should reside in the whole body of the people, or their representatives." But it has never been alledged that those who are not free agents, can, upon any rational principle, have any thing to do in government, either by themselves or others. If they have no share in government, why is the number of members in the assembly, to be increased on their account? Is it because in some of the states, a considerable part of the property of the inhabitants consists in a number of their fellow men, who are held in bondage, in defiance of every idea of benevolence, justice, and religion, and contrary to all the principles of liberty, which have been publickly avowed in the late glorious revolution? If this be a just ground for representation, the horses in some of the states, and the oxen in others, ought to be represented—for a great share of property in some of them, consists in these animals; and they have as much controul over their own actions, as these poor unhappy creatures, who are intended to be described in the above recited clause, by the words, "all other persons." By this mode of apportionment, the representatives of the different parts of the union, will be extremely unequal; in some of the southern states, the slaves are nearly equal in number to the free men; and for all these slaves, they will be entitled to a proportionate share in the legislature—this will give them an unreasonable weight in the government, which can derive no additional strength, protection, nor defence from the slaves, but the contrary. Why then should they be represented? What adds to the evil is, that these states are to be permitted to continue the inhuman traffic of importing slaves, until the year 1808—and for every cargo of these unhappy people, which unfeeling, unprincipled, barbarous, and avaricious wretches, may tear from their country, friends and tender connections, and bring into those states, they are to be rewarded by having an increase of members in the general assembly. . . .

FROM
IV
November 29, 1787

To the People of the State of New-York.

There can be no free government where the people are not possessed of the power of making the laws by which they are governed, either in their own persons, or by others substituted in their stead.

Experience has taught mankind, that legislation by representatives is the most eligible, and the only practicable mode in which the people of any country can exercise this right, either prudently or beneficially. But then, it is a matter of the highest importance, in forming this representation, that it be so constituted as to be capable of understanding the true interests of the society for which it acts, and so disposed as to pursue the good and happiness of the people as its ultimate end. The object of every free government is the public good, and all lesser interests yield to it. That of every tyrannical government, is the happiness and aggrandisement of one, or a few, and to this the public felicity, and every other interest must submit.—The reason of this difference in these governments is obvious. The first is so constituted as to collect the views and wishes of the whole people in that of their rulers, while the latter is so framed as to separate the interests of the governors from that of the governed. The principle of self love, therefore, that will influence the one to promote the good of the whole, will prompt the other to follow its own private advantage. The great art, therefore, in forming a good constitution, appears to be this, so to frame it, as that those to whom the power is committed shall be subject to the same feelings, and aim at the same objects as the people do, who transfer to them their authority. There is no possible way to effect this but by an equal, full and fair representation; this, therefore, is the great desideratum in politics. However fair an appearance any government may make, though it may possess a thousand plausible articles and be decorated with ever so many ornaments, yet if it is deficient in this essential principle of a full and just representation of the people, it will be only like a painted sepulcher—For, without this it cannot be a free government; let the administration of it be good or ill, it still will be a government, not according to the will of the people, but according to the will of a few.

To test this new constitution then, by this principle, is of the last importance—It is to bring it to the touch-stone of national liberty, and I hope I shall be excused, if, in this paper, I pursue the subject commenced in my last number, to wit, the necessity of an equal and full representation in the legislature.—In that, I showed that it was not equal, because the smallest states are to send the same number of members to the senate as the largest, and, because the slaves, who afford neither aid or defence to the government, are to encrease the proportion of members. To prove that it was not a just or adequate representation, it was urged, that so small a number could not resemble the people, or possess their sentiments and dispositions. That the choice of members would commonly fall upon the rich and great, while the middling class of the community would be excluded. That in so small a representation there was no security against bribery and corruption.

The small number which is to compose this legislature, will not only expose it to the danger of that kind of corruption, and undue influence, which will arise from the gift of places of honor and emolument, or the more direct one of bribery, but it will also subject it to another kind of influence no less fatal to the liberties of the people, though it be not so flagrantly repugnant to the principles of rectitude. It is not to be expected that a legislature will be found in any country that will not have some of its members, who will pursue their private ends, and for which they will sacrifice the public good. Men of this character are, generally, artful and designing, and frequently possess brilliant talents and abilities; they commonly act in concert, and agree to share the spoils of their country among them; they will keep their object ever in view, and follow it with constancy. To effect their purpose, they will assume any shape, and, Proteus like, mould themselves into any form—where they find members proof against direct bribery or gifts of offices, they will endeavor to mislead their minds by specious and false reasoning, to impose upon their unsuspecting honesty by an affectation of zeal for the public good; they will form juntos, and hold out-door meetings; they will operate upon the good nature of their opponents, by a thousand little attentions, and teize them into compliance by the earnestness of solicitation. Those who are acquainted with the manner of conducting business in public assemblies, know how prevalent art and address are in carrying a measure, even over men of the best intentions, and of good understanding. The firmest security against this kind of improper and dangerous influence, as well as all other, is a strong and numerous representation: in such a house of assembly, so great a number must be gained over, before the private views of individuals could be gratified that there could be scarce a hope of success. But in the foederal assembly, seventeen men are all that is necessary to pass a law. It is probable, it will seldom happen that more than twenty-five will be requisite to form a majority, when it is considered what a number of places of honor and emolument will be in the gift of the executive, the powerful influence that great and designing men have over the honest and unsuspecting, by their art and address, their soothing manners and civilities, and their cringing flattery, joined with their affected patriotism; when these different species of influence are combined, it is scarcely to be hoped that a legislature, composed of so small a number, as the one proposed by the new constitution, will long resist their force.

A farther objection against the feebleness of the representation is, that it will not possess the confidence of the people. The execution of the laws in a free government must rest on this confidence, and this must be founded on the good opinion they entertain of the framers of the laws. Every government must be supported, either by the people having such an attachment to it, as to be ready, when called upon, to support it, or by a force at the command of the government, to compel obedience. The latter mode destroys every idea of a free government; for the same force that may be employed to compel obedience to good laws, might, and probably would be used to wrest from the people their constitutional liberties.—Whether it is practicable to have a representation for the whole union sufficiently numerous to obtain that confidence which is necessary for the purpose of internal taxation, and other powers to which this proposed government extends, is an important question. I am clearly of opinion, it is not, and therefore I have stated this in my first number, as one of the reasons against going into an entire consolidation of the states—one of the most capital errors in the system, is that of extending the powers of the foederal government to objects to which it is not adequate, which it cannot exercise without endangering public liberty, and which it is not necessary they should possess, in order to preserve the union and manage our national concerns: of this, however, I shall treat more fully in some future paper—But, however this may be, certain it is, that the representation in the legislature is not so formed as to give reasonable ground for public trust. . . .

VIII
January 10, 1788

The next powers vested by this constitution in the general government, which we shall consider, are those, which authorise them to "borrow money on the credit of the United States, and to raise and support armies." I take these two together and connect them with the power to lay and collect taxes, duties, imposts and excises, because their extent, and the danger that will arise from the exercise of these powers, cannot be fully understood, unless they are viewed in relation to each other.

The power to borrow money is general and unlimited, and the clause so often before referred to, authorises the passing any laws proper and necessary to carry this into execution. Under this authority, the Congress may mortgage any or all the revenues of the union, as a fund to loan money upon, and it is probably, in this way, they may borrow of foreign nations, a principal sum, the interest of which will be equal to the annual revenues of the country.—By this means, they may create a national debt, so large, as to exceed the ability of the country ever to sink. I can scarcely contemplate a greater calamity that could befal this country, than to be loaded with a debt exceeding their ability ever to discharge.

If this be a just remark, it is unwise and improvident to vest in the general government a power to borrow at discretion, without any limitation or restriction.

It may possibly happen that the safety and welfare of the country may require, that money be borrowed, and it is proper when such a necessity arises that the power should be exercised by the general government.—But it certainly ought never to be exercised, but on the most urgent occasions, and then we should not borrow of foreigners if we could possibly avoid it.

The constitution should therefore have so restricted, the exercise of this power as to have rendered it very difficult for the government to practise it. The present confederation requires the assent of nine states to exercise this, and a number of the other important powers of the confederacy—and it would certainly have been a wise provision in this constitution, to have made it necessary that two thirds of the members should assent to borrowing money—when the necessity was indispensible, this assent would always be given, and in no other cause ought it to be.

The power to raise armies, is indefinite and unlimited, and authorises the raising forces, as well in peace as in war. Whether the clause which impowers the Congress to pass all laws which are proper and necessary, to carry this into execution, will not authorise them to impress men for the army, is a question well worthy consideration? If the general legislature deem it for the general welfare to raise a body of troops, and they cannot be procured by voluntary enlistments, it seems evident, that it will be proper and necessary to effect it, that men be impressed from the militia to make up the deficiency.

These powers taken in connection, amount to this: that the general government have unlimited authority and controul over all the wealth and all the force of the union. The advocates for this scheme, would favor the world with a new discovery, if they would shew, what kind of freedom or independency is left to the state governments, when they cannot command any part of the property or of the force of the country, but at the will of the Congress. It seems to me as absurd, as it would be to say, that I was free and independent, when I had conveyed all my property to another, and was tenant to will to him, and had beside, given an indenture of myself to serve him during life.—The power to keep up standing armies in time of peace, has been justly objected, to this system, as dangerous and improvident. The advocates who have wrote in its favor, have some of them ridiculed the objection, as though it originated in the distempered brain of its opponents, and others have taken pains to shew, that it is a power that was proper to be granted to the rulers in this constitution. That you may be enabled to form a just opinion on this subject, I shall first make some remarks, tending to prove, that this power ought to be restricted, and then animadvert on the arguments which have been adduced to justify it.

I take it for granted, as an axiom in politic, that the people should never authorise their rulers to do any thing, which if done, would operate to their injury.

It seems equally clear, that in a case where a power, if given and exercised, will generally produce evil to the community, and seldom good—and which, experience has proved, has most frequently been exercised to the great injury, and very often to the total destruction of the government; in such a case, I say, this power, if given at all, should if possible be so restricted, as to prevent the ill effect of its operation.

Let us then enquire, whether standing armies in time of peace, would be ever beneficial to our country—or if in some extraordinary cases, they might be necessary; whether it is not true, that they have generally proved a scourge to a country, and destructive of their liberty.

I shall not take up much of your time in proving a point, in which the friends of liberty, in all countries, have so universally agreed. The following extract from Mr. Pultney's speech, delivered in the house of commons of Great-Britain, on a motion for reducing the army, is so full to the point, and so much better than any thing I can say, that I shall be excused for inserting it. He says, "I have always been, and always shall be against a standing army of any kind; to me it is a terrible thing, whether under that of a parliamentary, or any other designation; a standing army is still a standing army by whatever name it is called; they are a body of men distinct from the body of the people; they are governed by different laws, and blind obedience, and an entire submission to the orders of their commanding officer, is their only principle; the nations around us, sir, are already enslaved, and have been enslaved by those very means; by means of their standing armies they have every one lost their liberties; it is indeed impossible that the liberties of the people in any country can be preserved where a numerous standing army is kept up. Shall we then take our measures from the example of our neighbours? No, sir, on the contrary, from their misfortunes we ought to learn to avoid those rocks upon which they have split.

"It signifies nothing to tell me that our army is commanded by such gentlemen as cannot be supposed to join in any measures for enslaving their country; it may be so; I have a very good opinion of many gentlemen now in the army; I believe they would not join in any such measures; but their lives are uncertain, nor can we be sure how long they will be kept in command, they may all be dismissed in a moment, and proper tools of power put in their room. Besides, sir, we know the passions of men, we know how dangerous it is to trust the best of men with too much power. Where was a braver army than that under Jul. Caesar? Where was there ever an army that had served their country more faithfully? That army was commanded generally by the best citizens of Rome, by men of great fortune and figure in their country, yet that army enslaved their country. The affections of the soldiers towards their country, the honor and integrity of the under officers, are not to be depended on. By the military law the administration of justice is so quick, and the punishment so severe, that neither the officer nor soldier dare dispute the orders of his supreme commander; he must not consult his own inclination. If an officer were commanded to pull his own father out of this house, he must do it; he dares not disobey; immediate death would be the sure consequence of the least grumbling: and if an officer were sent into the court of request, accompanied by a body of musketeers with screwed bayonets, and with orders to tell us what we ought to do, and how we were to vote: I know what would be the duty of this house; I know it would be our duty to order the officer to be hanged at the door of the lobby; but I doubt, sir, I doubt much, if such a spirit could be found in the house, or in any house of commons that will ever be in England.

"Sir, I talk not of imaginary things? I talk of what has happened to an English house of commons, from an English army; not only from an English army, but an army that was raised by that very house of commons, an army that was paid by them; therefore do not let us vainly imagine, that an army, raised and maintained by authority of parliament, will always be so submissive to them. If an army be so numerous as to have it in their power to overawe the parliament, they will be submissive as long as the parliament does nothing to disoblige their favourite general; but when that case happens, I am afraid, that in place of the parliament's dismissing the army, the army will dismiss the parliament."—If this great man's reasoning be just, it follows, that keeping up a standing army, would be in the highest degree dangerous to the liberty and happiness of the community—and if so, the general government ought not to have authority to do it; for no government should be empowered to do that which if done, would tend to destroy public liberty.

Brutus.

IX
January 17, 1788

The design of civil government is to protect the rights and promote the happiness of the people.

For this end, rulers are invested with powers. But we cannot from hence justly infer that these powers should be unlimited. There are certain rights which mankind possess, over which government ought not to have any controul, because it is not necessary they should, in order to attain the end of its institution. There are certain things which rulers should be absolutely prohibited from doing, because, if they should do them, they would work an injury, not a benefit to the people. Upon the same principles of reasoning, if the exercise of a power, is found generally or in most cases to operate to the injury of the community, the legislature should be restricted in the exercise of that power, so as to guard, as much as possible, against the danger. These principles seem to be the evident dictates of common sense, and what ought to give sanction to them in the minds of every American, they are the great principles of the late revolution, and those which governed the framers of all our state constitutions. Hence we find, that all the state constitutions, contain either formal bills of rights, which set bounds to the powers of the legislature, or have restrictions for the same purpose in the body of the constitutions. Some of our new political Doctors, indeed, reject the idea of the necessity, or propriety of such restrictions in any elective government, but especially in the general one.

But it is evident, that the framers of this new system were of a contrary opinion, because they have prohibited the general government, the exercise of some powers, and restricted them in that of others.

I shall adduce two instances, which will serve to illustrate my meaning, as well as to confirm the truth of the preceeding remark.

In the 9th section, it is declared, "no bill of attainder shall be passed." This clause takes from the legislature all power to declare a particular person guilty of a crime by law. It is proper the legislature should be deprived of the exercise of this power, because it seldom is exercised to the benefit of the community, but generally to its injury.

In the same section it is provided, that "the privilege of the writ of habeas corpus shall not be suspended, unless when in cases of rebellion and invasion, the public safety may require it." This clause limits the power of the legislature to deprive a citizen of the right of habeas corpus, to particular cases viz. those of rebellion and invasion; the reason is plain, because in no other cases can this power be exercised for the general good.

Let us apply these remarks to the case of standing armies in times of peace. If they generally prove the destruction of the happiness and liberty of the people, the legislature ought not to have power to keep them up, or if they had, this power should be so restricted, as to secure the people against the danger arising from the exercise of it.

That standing armies are dangerous to the liberties of a people was proved in my last number—If it was necessary, the truth of the position might be confirmed by the history of almost every nation in the world. A cloud of the most illustrious patriots of every age and country, where freedom has been enjoyed, might be adduced as witnesses in support of the sentiment. But I presume it would be useless, to enter into a laboured argument, to prove to the people of America, a position, which has so long and so generally been received by them as a kind of axiom.

Some of the advocates for this new system controvert this sentiment, as they do almost every other that has been maintained by the best writers on free goverment.—Others, though they will not expressly deny, that standing armies in times of peace are dangerous, yet join with these in maintaining, that it is proper the general government should be vested with the power to do it. I shall now proceed to examine the arguments they adduce in support of their opinions.

A writer, in favor of this system, treats this objection as a ridiculous one. He supposes it would be as proper to provide against the introduction of Turkish janizaries, or against making the Alcoran a rule of faith.

From the positive, and dogmatic manner, in which this author delivers his opinions, and answers objections made to his sentiments—one would conclude, that he was some pedantic pedagogue who had been accustomed to deliver his dogmas to pupils, who always placed implicit faith in what he delivered.

But, why is this provision so ridiculous? because, says this author, it is unnecessary. But, why is it unnecessary? "because, the principles and habits, as well as the power of the Americans are directly opposed to standing armies; and there is as little necessity to guard against them by positive constitutions, as to prohibit the establishment of the Mahometan religion." It is admitted then, that a standing army in time of peace, is an evil. I ask then, why should this government be authorised to do evil? If the principles and habits of the people of this country are opposed to standing armies in time of peace, if they do not contribute to the public good, but would endanger the public liberty and happiness, why should the government be vested with the power? No reason can be given, why rulers should be authorised to do, what, if done, would oppose the principles and habits of the people, and endanger the public safety, but there is every reason in the world, that they should be prohibited from the exercise of such a power. But this author supposes, that no danger is to be apprehended from the exercise of this power, because, if armies are kept up, it will be by the people themselves, and therefore, to provide against it, would be as absurd as for a man to "pass a law in his family, that no troops should be quartered in his family by his consent." This reasoning supposes, that the general government is to be exercised by the people of America themselves—But such an idea is groundless and absurd. There is surely a distinction between the people and their rulers, even when the latter are representatives of the former.—They certainly are not identically the same, and it cannot be disputed, but it may and often does happen, that they do not possess the same sentiments or pursue the same interests. I think I have shewn, that as this government is constituted, there is little reason to expect, that the interest of the people and their rulers will be the same.

Besides, if the habits and sentiments of the people of America are to be relied upon, as the sole security against the encroachment of their rulers, all restrictions in constitutions are unnecessary; nothing more is requisite, than to declare who shall be authorized to exercise the powers of government, and about this we need not be very careful—for the habits and principles of the people will oppose every abuse of power. This I suppose to be the sentiments of this author, as it seems to be of many of the advocates of this new system. An opinion like this, is as directly opposed to the principles and habits of the people of America, as it is to the sentiments of every writer of reputation on the science of government, and repugnant to the principles of reason and common sense.

The idea that there is no danger of the establishment of a standing army, under the new constitution, is without foundation.

It is a well known fact, that a number of those who had an agency in producing this system, and many of those who it is probable will have a principal share in the administration of the government under it, if it is adopted, are avowedly in favour of standing armies. It is a language common among them, "That no people can be kept in order, unless the government have an army to awe them into obedience; it is necessary to support the dignity of government, to have a military establishment." And there will not be wanting a variety of plausible reason to justify the raising one, drawn from the danger we are in from the Indians on our frontiers, or from the European provinces in our neighbourhood. If to this we add, that an army will afford a decent support, and agreeable employment to the young men of many families, who are too indolent to follow occupations that will require care and industry, and too poor to live without doing any business we can have little reason to doubt, but that we shall have a large standing army, as soon as this government can find money to pay them, and perhaps sooner.

A writer, who is the boast of the advocates of this new constitution, has taken great pains to shew, that this power was proper and necessary to be vested in the general government.

He sets out with calling in question the candour and integrity of those who advance the objection, and with insinuating, that it is their intention to mislead the people, by alarming their passions, rather than to convince them by arguments addressed to their understandings.

The man who reproves another for a fault, should be careful that he himself be not guilty of it. How far this writer has manifested a spirit of candour, and has pursued fair reasoning on this subject, the impartial public will judge, when his arguments pass before them in review.

He first attempts to shew, that this objection is futile and disingenuous, because the power to keep up standing armies, in time of peace, is vested, under the present government, in the legislature of every state in the union, except two. Now this is so far from being true, that it is expressly declared, by the present articles of confederation, that no body of forces "shall be kept up by any state, in time of peace, except such number only, as in the judgment of the United States in Congress assembled, shall be deemed requisite to garrison the forts necessary for the defence of such state." Now, was it candid and ingenuous to endeavour to persuade the public, that the general government had no other power than your own legislature have on this head; when the truth is, your legislature have no authority to raise and keep up any forces?

He next tells us, that the power given by this constitution, on this head, is similar to that which Congress possess under the present confederation. As little ingenuity is manifested in this representation as in that of the former.

I shall not undertake to enquire whether or not Congress are vested with a power to keep up a standing army in time of peace; it has been a subject warmly debated in Congress, more than once, since the peace; and one of the most respectable states in the union, were so fully convinced that they had no such power, that they expressly instructed their delegates to enter a solemn protest against it on the journals of Congress, should they attempt to exercise it.

But should it be admitted that they have the power, there is such a striking dissimilarity between the restrictions under which the present Congress can exercise it, and that of the proposed government, that the comparison will serve rather to shew the impropriety of vesting the proposed government with the power, than of justifying it.

It is acknowledged by this writer, that the powers of Congress, under the present confederation, amount to little more than that of recommending. If they determine to raise troops, they are obliged to effect it through the authority of the state legislatures. This will, in the first instance, be a most powerful restraint upon them, against ordering troops to be raised. But if they should vote an army, contrary to the opinion and wishes of the people, the legislatures of the respective states would not raise them. Besides, the present Congress hold their places at the will and pleasure of the legislatures of the states who send them, and no troops can be raised, but by the assent of nine states out of the thirteen. Compare the power proposed to be lodged in the legislature on this head, under this constitution, with that vested in the present Congress, and every person of the least discernment, whose understanding is not totally blinded by prejudice, will perceive, that they bear no analogy to each other. Under the present confederation, the representatives of nine states, out of thirteen, must assent to the raising of troops, or they cannot be levied: under the proposed constitution, a less number than the representatives of two states, in the house of representatives, and the representatives of three states and an half in the senate, with the assent of the president, may raise any number of troops they please. The present Congress are restrained from an undue exercise of this power, from this consideration, they know [that] the state legislatures, through whose authority it must be carried into effect, would not comply with the requisition for the purpose, if it was evidently opposed to the public good: the proposed constitution authorizes the legislature to carry their determinations into execution, without the intervention of any other body between them and the people. The Congress under the present form are amenable to, and removable by, the legislatures of the respective states, and are chosen for one year only: the proposed constitution does not make the members of the legislature accountable to, or removeable by the state legislatures at all; and they are chosen, the one house for six, and the other for two years; and cannot be removed until their time of service is expired, let them conduct ever so badly.—The public will judge, from the above comparison, how just a claim this writer has to that candour he affects to possess. In the mean time, to convince him, and the advocates for this system, that I possess some share of candor, I pledge myself to give up all opposition to it, on the head of standing armies, if the power to raise them be restricted as it is in the present confederation; and I believe I may safely answer, not only for myself, but for all who make the objection, that they will be satisfied with less.

Brutus.

XI
January 31, 1788

The nature and extent of the judicial power of the United States, proposed to be granted by this constitution, claims our particular attention. . . .

Much has been said and written upon the subject of this new system on both sides, but I have not met with any writer, who has discussed the judicial powers with any degree of accuracy. And yet it is obvious, that we can form but very imperfect ideas of the manner in which this government will work, or the effect it will have in changing the internal police and mode of distributing justice at present subsisting in the respective states, without a thorough investigation of the powers of the judiciary and of the manner in which they will operate. This government is a complete system, not only for making, but for executing laws. And the courts of law, which will be constituted by it, are not only to decide upon the constitution and the laws made in pursuance of it, but by officers subordinate to them to execute all their decisions. The real effect of this system of government, will therefore be brought home to the feelings of the people, through the medium of the judicial power. It is, moreover, of great importance, to examine with care the nature and extent of the judicial power, because those who are to be vested with it, are to be placed in a situation altogether unprecedented in a free country. They are to be rendered totally independent, both of the people and the legislature, both with respect to their offices and salaries. No errors they may commit can be corrected by any power above them, if any such power there be, nor can they be removed from office for making ever so many erroneous adjudications.

The only causes for which they can be displaced is, conviction of treason, bribery, and high crimes and misdemeanors.

This part of the plan is so modelled, as to authorise the courts, not only to carry into execution the powers expressly given, but where these are wanting or ambiguously expressed, to supply what is wanting by their own decisions.

That we may be enabled to form a just opinion on this subject, I shall, in considering it,

1st. Examine the nature and extent of the judicial powers—and

2d. Enquire, whether the courts who are to exercise them, are so constituted as to afford reasonable ground of confidence, that they will exercise them for the general good.

With a regard to the nature and extent of the judicial powers, I have to regret my want of capacity to give that full and minute explanation of them that the subject merits. To be able to do this, a man should be possessed of a degree of law knowledge far beyond what I pretend to. A number of hard words and technical phrases are used in this part of the system, about the meaning of which gentlemen learned in the law differ.

Its advocates know how to avail themselves of these phrases. In a number of instances, where objections are made to the powers given to the judicial, they give such an explanation to the technical terms as to avoid them.

Though I am not competent to give a perfect explanation of the powers granted to this department of the government, I shall yet attempt to trace some of the leading features of it, from which I presume it will appear, that they will operate to a total subversion of the state judiciaries, if not, to the legislative authority of the states.

In article 3d, sect. 2d, it is said, "The judicial power shall extend to all cases in law and equity arising under this constitution, the laws of the United States, and treaties made, or which shall be made, under their authority, &c."

The first article to which this power extends, is, all cases in law and equity arising under this constitution.

What latitude of construction this clause should receive, it is not easy to say. At first view, one would suppose, that it meant no more than this, that the courts under the general government should exercise, not only the powers of courts of law, but also that of courts of equity, in the manner in which those powers are usually exercised in the different states. But this cannot be the meaning, because the next clause authorises the courts to take cognizance of all cases in law and equity arising under the laws of the United States; this last article, I conceive, conveys as much power to the general judicial as any of the state courts possess.

The cases arising under the constitution must be different from those arising under the laws, or else the two clauses mean exactly the same thing.

The cases arising under the constitution must include such, as bring into question its meaning, and will require an explanation of the nature and extent of the powers of the different departments under it.

This article, therefore, vests the judicial with a power to resolve all questions that may arise on any case on the construction of the constitution, either in law or in equity.

1st. They are authorised to determine all questions that may arise upon the meaning of the constitution in law. This article vests the courts with authority to give the constitution a legal construction, or to explain it according to the rules laid down for construing a law.—These rules give a certain degree of latitude of explanation. According to this mode of construction, the courts are to give such meaning to the constitution as comports best with the common, and generally received acceptation of the words in which it is expressed, regarding their ordinary and popular use, rather than their grammatical propriety. Where words are dubious, they will be explained by the context. The end of the clause will be attended to, and the words will be understood, as having a view to it; and the words will not be so understood as to bear no meaning or a very absurd one.

2d. The judicial are not only to decide questions arising upon the meaning of the constitution in law, but also in equity.

By this they are empowered, to explain the constitution according to the reasoning spirit of it, without being confined to the words or letter.

"From this method of interpreting laws (says Blackstone) by the reason of them, arises what we call equity;" which is thus defined by Grotius, "the correction of that, wherein the law, by reason of its universality, is deficient["]; for since in laws all cases cannot be foreseen, or expressed, it is necessary, that when the decrees of the law cannot be applied to particular cases, there should some where be a power vested of defining those circumstances, which had they been foreseen the legislator would have expressed; and these are the cases, which according to Grotius, ["]lex non exacte definit, sed arbitrio boni viri permittet."

The same learned author observes, "That equity, thus depending essentially upon each individual case, there can be no established rules and fixed principles of equity laid down, without destroying its very essence, and reducing it to a positive law."

From these remarks, the authority and business of the courts of law, under this clause, may be understood.

They will give the sense of every article of the constitution, that may from time to time come before them. And in their decisions they will not confine themselves to any fixed or established rules, but will determine, according to what appears to them, the reason and spirit of the constitution. The opinions of the supreme court, whatever they may be, will have the force of law; because there is no power provided in the constitution, that can correct their errors, or controul their adjudications. From this court there is no appeal. And I conceive the legislature themselves, cannot set aside a judgment of this court, because they are authorised by the constitution to decide in the last resort. The legislature must be controuled by the constitution, and not the constitution by them. They have therefore no more right to set aside any judgment pronounced upon the construction of the constitution, than they have to take from the president, the chief command of the army and navy, and commit it to some other person. The reason is plain; the judicial and executive derive their authority from the same source, that the legislature do theirs; and therefore in all cases, where the constitution does not make the one responsible to, or controulable by the other, they are altogether independent of each other.

The judicial power will operate to effect, in the most certain, but yet silent and imperceptible manner, what is evidently the tendency of the constitution:—I mean, an entire subversion of the legislative, executive and judicial powers of the individual states. Every adjudication of the supreme court, on any question that may arise upon the nature and extent of the general government, will affect the limits of the state jurisdiction. In proportion as the former enlarge the exercise of their powers, will that of the latter be restricted.

That the judicial power of the United States, will lean strongly in favour of the general government, and will give such an explanation to the constitution, as will favour an extension of its jurisdiction, is very evident from a variety of considerations.

1st. The constitution itself strongly countenances such a mode of construction. Most of the articles in this system, which convey powers of any considerable importance, are conceived in general and indefinite terms, which are either equivocal, ambiguous, or which require long definitions to unfold the extent of their meaning. The two most important powers committed to any government, those of raising money, and of raising and keeping up troops, have already been considered, and shewn to be unlimited by any thing but the discretion of the legislature. The clause which vests the power to pass all laws which are proper and necessary, to carry the powers given into execution, it has been shewn, leaves the legislature at liberty, to do every thing, which in their judgment is best. It is said, I know, that this clause confers no power on the legislature, which they would not have had without it—though I believe this is not the fact, yet, admitting it to be, it implies that the constitution is not to receive an explanation strictly, according to its letter; but more power is implied than is expressed. And this clause, if it is to be considered, as explanatory of the extent of the powers given, rather than giving a new power, is to be understood as declaring, that in construing any of the articles conveying power, the spirit, intent and design of the clause, should be attended to, as well as the words in their common acceptation.

This constitution gives sufficient colour for adopting an equitable construction, if we consider the great end and design it professedly has in view—these appear from its preamble to be, "to form a more perfect union, establish justice, insure domestic tranquility, provide for the common defence, promote the general welfare, and secure the blessings of liberty to ourselves and posterity." The design of this system is here expressed, and it is proper to give such a meaning to the various parts, as will best promote the accomplishment of the end; this idea suggests itself naturally upon reading the preamble, and will countenance the court in giving the several articles such a sense, as will the most effectually promote the ends the constitution had in view—how this manner of explaining the constitution will operate in practice, shall be the subject of future enquiry.

2d. Not only will the constitution justify the courts in inclining to this mode of explaining it, but they will be interested in using this latitude of interpretation. Every body of men invested with office are tenacious of power; they feel interested, and hence it has become a kind of maxim, to hand down their offices, with all its rights and privileges, unimpaired to their successors; the same principle will influence them to extend their power, and increase their rights; this of itself will operate strongly upon the courts to give such a meaning to the constitution in all cases where it can possibly be done, as will enlarge the sphere of their own authority. Every extension of the power of the general legislature, as well as of the judicial powers, will increase the powers of the courts; and the dignity and importance of the judges, will be in proportion to the extent and magnitude of the powers they exercise. I add, it is highly probable the emolument of the judges will be increased, with the increase of the business they will have to transact and its importance. From these considerations the judges will be interested to extend the powers of the courts, and to construe the constitution as much as possible, in such a way as to favour it; and that they will do it, appears probable.

3d. Because they will have precedent to plead, to justify them in it. It is well known, that the courts in England, have by their own authority, extended their jurisdiction far beyond the limits set them in their original institution, and by the laws of the land.

The court of exchequer is a remarkable instance of this. It was originally intended principally to recover the king's debts, and to order the revenues of the crown. It had a common law jurisdiction, which was established merely for the benefit of the king's accomptants. We learn from Blackstone, that the proceedings in this court are grounded on a writ called quo minus, in which the plaintiff suggests, that he is the king's farmer or debtor, and that the defendant hath done him the damage complained of, by which he is less able to pay the king. These suits, by the statute of Rutland, are expressly directed to be confined to such matters as specially concern the king, or his ministers in the exchequer. And by the articuli super cartas, it is enacted, that no common pleas be thenceforth held in the exchequer contrary to the form of the great charter: but now any person may sue in the exchequer. The surmise of being debtor to the king being matter of form, and mere words of course; and the court is open to all the nation.

When the courts will have a precedent before them of a court which extended its jurisdiction in opposition to an act of the legislature, is it not to be expected that they will extend theirs, especially when there is nothing in the constitution expressly against it? and they are authorised to construe its meaning, and are not under any controul?

This power in the judicial, will enable them to mould the government, into almost any shape they please.—The manner in which this may be effected we will hereafter examine.

Brutus.

FROM
XVI
April 10, 1788

. . . The apportionment of members of Senate among the States is not according to numbers, or the importance of the States; but is equal. This, on the plan of a consolidated government, is unequal and improper; but is proper on the system of confederation—on this principle I approve of it. It is indeed the only feature of any importance in the constitution of a confederated government. It was obtained after a vigorous struggle of that part of the Convention who were in favor of preserving the state governments. It is to be regretted, that they were not able to have infused other principles into the plan, to have secured the government of the respective states, and to have marked with sufficient precision the line between them and the general government.

The term for which the senate are to be chosen, is in my judgment too long, and no provision being made for a rotation will, I conceive, be of dangerous consequence.

It is difficult to fix the precise period for which the senate should be chosen. It is a matter of opinion, and our sentiments on the matter must be formed, by attending to certain principles. Some of the duties which are to be performed by the senate, seem evidently to point out the propriety of their term of service being extended beyond the period of that of the assembly. Besides as they are designed to represent the aristocracy of the country, it seems fit they should possess more stability, and so continue a longer period than that branch who represent the democracy. The business of making treaties and some other which it will be proper to commit to the senate, requires that they should have experience, and therefore that they should remain some time in office to acquire it.—But still it is of equal importance that they should not be so long in office as to be likely to forget the hand that formed them, or be insensible of their interests. Men long in office are very apt to feel themselves independent [and] to form and pursue interests separate from those who appointed them. And this is more likely to be the case with the senate, as they will for the most part of the time be absent from the state they represent, and associate with such company as will possess very little of the feelings of the middling class of people. For it is to be remembered that there is to be a *federal city*, and the inhabitants of it will be the great and the mighty of the earth. For these reasons I would shorten the term of their service to four years. Six years is a long period for a man to be absent from his home, it would have a tendency to wean him from his constitutents.

A rotation in the senate, would also in my opinion be of great use. It is probable that senators once chosen for a state will, as the system now stands, continue in office for life. The office will be honorable if not lucrative. The persons who occupy it will probably wish to continue in it, and therefore use all their influence and that of their friends to continue in office.—Their friends will be numerous and powerful, for they will have it in their power to confer great favors; besides it will before long be considered as disgraceful not to be re-elected. It will therefore be considered as a matter of delicacy to the character of the senator not to return him again.—Every body acquainted with public affairs knows how difficult it is to remove from office a person who is [has?] long been in it. It is seldom done except in cases of gross misconduct. It is rare that want of competent ability procures it. To prevent this inconvenience I conceive it would be wise to determine, that a senator should not be eligible after he had served for the period assigned by the constitution for a certain number of years; perhaps three would be sufficient. A farther benefit would be derived from such an arrangement; it would give opportunity to bring forward a greater number of men to serve their country, and would return those, who had served, to their state, and afford them the advantage of becoming better acquainted with the condition and politics of their constituents. It farther appears to me proper, that the legislatures should retain the right which they now hold under the confederation, of recalling their members. It seems an evident dictate of reason, that when a person authorises another to do a piece of business for him, he should retain the power to displace him, when he does not conduct according to his pleasure. This power in the state legislatures, under confederation, has not been exercised under the new system. It may operate much to the public benefit.

These brief remarks are all I shall make on the organization of the senate. The powers with which they are invested will require a more minute investigation.

This body will possess a strange mixture of legislative, executive and judicial powers, which in my opinion will in some cases clash with each other.

1. They are one branch of the legislature, and in this respect will possess equal powers in all cases with the house of representatives; for I consider the clause which gives the house of representatives the right of originating bills for raising a revenue as merely nominal, seeing the senate be authorised to propose or concur with amendments.

2. They are a branch of the executive in the appointment of ambassadors and public ministers, and in the appointment of all other officers, not otherwise provided for; whether the forming of treaties, in which they are joined with the president, appertains to the legislative or the executive part of the government, or to neither, is not material.

3. They are part of the judicial, for they form the court of impeachments.

It has been a long established maxim, that the legislative, executive and judicial departments in government should be kept distinct. It is said, I know, that this cannot be done. And therefore that this maxim is not just, or at least that it should only extend to certain leading features in a government. I admit that this distinction cannot be perfectly preserved. In a due ballanced government, it is perhaps absolutely necessary to give the executive qualified legislative powers, and the legislative or a branch of them judicial powers in the last resort. It may possibly also, in some special cases, be advisable to associate the legislature, or a branch of it, with the executive, in the exercise of acts of great national importance. But still the maxim is a good one, and a separation of these powers should be sought as far as is practicable. I can scarcely imagine that any of the advocates of the system will pretend, that it was necessary to accumulate all these powers in the senate.

There is a propriety in the senate's possessing legislative powers; this is the principal end which should be held in view in their appointment. I need not here repeat what has so often and ably been advanced on the subject of a division of the legislative power into two branches—The arguments in favor of it I think conclusive. But I think it equally evident, that a branch of the legislature should not be invested with the power of appointing officers. This power in the senate is very improperly lodged for a number of reasons—These shall be detailed in a future number.

Brutus.

FROM

The Address and Reasons of Dissent of the Minority of the Convention of Pennsylvania to their Constituents

Pennsylvania Packet and Daily Advertiser
December 18, 1787

The dissenting minority of the Pennsylvania ratifying convention published its objections after failing to secure space for them in the pages of the official journal of the convention.

. . . The election for members of the convention was held at so early a period and the want of information was so great, that some of us did not know of it until after it was over, and we have reason to believe that great numbers of the people of Pennsylvania have not yet had an opportunity of sufficiently examining the proposed constitution.—We apprehend that no change can take place that will affect the internal government or constitution of this commonwealth, unless a majority of the people should evidence a wish for such a change; but on examining the number of votes given for members of the present state convention, we find that of upwards of *seventy thousand* freemen who are intitled to vote in Pennsylvania, the whole convention has been elected by about *thirteen thousand* voters, and though *two thirds* of the members of the convention have thought proper to ratify the proposed constitution, yet those *two thirds* were elected by the votes of only *six thousand and eight hundred* freemen.

In the city of Philadelphia and some of the eastern counties, the junto that took the lead in the business agreed to vote for none but such as would solemnly promise to adopt the system *in toto*, without exercising their judgment. In many of the counties the people did not attend the elections as they had not an opportunity of judging of the plan. Others did not consider themselves bound by the call of a set of men who assembled at the statehouse in Philadelphia, and assumed the name of the legislature of Pennsylvania; and some were prevented from voting by the violence of the party who were determined at all events to force down the measure. To such lengths did the tools of despotism carry their outrage, that in the night of the election for members of convention, in the city of Philadelphia, several of the subscribers (being then in the city to transact your business) were grossly abused, ill-treated and insulted while they were quiet in their lodgings, though they did not interfere, nor had any thing to do with the said election, but as they apprehend, because they were supposed to be adverse to the proposed constitution, and would not tamely surrender those sacred rights, which you had committed to their charge.

The convention met, and the same disposition was soon manifested in considering the proposed constitution, that had been exhibited in every other stage of the business. We were prohibited by an express vote of the convention, from taking any question on the separate articles of the plan, and reduced to the necessity of adopting or rejecting *in toto*.—'Tis true the majority permitted us to debate on each article, but restrained us from proposing amendments.—They also determined not to permit us to enter on the minutes our reasons of dissent against any of the articles, nor even on the final question our reasons of dissent against the whole. Thus situated we entered on the examination of the proposed system of government, and found it to be such as we could not adopt, without, as we conceived, surrendering up your dearest rights. We offered our objections to the convention, and opposed those parts of the plan, which, in our opinion, would be injurious to you, in the best manner we were able; and closed our arguments by offering the following propositions to the convention.

1. The right of conscience shall be held inviolable; and neither the legislative, executive nor judicial powers of the United States shall have authority to alter, abrogate, or infringe any part of the constitution of the several states, which provide for the preservation of liberty in matters of religion.

2. That in controversies respecting property, and in suits be-

tween man and man, trial by jury shall remain as heretofore, as well in the federal courts, as in those of the several states.

3. That in all capital and criminal prosecutions, a man has a right to demand the cause and nature of his accusation, as well in the federal courts, as in those of the several states; to be heard by himself and his counsel; to be confronted with the accusers and witnesses; to call for evidence in his favor, and a speedy trial by an impartial jury of his vicinage, without whose unanimous consent, he cannot be found guilty, nor can he be compelled to give evidence against himself; and that no man be deprived of his liberty, except by the law of the land or the judgment of his peers.

4. That excessive bail ought not to be required, nor excessive fines imposed, nor cruel nor unusual punishments inflicted.

5. That warrants unsupported by evidence, whereby any officer or messenger may be commanded or required to search suspected places, or to seize any person or persons, his or their property, not particularly described, are grievous and oppressive, and shall not be granted either by the magistrates of the federal government or others.

6. That the people have a right to the freedom of speech, of writing and publishing their sentiments, therefore, the freedom of the press shall not be restrained by any law of the United States.

7. That the people have a right to bear arms for the defence of themselves and their own state, or the United States, or for the purpose of killing game; and no law shall be passed for disarming the people or any of them, unless for crimes committed, or real danger of public injury from individuals; and as standing armies in the time of peace are dangerous to liberty, they ought not to be kept up: and that the military shall be kept under strict subordination to and be governed by the civil powers.

8. The inhabitants of the several states shall have liberty to fowl and hunt in seasonable times, on the lands they hold, and on all other lands in the United States not inclosed, and in like manner to fish in all navigable waters, and others not private property, without being restrained therein by any laws to be passed by the legislature of the United States.

9. That no law shall be passed to restrain the legislatures of the several states from enacting laws for imposing taxes, except imposts and duties on goods imported or exported, and that no taxes, except imposts and duties upon goods imported and exported,

and postage on letters shall be levied by the authority of Congress.

10. That the house of representatives be properly increased in number; that elections shall remain free; that the several states shall have power to regulate the elections for senators and representatives, without being controuled either directly or indirectly by any interference on the part of the Congress; and that elections of representatives be annual.

11. That the power of organizing, arming and disciplining the militia (the manner of disciplining the militia to be prescribed by Congress) remain with the individual states, and that Congress shall not have authority to call or march any of the militia out of their own state, without the consent of such state, and for such length of time only as such state shall agree.

That the sovereignty, freedom and independency of the several states shall be retained, and every power, jurisdiction and right which is not by this constitution expressly delegated to the United States in Congress assembled.

12. That the legislative, executive, and judicial powers be kept separate; and to this end that a constitutional council be appointed, to advise and assist the president, who shall be responsible for the advice they give, hereby the senators would be relieved from almost constant attendance; and also that the judges be made completely independent.

13. That no treaty which shall be directly opposed to the existing laws of the United States in Congress assembled, shall be valid until such laws shall be repealed, or made conformable to such treaty; neither shall any treaties be valid which are in contradiction to the constitution of the United States, or the constitutions of the several states.

14. That the judiciary power of the United States shall be confined to cases affecting ambassadors, other public ministers and consuls; to cases of admiralty and maritime jurisdiction; to controversies to which the United States shall be a party; to controversies between two or more states—between a state and citizens of different states—between citizens claiming lands under grants of different states; and between a state or the citizen thereof and foreign states, and in criminal cases, to such only as are expressly enumerated in the constitution, and that the United States in Congress assembled, shall not have power to enact laws, which shall alter the laws of descents and distribution of the effects of deceased

persons, the titles of lands or goods, or the regulation of contracts in the individual states.

After reading these propositions, we declared our willingness to agree to the plan, provided it was so amended as to meet these propositions, or something similar to them: and finally moved the convention to adjourn, to give the people of Pennsylvania time to consider the subject, and determine for themselves; but these were all rejected, and the final vote was taken, when our duty to you induced us to vote against the proposed plan, and to decline signing the ratification of the same.

During the discussion we met with many insults, and some personal abuse; we were not even treated with decency, during the sitting of the convention, by the persons in the gallery of the house; however, we flatter ourselves that in contending for the preservation of those invaluable rights you have thought proper to commit to our charge, we acted with a spirit becoming freemen, and being desirous that you might know the principles which actuated our conduct, and being prohibited from inserting our reasons of dissent on the minutes of the convention, we have subjoined them for your consideration, as to you alone we are accountable. It remains with you whether you will think those inestimable privileges, which you have so ably contended for, should be sacrificed at the shrine of despotism, or whether you mean to contend for them with the same spirit that has so often baffled the attempts of an aristocratic faction, to rivet the shackles of slavery on you and your unborn posterity.

Our objections are comprised under three general heads of dissent, viz.

We dissent, first, because it is the opinion of the most celebrated writers on government, and confirmed by uniform experience, that a very extensive territory cannot be governed on the principles of freedom, otherwise than by a confederation of republics, possessing all the powers of internal government; but united in the management of their general, and foreign concerns.

If any doubt could have been entertained of the truth of the foregoing principle, it has been fully removed by the concession of *Mr. Wilson*, one of majority on this question; and who was one of the deputies in the late general convention. In justice to him, we will give his own words; they are as follows, viz. "The extent of country for which the new constitution was required, produced another difficulty in the business of the federal convention. It is the opinion of some celebrated writers, that to a small territory, the democratical; to a middling territory (as Montesquieu has termed it) the monarchial; and to an extensive territory, the despotic form of government is best adapted. Regarding then the wide and almost unbounded jurisdiction of the United States, at first view, the hand of despotism seemed necessary to controul, connect, and protect it; and hence the chief embarrassment rose. For, we know that, altho' our constituents would chearfully submit to the legislative restraints of a free government, they would spurn at every attempt to shackle them with despotic power."—And again in another part of his speech he continues.—"Is it probable that the dissolution of the state governments, and the establishment of one *consolidated empire* would be eligible in its nature, and satisfactory to the people in its administration? I think not, as I have given reasons to shew that so extensive a territory could not be governed, connected, and preserved, but by the *supremacy of despotic power.* All the exertions of the most potent emperors of Rome were not capable of keeping that empire together, which in extent was far inferior to the dominion of America."

We dissent, secondly, because the powers vested in Congress by this constitution, must necessarily annihilate and absorb the legislative, executive, and judicial powers of the several states, and produce from their ruins one consolidated government, which from the nature of things will be *an iron handed despotism*, as nothing short of the supremacy of despotic sway could connect and govern these United States under one government.

As the truth of this position is of such decisive importance, it ought to be fully investigated, and if it is founded to be clearly ascertained; for, should it be demonstrated, that the powers vested by this constitution in Congress, will have such an effect as necessarily to produce one consolidated government, the question then will be reduced to this short issue, viz. whether satiated with the blessings of liberty; whether repenting of the folly of so recently asserting their unalienable rights, against foreign despots at the expence of so much blood and treasure, and such painful and arduous struggles, the people of America are now willing to resign every privilege of freemen, and submit to the dominion of an absolute government, that will embrace all America in one chain of despotism; or whether they will with virtuous indignation, spurn at the shackles prepared for them, and confirm their liberties by a conduct becoming freemen.

That the new government will not be a confederacy of states, as it ought, but one consolidated government, founded upon the destruction of the several governments of the states, we shall now shew.

The powers of Congress under the new constitution, are complete and unlimited over the *purse* and the *sword*, and are perfectly independent of, and supreme over, the state governments; whose intervention in these great points is entirely destroyed. By virtue of their power of taxation. Congress may command the whole, or any part of the property of the people. They may impose what imposts upon commerce; they may impose what land taxes, poll taxes, excises, duties on all written instruments, and duties on every other article that they may judge proper; in short, every species of taxation, whether of an external or internal nature is comprised in section the 8th, of article the 1st, viz. "The Congress shall have power to lay and collect taxes, duties, imposts, and excises, to pay the debts, and provide for the common defence and general welfare of the United States."

As there is no one article of taxation reserved to the state governments, the Congress may monopolise every source of revenue, and thus indirectly demolish the state governments, for without funds they could not exist, the taxes, duties and excises imposed by Congress may be so high as to render it impracticable to levy further sums on the same articles; but whether this should be the case or not, if the state governments should presume to impose taxes, duties or excises, on the same articles with Congress, the latter may abrogate and repeal the laws whereby they are imposed, upon the allegation that they interfere with the due collection of their taxes, duties or excises, by virtue of the following clause. Part of section 8th, article 1st. viz. "To make all laws which shall be necessary and proper for carrying into execution the foregoing powers, and all other powers vested by this constitution in the government of the United States, or in any department or officer thereof."

The Congress might gloss over this conduct by construing every purpose for which the state legislatures now lay taxes, to be for the *"general welfare,"* and therefore as of their ju[ris]diction.

And the supremacy of the laws of the United States is established by article 6th, viz. "That this constitution and the laws of the United States, which shall be made in pursuance thereof, and *all treaties* made, or which shall be made, under the authority of the United States, shall be the *supreme law* of the *land;* and *the judges in every state shall be bound thereby; any thing in the constitution or laws of any state to the contrary notwithstanding.*" It has been alledged that the words "pursuant to the constitution," are a restriction upon the authority of Congress, but when it is considered that by other sections they are invested with every efficient power of government, and which may be exercised to the absolute destruction of the state governments, without any violation of even the forms of the constitution, this seeming restriction, as well as every other restriction in it, appears to us to be nugatory and delusive; and only introduced as a blind upon the real nature of the government. In our opinion, "pursuant to the constitution," will be co-extensive with the *will* and *pleasure* of Congress, which, indeed, will be the only limitation of their powers.

We apprehend that two co-ordinate sovereignties would be a solecism in politics. That therefore as there is no line of distinction drawn between the general, and state governments; as the sphere of their jurisdiction is undefined, it would be contrary to the nature of things, that both should exist together, one or the other would necessarily triumph in the fullness of dominion. However the contest could not be of long continuance, as the state governments are divested of every means of defence, and will be obliged by "the supreme law of the land" *to yield at discretion.*

It has been objected to this total destruction of the state governments, that the existence of their legislatures is made essential to the organization of Congress; that they must assemble for the appointment of the senators and president general of the United States. True, the state legislatures may be continued for some years, as boards of appointment, merely, after they are divested of every other function, but the framers of the constitution foreseeing that the people will soon be disgusted with this solemn mockery of a government without power and usefulness, have made a provision for relieving them from the imposition, in section 4th, of article 1st, viz. "The times, places, and manner of holding elections for senators and representatives, shall be prescribed in each state by the legislature thereof; *but the Congress may at any time, by law make or alter such regulations; except as to the place of chusing senators.*"

As Congress have the controul over the time of the appointment of the president general, of the senators and of the representatives of the United States, they may prolong their existence in office, for life, by postponing the time of their election and appointment, from period to period, under various pretences, such as an apprehension of invasion, the factious disposition of the people, or any other plausible pretence that the occasion may suggest; and having thus obtained life-estates in the government, they may fill up the vacancies themselves, by their controul over the mode of appointment; with this exception in regard to the senators, that as the place of appointment for them, must, by the constitution, be in the particular state, they may depute some body in the respective states, to fill up the vacancies in the senate, occasioned by death, until they can venture to assume it themselves. In this manner, may the only restriction in this clause be evaded. By virtue of the foregoing section, when the spirit of the people shall be gradually broken; when the general government shall be firmly established, and when a numerous standing army shall render opposition vain, the Congress may compleat the system of despotism, in renouncing all dependance on the people, by continuing themselves, and children in the government.

The celebrated *Montesquieu*, in his Spirit of Laws, vol. 1, page 12th, says, "That in a democracy there can be no exercise of sovereignty, but by the suffrages of the people, which are their will; now the sovereigns will is the sovereign himself; the laws therefore, which establish the right of suffrage, are fundamental to this government. In fact, it is as important to regulate in a republic in what manner, by whom, and concerning what suffrages are to be given, as it is in a monarchy to know who is the prince, and after what manner he ought to govern." The *time, mode* and *place* of the election of representatives, senators and president general of the United States, ought not to be under the controul of Congress, but fundamentally ascertained and established.

The new constitution, consistently with the plan of consolidation, contains no reservation of the rights and privileges of the state governments, which was made in the confederation of the year 1778, by article the 2d, viz. "That each state retains its sovereignty, freedom and independence, and every power, jurisdiction and right, which is not by this confederation expressly delegated to the United States in Congress assembled."

The legislative power vested in Congress by the foregoing recited sections is so unlimited in its nature; may be so comprehensive and boundless [in] its exercise, that this alone would be amply sufficient to annihilate the state governments, and swallow them up in the grand vortex of general empire.

The judicial powers vested in Congress are also so various and extensive, that by legal ingenuity they may be extended to every case, and thus absorb the state judiciaries, and when we consider the decisive influence that a general judiciary would have over the civil polity of the several states, we do not hesitate to pronounce that this power, unaided by the legislative, would effect a consolidation of the states under one government.

The powers of a court of equity, vested by this constitution, in the tribunals of Congress; powers which do not exist in Pennsylvania, unless so far as they can be incorporated with jury trial, would, in this state, greatly contribute to this event. The rich and wealthy suitors would eagerly lay hold of the infinite mazes, perplexities and delays, which a court of chancery, with the appellate powers of the supreme court in fact as well as law would furnish him with, and thus the poor man being plunged in the bottomless pit of legal discussion, would drop his demand in despair.

In short, consolidation pervades the whole constitution. It begins with an annunciation that such was the intention. The main pillars of the fabric correspond with it, and the concluding paragraph is a confirmation of it. The preamble begins with the words, "We the people of the United States," which is the style of a compact between individuals entering into a state of society, and not that of a confederation of states. The other features of consolidation, we have before noticed.

Thus we have fully established the position, that the powers vested by this constitution in Congress, will effect a consolidation of the states under one government, which even the advocates of this constitution admit, could not be done without the sacrifice of all liberty. . . .

Agrippa

Agrippa's letters, generally attributed to James Winthrop, are addressed to the interests and prejudices of the people of Massachusetts. They appeared in *The Massachusetts Gazette* between November 1787 and January 1788. Winthrop was librarian of Harvard College in 1770; Register of Probate in Middlesex County in 1787; later, in 1791, Judge of Common Pleas.

The name Agrippa has popular, anti-tyranny connotations. Agrippa appears as a minor conspirator against Caesar.

IV
December 3, 1787

To the People.

Having considered some of the principal advantages of the happy form of government under which it is our peculiar good fortune to live, we find by experience, that it is the best calculated of any form hitherto invented, to secure to us the rights of our persons and of our property, and that the general circumstances of the people shew an advanced state of improvement never before known. We have found the shock given by the war in a great measure obliterated, and the publick debt contracted at that time to be considerably reduced in the nominal sum. The Congress lands are fully adequate to the redemption of the principal of their debt, and are selling and populating very fast. The lands of this state, at the west, are, at the moderate price of eighteen pence an acre, worth near half a million pounds in our money. They ought, therefore, to be sold as quick as possible. An application was made lately for a large tract at that price, and continual applications are made for other lands in the eastern part of the state. Our resources are daily augmenting.

We find, then, that after the experience of near two centuries our separate governments are in full vigour. They discover, for all the purposes of internal regulation, every symptom of strength, and none of decay. The new system is, therefore, for such purposes, useless and burdensome.

Let us now consider how far it is practicable consistent with the happiness of the people and their freedom. It is the opinion of the ablest writers on the subject, that no extensive empire can be governed upon republican principles, and that such a government will degenerate to a despotism, unless it be made up of a confederacy of smaller states, each having the full powers of internal regulation. This is precisely the principle which has hitherto preserved our freedom. No instance can be found of any free government of considerable extent which has been supported upon any other plan. Large and consolidated empires may indeed dazzle the eyes of a distant spectator with their splendour, but if examined more nearly are always found to be full of misery. The reason is obvious. In large states the same principles of legislation will not apply to all the parts. The inhabitants of warmer climates are more dissolute in their manners, and less industrious, than in colder countries. A degree of severity is, therefore, necessary with one which would cramp the spirit of the other. We accordingly find that the very great empires have always been despotick. They have indeed tried to remedy the inconveniences to which the people were exposed by local regulations; but these contrivances have never answered the end. The laws not being made by the people, who felt the inconveniences, did not suit their circumstances. It is under such tyranny that the Spanish provinces languish, and such would be our misfortune and degradation, if we should submit to have the concerns of the whole empire managed by one legislature. To promote the happiness of the people it is necessary that there should be local laws; and it is necessary that those laws should be made by the representatives of those who are immediately subject to the want of them. By endeavouring to suit both extremes, both are injured.

It is impossible for one code of laws to suit Georgia and Massachusetts. They must, therefore, legislate for themselves. Yet there is, I believe, not one point of legislation that is not surrendered in the proposed plan. Questions of every kind respecting property are determinable in a continental court, and so are all kinds of criminal causes. The continental legislature has, therefore, a right to make rules *in all cases* by which their judicial courts shall proceed and decide causes. No rights are reserved to the citizens. The laws of Congress are in all cases to be the supreme law of the land, and paramount to the constitutions of the individual states. The Congress may institute what modes of trial they please, and no plea drawn from the constitution of any state can avail. This new system is, therefore, a consolidation of all the states into one large mass, however diverse the parts may be of which it is to be composed. The idea of an uncompounded republick, on an average, one thousand miles in length, and eight hundred in breadth, and containing six millions of white inhabitants all reduced to the same standard of morals, or habits, and of laws, is in itself an absurdity, and contrary to the whole experience of mankind. The attempt made by Great-Britain to introduce such a system, struck us with horrour, and when it was proposed by some theorist that we should be represented in parliament, we uniformly declared that one legislature could not represent so many different interests for the purposes of legislation and taxation. This was the leading principle of the revolution, and makes an essential article in our creed. All that part, therefore, of the new system, which relates to the internal government of the states, ought at once to be rejected.

Agrippa.

IX
December 28, 1787

To the People.

We come now to the second and last article of complaint against the present confederation, which is, that Congress has not the sole power to regulate the intercourse between us and foreigners. Such a power extends not only to war and peace, but to trade and naturalization. This last article ought never to be given them; for though most of the states may be willing for certain reasons to receive foreigners as citizens, yet reasons of equal weight may induce other states, differently circumstanced, to keep their blood pure. Pennsylvania has chosen to receive all that would come there. Let any indifferent person judge whether that state in point of morals, education, energy is equal to any of the eastern states; the small state of Rhode-Island only excepted. Pennsylvania in the course of a century has acquired her present extent and population at the expense of religion and good morals. The eastern states have, by keeping separate from the foreign mixtures, acquired, their present greatness in the course of a century and an half, and have preserved their religion and morals. They have also preserved that manly virtue which is equally fitted for rendering them respectable in war, and industrious in peace.

The remaining power for peace and trade might perhaps be safely enough lodged with Congress under some limitations. Three restrictions appear to me to be essentially necessary to preserve the equality of rights to the states, which it is the object of the state governments to secure to each citizen. 1st. It ought not to be in the power of Congress either by treaty or otherwise to alienate part of any state without the consent of the legislature. 2d. They ought not to be able by treaty or other law to give any legal preference to one part above another. 3d. They ought to be restrained from creating any monopolies. Perhaps others may propose different regulations and restrictions. One of these is to be found in the old confederation, and another in the newly proposed plan. The third seems to be equally necessary.

After all that has been said and written on this subject, and on the difficulty of amending our old constitution so as to render it adequate to national purposes, it does not appear that anything more was necessary to be done, than framing two new articles. By one a limited revenue would be given to Congress with a right to collect it, and by the other a limited right to regulate our intercourse with foreign nations. By such an addition we should have preserved to each state its power to defend the rights of the citizens, and the whole empire would be capable of expanding, and receiving additions without altering its former constitution. Congress, at the same time, by the extent of their jurisdiction, and the number of their officers, would have acquired more respectability at home, and a sufficient influence abroad. If any state was in such a case to invade the rights of the Union, the other states would join in defence of those rights, and it would be in the power of Congress to direct the national force to that object. But it is certain that the powers of Congress over the citizens should be small in proportion as the empire is extended; that, in order to preserve the balance, each state may supply by energy what is wanting in numbers. Congress would be able by such a system as we have proposed to regulate trade with foreigners by such duties as should effectually give the preference to the produce and manufactures of our own country. We should then have a friendly intercourse established between the states, upon the principles of mutual interest. A moderate duty upon foreign vessels would give an advantage to our own people, while it would avoid all the [dis]advantages arising from a prohibition, and the consequent deficiency of vessels to transport the produce of the southern states.

Our country is at present upon an average a thousand miles long from north to south, and eight hundred broad from the Mississippi to the Ocean. We have at least six millions of white inhabitants, and the annual increase is about two hundred and fifty thousand souls, exclusive of emigrants from Europe. The greater part of our increase is employed in settling the new lands, while the older settlements are entering largely into manufactures of various kinds. It is probable, that the extraordinary exertions of this state in the way of industry for the present year only, exceed in value five hundred thousand pounds. The new settlements, if all made in the same tract of country, would form a large state annually; and the time seems to be literally accomplished when a nation shall be born in a day. Such an immense country is not only capable of yielding all the produce of Europe, but actually does produce by far the greater part of the raw materials. The restrictions on our trade in Europe, necessarily oblige us to make use of those materials, and the high price of labour operates as an encouragement to mechanical improvements. In this way we daily make rapid advancements towards independence in resources as well as in empire. If we adopt the new system of government we shall by one rash vote lose the fruit of the toil and expense of thirteen years, at the time when the benefits of that toil and expense are rapidly increasing. Though the imposts of Congress on foreign trade may tend to encourage manufactures, the excise and dry tax will destroy all the beneficial effects of the impost, at the same time that they diminish our capital. Be careful then to give only a limited revenue, and the limited power of managing foreign concerns. Once surrender the rights of internal legislation and taxation, and instead of being respected abroad, foreigners will laugh at us, and posterity will lament our folly.

Agrippa.

A Farmer

Generally "The (Maryland) Farmer," to distinguish him from the other writer claiming that vocation. Thought to have been John Francis Mercer, a member of the Constitutional Convention who refused to sign, and an active Anti-Federalist in the state. He was also elected to the Maryland House of Delegates.

The essays appeared in *The Maryland Gazette*, Baltimore, in February, March, and April 1788.

FROM
V
March 25, 1788

. . . Is it then possible that governments of simplicity and equal right, can have been fairly dealt by in theory or practice? The votaries of tyranny and usurpation stand not alone—in bitter opposition; every man of enterprize, of superior talents and fortune, is interested to debase them; their banners have ever been deserted because they never can pay their troops.—The most amiable and sensible of mankind seem to have made a stand in favour of a mixed government founded on the permanent orders and objects of men.—Thither I suspect the American government is now tending. If it must be so—Let it go gently then—with slow and equal steps.—Let each gradation and experiment have a full and fair trial—Let there be no effect without a good, apparent and well considered cause—Let us live all the days of our lives, and as happily as circumstances will permit.—Finally, let moderation be our guide and the influence of manners will conduct us (I hope without injury) to some permanent, fixed establishment, where we may repose a while, unagitated by alteration or revolution—For in sudden and violent changes, how many of the most worthy of our fellow-citizens must get their bones crushed?

I cannot think that any *able and virtuous citizen*, would in his cool and dispationate moments, wish to blend or risque the fundamental rights of men, with any organization of society that the Americans can or will make for fifty years to come.—Let us keep these rights of individuals—these unalienable blessings[—]reserved and separated from every constitution and form—If they are unmingled, the attentive eyes of every citizen will be kept fixed upon them. We shall watch them as a sacred deposit, and we may carry them uninjured and unimpaired through every vicissitude and change, from the government we have left, into some other that may be established on the fixed and solid principles of reason.—Nor can there be, I imagine, any *prudent man*, who would trust the whimsical inventions of the day, with that dangerous weapon *a standing army*, in our present unsettled circumstances—striving to substantiate inefficient and unnatural forms—it would wield us into despotism in a moment, and we have surely had throat-cutting enough in our day.

Throughout the world government by representation, seems only to have been established to disgrace itself and be abolished—its very principle is change, and it sets all system at defiance—it perishes by speedy corruption.—The few representatives can always corrupt themselves by legislative speculations, from the pockets of their numerous constituents—quick rotation, like a succession of terms tenants on a farm, only encreases the evil by rendering them more rapacious. If the executive is changeable, he can never oppose large decided majorities of influential individuals—or enforce on those powerful men, who may render his next election [nugatory] the rigor of *equal law, which is the grand and only object of human society*.—If the executive is to be rendered ineligible for a certain period, he will either *not do his duty*, or he will retire into the unprotected situation of a private individual, with all the sworn animosities of a powerful majority—aristocracy—junto—the cry of the populace, or perhaps the whole combined to pursue him to the grave, or a public execution. The considerate and good, who adorn private life, and such only can be safely trusted in high public station, will never commit themselves to a situation where a consciencious discharge of duty may embitter the evening of life, if not draw down ruin and infamy on themselves and families.—There never was but one man who stepped from the top to the bottom, without breaking his neck, and that was Sylla; and although it is true that whilst he was up, he broke the hearts of the Romans, yet his dying undisturbed in private life, is one of those miracles that must remain forever unexplained. If the aristocracy, or representation of wealth, (the principle of wh[i]ch order is to keep all things as they are, for by confusion they may lose more than they can gain) is also changeable, there then is nothing fixed and permanent in government.—Legislative tyranny commences, and exhibits a perpetual scene of plunder and confusion, fearlessly practised under the sanction of authority and law. It is true that the influence of manners may and will resist for a time; yet that must give way to a general and prevalent corruption—Those who are respectable at home and have permanent [ ] in life, and such only can give stability to government, will not suffer themselves to be mounted up on the wheel of fortune, to be let down again as it turns, the mockery of children and fools.—Where representation has been admitted as a component part of government, it has always proved defective, if not destructive. What then must be the consequence where the whole government is founded on representation? Every American can now answer, it will be at best but—*representation of government*—with us the influence of manners has been great—it is indeed declining fast; but aided by the solidity of the judiciary establishments, and the wisest code of civil laws, that ever mankind were blessed with, it has hitherto supported the forms of society: But the people are now weary of their representatives and their governments.—We may trace the progress.—One candidate, to recommend his pretensions, discloses and descants on the errors of the preceding administration—The people believe him and are deceived—they change men; but measures are still the same, or injured by the sudden and violent alteration of system—At least the next candidate asserts it is so—is again believed, and his constituents again deceived; a general disgust and sullen silence ensue; elections are deserted; government is first despised, and then cordially hated.

There can be no fixed and permanent government that does not rest *on the fixed and permanent orders and objects of mankind.*—Government on *paper* may amuse, but we pay dear for the amusement, the only fixed and permanent *order* with us at present are the YEOMANRY, and they have no power whatever,—unless the right of changing masters at a certain period, and devolving on their changeable representatives their whole political existence—may be called power—The order of GENTRY, with us, is not a fixed and permanent order at all, and if they attempt to erect themselves into one at present, it is usurpation, and they will be pulled down; and yet, in my opinion, such an order is essential to a perfect government, founded on representation.—Every other mode of introducing wealth into power, has proved vicious and abominable.—With us delegates become by selection, themselves a species of subaltern aristocracy—They intrigue with the senates, who by a refined mode of election are a misbegotten, side blow, representation of wealth, and they both form an imperfect aristocracy, on the worst principles on which that order can be admitted into government—and the democratic influence which is thus amalgomated and not divided, but unformed becomes vicious from its impotence.

These defects spring from our attempting to erect republican fabrics on the ruined and imperfect pillars of an old corrupt monarchy—not less absurd, than to expect the limbs to perform the functions of life, after cutting off the head.—The opposition which brought Charles the first to the block, was composed of some of the ablest and most virtuous characters that ever adorned any age or clime—Hampden, Pym, Selden, Sir Harry Vane, Sydney, Marvell and many others.—They pursued their old model—attempted to form a government by representation which was at first steadied and restrained by the best senate in the world, (the English House of Lords)—the two houses soon disagreed, and there being no third power to interpose, the representatives, voted the House of Lords useless—new modelled the government into a single branch, and then began to plunder most unmercifully—At last Cromwell kicked them all out of doors, and after his tyrannical usurpation and death, the nation were very happy to take shelter again under the regal government, and even restored an unworthy family (which they had irritated beyond forgiveness) to the throne.

A Farmer.

(*To be continued.*)

March 28, 1788

(*Continued from our last.*)

After every consideration I can give this subject, I am satisfied, that *government founded on representation*, indispensibly requires, at least an executive for life, whose person must be sacred from impeachment, and only his ostensible ministers responsible—A senate for life, the vacancies to be filled up and the number occasionally encreased but under a limitation, by the executive—the hand that holds the balance must have the power of adding weight and influence to the lightest scale, and of frequently removing turbulent men into an higher and inoffensive situation:—I am inclined to think that an important portion of American opinion leans that way at this moment—My fear is, that our general government may ultimate in an hereditary authority—if not despotism—to avoid the former, great attention should be paid to the important office of Vice-President—at present but little understood:—A Vice-President to succeed on a vacancy prevents those evils which have ruined Poland and all the northern kingdoms—thus we see the King of the Romans has secured Germany from every evil of elective monarchy, and had the golden bull prevented one of the family or kindred of the reigning Emperor from filling the office of the King of Romans, this part of the Germanic constitution would have been perfect, and the house of Austria would never have been enabled to usurp the imperial crown as a patrimony and desolate Europe with her ambitious views; she would have continued in that beggarly condition from which Rodolph of Hapsburg raised it—The American constitution is much better guarded but not by any means completely so.

If this is the best we can hope for—if this is the best reward we can expect for the sons of America slain, and the distresses we shall long continue to feel—is it not incumbent on us to examine minutely all its consequences?—Let us view government by representation in its favorite form—The constitution of England—its uncommon success and length of duration there, has drawn on it very unmerited encomiums from the enlightened Genevan Delolme—the only great political writer who does not seem to hold representation in contempt,—indeed the viewing it through this favorable medium has always animated our hopes, and led many sensible Americans to imagine, this old and universal experiment, to be peculiar to that isle—In pursuing my inquiry into the principles and effects of the British government, I shall first grant that it is a rational system, founded on solid, safe principles—and one of the best governments for the higher ranks of mankind in the world—but then I must insist that it was hardly a government at all, until it became simplified by the introduction and regular formation of the effective administration of responsible ministers, on its present system—which we cannot date higher up, than the appointment of Lord Strafford and others by Charles 1st.*—Moreover I do not know how far the system of bribery introduced by Sir Robert Walpole, and the influence of the numcrous body of public creditors, are not now absolutely necessary to its present stability—and after all, I am not satisfied how such a simplification as would produce a responsibility, can be effected in a government, complicated by so many subordinate and powerful corporations as the American States will be—and yet responsibility must be attained and an easy and certain mode adopted, of changing measures and men without commotion, or liberty will be lost in the attempt—I am confused and bewildered when I arrive at this point of reflection, and despotism meets me at every turn.—There are but *two* modes of governing mankind, by just and equal law, enforced impartially on all ranks of society, or by the sword:—If such laws cannot be obtained, or the attainment is attended with too much difficulty, the sword will supply their place; *et inter arma leges silent. When arms command the laws are disobeyed.* Shall we have patience, with the disorders of our complicated machine? As Alexander dissolved the gordian knot with the sword—so I fear a standing army will simplify the governments of America—I have said that the government of England afforded firm protection of property—it certainly does so, comparatively speaking—yet the history of its frequent revolutions, will discover that even property is insecure there. During the civil wars, in which the Stuarts involved this nation, two-thirds of the property of the kingdom changed masters; and in those between Lancaster and York, and before the firm establishment of the line of Tuder, almost all the old families perished and their property became dissipated:—And yet its protection of property is its favorable side; turn your eyes

* Before that period they were minions and favorites, who by plundering and oppressing the people excited constant commotion, and were seldom changed but with their masters, and by the axe or halter.

to the lower order of citizens, and they are pressed into the earth by taxation and imposition—very rarely will industry enable the husbandman to rear a family—where the sons of agriculture are so poorly rewarded, government must be ulcerated to the heart—the miserable poor who pursue the dictates of nature and religion, in that connection which is destined to sweeten the bitter draught of life, are commonly handed from constable to constable, until their unfortunate birth compels some parish to own them.—The people of England have always and forever will emigrate—The people of England never repair to arms to repel foreign invasion—and they never will unless compelled—to conquer England, it would only seem necessary from past example, to escape their floating defences and land on the island; passing by former invasions and conquests. As late as the year 1745, Prince Charles Edward, at the head of an undisciplined rabble, belonging to some Highland clans attached to his family, marched undisturbed, through the most populous counties into the heart of the kingdom, and the capital containing 200,000 fighting men trembled for its safety at the approach of an unexperienced boy, followed by 4 or 5000 half armed peasants—scarcely a man in the kingdom shouldered a musquet until the danger disappeared, and government owed its safety to the protection of foreign mercenaries, or rather the weakness and irresolution of the assailant—The fact is, the people will never fight (if they can help it) for representatives, taxes and rags.

Let us now contrast this scene with one, where the people *personally* exercise the powers of government—The three small democratic Cantons of Uri, Schuitz and Underwald, broke the chains of their former servitude, and laid the foundation of the Swiss confederacy—they effected the revolution, and in conjunction with the other democratic Cantons and their democratic allies the Grisons, have supported the grand fabric of Helvetic liberty to this day. Every Swiss farmer is by birth a legislator, and he becomes a voluntary soldier to defend his power and his property; their fathers have been so before them for near 500 years, without revolution, and almost without commotion—they have been the secure spectators of the constant and universal destruction of the human species, which the usurpations of the *few* have ever created, and must I fear forever perpetuate:—Whilst all Europe were butchering each other for the love of God, and defending the usurpations of the clergy, under the masque of religion, the malignant evil crept into this sacred asylum of liberty; (but where the government resides in the body of the people, they can never be corrupted by the artifice or the wealth of the *few*) they soon banished the daemon of discord, and Protestant and Papist sat down under the peaceful shade of the same tree, whilst in every surrounding State and kingdom, the son was dragging the father, and brothers, their brothers, to the scaffold, under the sanction of those distinctions:—Thus these happy Helvetians have in peace and security beheld all the rest of Europe become a common slaughterhouse.—A free Swiss acquires from his infancy, a knowledge of the fundamental laws of his country, and the leading principles of their national policy are handed down by tradition from father to son—the first of these is never to trust power to representatives, or a national government. A free Swiss pays no taxes, on the contrary he receives taxes; every male of 16 years, shares near ten shillings sterling annually, which the rich and powerful surrounding monarchies pay for the friendship of these manly farmers. Whenever their societies become too large, as government belongs to the citizens and the citizens are the property of no government, they divide amicably, and each separate part pursues the simple form, recommended by their ancestors and become venerable, by the glorious and happy experience of ages of prosperity—Their frugal establishments are chiefly supported by the pay which the officers of government receive for the services they render individuals. With a country the most unfriendly to industry in the world, they have become in a series of years, passed in uninterrupted but moderate labor, frugality, peace and happiness, the richest nation under the sun. I have seen a computation, by which it appeared, that the interest of the money they have before hand, and that which is due them from the rich nations of Europe, would support themselves and their posterity forever, without farther exertion; and this whilst every other government is actually as much or more in debt than it is worth.

An intelligent author has remarked, that passing from a democratic to an aristocratic Canton of Swisserland, you quit the society of men to contemplate the regular labor of brutes; they are compelled indeed in the aristocratic Cantons to be extremely moderate in their government, and to lay few or no taxes, or they would drive their subjects into the neighboring free States—as it is, they are well cloathed, well fed and taken good care of—The same author remarks, that the line which separates all Swisserland, from the countries around (where men like cattle are the property of their proud Lords and kept chained to the soil) is the line of division between light and darkness—between happiness and horror.

The love of the Switzers for their country is altogether romantic and surpasses the bounds of credibility—those memorable relations authenticated by the common consent of all historians, of their beating on all occasions the flower of the Austrian and French troops (who have invaded them) with numbers so unequal and trifling as scarce to exceed their enemies out-guards; the instances of hundreds of citizens devoting their lives for the safety of their country; of their frequently disdaining life and refusing quarter when overpowered by numbers, have astonished and terrified the neighbouring powers, and seem incomprehensible to a people dispirited by taxes, overloaded with debts and disgusted with government. I cannot omit a striking characteristic, authenticated by Coxe and others, whose authority will not be questioned; they relate that there is a rustic tune familiar in the mountains of Swisserland—it is called the *Rantz des vacques*—it consists of a few simple notes of native wild melody. The French and Dutch governments have been compelled to forbid under very severe penalties, the playing this woodland music, to those Swiss troops, which they hire for a limited time; the well-known notes revive instantly all the fond images, which were impressed on their youthful bosoms, their friends, their parents, their relations and their beloved country, rush into their imaginations in a full tide of affection—no persuasion can detain them, they desert home in regiments, or if retained by force, they pine away in the deepest melancholy—no instance has yet occurred of Swiss troops serving in any part of Europe, who have not returned, with the diligence and anxiety of affectionate children, on the first appearance of danger to their parent country:—The same amor-patriae, the same divine love of their country, universally pervades the bosom of every citizen, who in right of his birth, legislates for himself:—Grosley relates that he saw in Rome a poor fellow (who had travelled through great part of Europe and Asia afoot) declaiming to a crowd with the most passionate zeal, in praise of his own country, boasting of her happiness and prefering San Marino to all the world besides—This democratic republic, is a little beehive of free citizens, who have made a delicious garden of the top of a bleak barren mountain, situated in the midst of the finest and most fruitful plains of Italy, which tyranny has depopulated around them.—Look into the human breast—We love that power, which we exercise ourselves, but we detest that which others exercise over us, be they Representatives, Lords or Kings; and to this source we may trace the abuse, which the Americans bestow on their country and their governments.

But we are told that Swisserland, *should be no example for us*—I am very sorry for it—they are the only, the only part of the human species that sustain the dignity of character, belonging to the divine resemblance we bear,—*they are few in number it is said*—This is not true—they are more numerous than we are—*They cover a small spot of territory*—this is also not true—they possess a large tract of country in the very heart of Europe—but this is not all—The Helvetic confederacy, including the three leagues of the Grisons comprehends one hundred perhaps two hundred, independent governments and States—nor is there any reason from their history or present state to doubt, that the same plan of confederation might not be extended with as lasting and happy effects to one thousand independent governments—But it is also said *they are a poor, frugal* people—As to their poverty that is likewise untrue—they have great sums of money before hand and owe not a six-pence—they indeed are a wise and consequently a frugal people—though they still have great estates and even luxury among them too—But should we despise their poverty or their frugality? We who are so many millions worse than nothing? *But still we are told we must not take example from them—we must take example from Holland and Germany*—They had better at once tell us, that we must desert the worship of God and follow that of the devil.

From the first dawn of light, that broke in upon my reason, I became devoted to governments of simplicity and equal right—The names of heroes, whose blood has bedewed the altars of freedom, vibrate like the shock of electricity, on my frame; and when I read the story of Brutus and Cassius, the most noble and the last of the Romans, tears of admiration gush from my eyes.—Under these impressions which only the grave can erase, I feel unspeakable horror at every step, which removes power and rights, at a greater distance from the body of the people, to whom they belong, and confines them to the hands of *the few*. I have proposed to myself this question: If representatives cannot govern the people—If they abuse the power entrusted to them, shall they devolve this power on a still smaller number, who must be more liable to corruption from the encrease of temptation? Or should they restore it into the hands of the people, from whom they received it? who alone are incorruptible, because the wealth of the few can never bribe the many, against the duty they owe to themselves. If I am told that the people are incapable of governing themselves—I shall answer that they have never been tried in America, except among the native Indians, who are free and happy, and who prove that self-government is the growth of our soil—And I also answer that they are more fit for self-government, than they are at present for any of the safe and solid governments, founded on representation.—When I see all these principles established by the example of the Swiss, who have remained under the simplest of all forms of government for near five hundred years, in uninterrupted tranquility and happiness—whilst every other invention of genius, devise of art, or imposition of force, has been torn up by the roots, with every aggravated circumstance of horror—I can no longer doubt—All the mists of theory and speculation vanish before an experiment like this.

The greatest human discernment, ever concentrated in the mind of one man, was the portion of the celebrated Nicholas Machiavelli—a name loaded with abuse by tyrants, flatterers and the mushrooms of science, because he told the truth; because he was a republican and the friend of mankind in times of usurpation; or because, they have never read or do not understand his works. After every inquiry which the most unbounded information and reflection, with a long experience in high public office afforded, Machiavelli, delivers his deliberate opinion in favour of the body of the people, as the only safe depository of liberty and power—He prefers it to the aristocracy and the Prince; but he does not disgrace the inquiry by mentioning representation. If this was the opinion of Machiavelli, a citizen of Florence, where a numerous populace confined and crowded within the walls of a city, formed the most turbulent republic, that ever disgraced the cause of freedom by cruelty and anarchy—How much more favourably must his decision apply to the yeomanry of America—Landholders and consequently the most independent of mankind, mild by nature, moderate by manners, and persevering in every honest pursuit:—Surely if ever men were worthy of being entrusted with their own rights, the freeholders of America are—*Make them then and their posterity legislators by birth*—I mean not the lowest populace—I mean that class of citizens to whom this country belongs:—Numbers unqualified by property, should have their influence—they should be protected—they might preserve the right of election—But they who hold the property of the soil, are alone entitled to govern it:—to effect this there would need but little change in the present forms—They might all stand—but the laws which pass the legislature before they become binding, should be referred to the different counties and cities—printed reasons drawn by committees, might if necessary, accompany each, together with an annual estimate of public wants and a detail of the expenditures of the former sums granted. Let these laws then be submitted to the free deliberation of the *freeholders* of the counties and cities—the numbers of the yeas and nays be taken on each by the presiding magistrate, and transmitted to the executive, who may then upon comparing the returns from the several counties and corporations, declare what laws are the will of the people. On the appearance of any sudden danger the two houses or indeed a majority of one house, might invest the Executive with that authority, exigency might require for the safety of the republic, until remedy should be provided by law.

The number of representatives might be decreased and an expence saved—this would at one blow destroy all legislative speculations—the influence of demagogues, or oligarchic juntos must then cease—The assemblage of the freeholders, separate in different counties would prevent disturbance—As no new law could be made in them, little confusion could ensue—After some years, or even immediately if confined to future cases—the celebrated law of Geneva might be introduced, and no freeholder admitted to the assembly until he had paid his father's debts. Sumptuary laws, permitting the use, but prohibiting the abuse of wealth, might be interposed to guard the public manners.—The Governor and two members of the senate might constitute a council of censors, to punish offenders against the sumptuary laws and the laws of morality, by a removal from office, and even disfranchisement, if necessary, with an appeal to the people of the county where the offender resided, in the latter case, and to the people of the State in the former.—Seminaries of useful learning, with prefessorships of political and domestic œconomy might be established in every county, discarding the philosophy of the moon and skies, we might descend to teach our citizens what is useful in this world—the principles of free government, illustrated by the history of mankind—the sciences of morality, agriculture, commerce, the management of farms and household affairs—The light would then penetrate, where mental darkness now reigns.—Do these things and in a very few years, the people instead of abusing, would wake up to their knees in blood, to defend their governments.

For some years past this has been the darling object of my life—to which all my views have tended—And I now think that nothing intermediate would be lasting or worthy the pursuit—Whenever I fairly lose sight of this—As soon as I turn my back forever on these dear illusions, which will be as soon as the proposed fœderal government is adopted—I shall turn all my wishes to that social state, whither that government will lead us, and I both hope and expect that with those amendments and guards, which it seems to be the general disposition to provide—it will gradually maturate in a safe and reasonable government.—Until that adoption I speak to my fellow citizens in the words of the proverb—*Do not that by others, which you can do yourselves.*

A Farmer.

A Republican Federalist

These letters were addressed to the Massachusetts ratifying convention. The authorship is not known.

The pseudonym is significant: it claims the title of "Federalist," as a believer in the old Confederation, for the *opposition* to the new Constitution.

V
January 19, 1788

TO THE MEMBERS OF THE CONVENTION OF MASSACHUSETTS.

Honourable Friends, and Fellow Citizens,

The proceedings of the federal Convention, having, as has been shewn, originated in usurpation, and being founded in tyranny, cannot be ratified by the State Convention, *without breaking down the barriers of liberty; trampling on the authority of federal and State Constitutions, and annihilating in America, governments founded in compact.* In this predicament, there appears but two measures which can with safety be adopted by the Convention of this State. One has been hinted at, *an adjournment*, until the sense of Virginia can be known. The great danger in this business is, from *precipitation, not* from *delay*: The *latter* cannot injure whilst the *former* may *irretrievably* ruin us; an adjournment would not only ripen the judgment of our own citizens, but give them an opportunity of benefiting by the opinions of those States, which are attentive to, but not *extravagantly* zealous in this matter. The other measure is, to return the proceedings of the federal Convention to the legislature of this State, to be by them transmitted to Congress, and *amended* agreeably to the articles of Confederation: For the system being *improperly* before the State Convention, and they being *incompetent* to a ratification of it, cannot thereby bind the citizens of Massachusetts. Had the system been in itself unobjectionable, it is evident from what has been said, that the sentiments of the qualified voters *on the necessity* of a revision, *must* have been taken, and two thirds of them *must* have been in favour of it, before a State Convention could be called for amending the Constitution, much more for dissolving the government.

Let us once more particularly attend to the system itself. It begins, "We the People of the United States, in order to form a more perfect union," &c. "do ordain and establish this Constitution for the United States of America"—In other words, *We the people, do hereby publickly declare the violation of the faith which we have solemnly pledged to each other—do give the most unequivocal evidence, that we cannot ourselves, neither can any others, place the least confidence in our most solemn covenants, do effectually put an end in America, to governments founded in compact—do relinquish that security for life, liberty and property, which we had in the Constitutions of these States, and of the Union—do give up governments which we well understood, for a new system which we have no idea of—and we do, by this act of ratification and political suicide, destroy the new system itself, and prepare the way for a despotism, if agreeable to our rulers.* All this we do, for the *honour of having a system of consolidation formed by us the people.* This is not *magnifying*, for such are the facts, and such will be the consequences. Indeed we find *despotism* not only in contemplation of the Pennsylvanians, but openly avowed in their State Convention, in the words following—"Despotism, if wisely administered, is the best system invented by the ingenuity of man." This was declared by chief justice M'Kean; and in such an high office, we must suppose him a man of too much precaution to have made the declaration, had he not known, that a majority of the Convention, and of the citizens, who so highly applauded his speeches, were of his opinion. M. Montesquieu, in his "Spirit of Laws," 1st vol. book 3, chap. 9, says, "As *virtue* is necessary in a *republick*, and *honour* in a monarchy, so *fear* is necessary in a *despotick* government: With regard to *virtue*, there is no occasion for it, and *honour* would be extremely dangerous." Thus has a declaration been made in Pennsylvania, in favour of a government which substitues *fear* for *virtue*, and reduces men *from rational beings* to the *level of brutes*; and if the citizens of Massachusetts are disposed to follow the example, and *submit their necks to the yoke*, they must expect to be governed by the *whip* and goad. But it is remarkable, that the resolution of the federal Convention, for transmitting the system to the people, provided, "that the Constitution should *be laid before the United States in Congress assembled*, and afterwards submitted to a Convention of Delegates, chosen in each State by the people thereof, *under the recommendation of its legislature*["]; thus making Congress and the legislatures, *vehicles of conveyance*, but precluding them from passing their judgments on the system. Had it been submitted to their consideration, their members were men of such discernment, that the *defects* as well as *excellencies* of the plan, would have been clearly explained to the people; but immediately on the publication of it, we find measures were taken to prejudice the people against all persons in the legislative, executive and judicial departments of the States and Confederacy (if opposed to the plan) as being actuated by motives of private interest. Mr. Wilson, a member of the federal and Pennsylvania Convention, in his town meeting speech, adopted this practice, which, to say the least of it, was very illiberal. Indeed, it is but justice to observe, that many artful advocates of this plan, to cover their designs of creating a government which will afford *abundance of legislative offices for placemen and pensioners, proclaimed suspicions* of others, and diverted the attention of the people from themselves, on whom the odium should fall.

Let us now proceed to the provision in the system for a representation of the people, which is the *corner stone* of a free government. The Constitution provides, art. 1st, sect. 2, "that representatives and direct taxes shall be apportioned among the several States, which may be included within this union, according to their respective numbers, which shall be determined by adding to the whole number of free persons, including those bound to service for a term of years, and excluding Indians not taxed, three fifths of all other persons." Representatives "then are to be apportioned among the several States, according to their respective numbers," and *five* slaves, in computing those numbers, are to be classed with three freemen—By which rule, fifty thousand slaves, having neither *liberty* or *property*, will have a representative in that branch of the legislature—to which more especially will be committed, the *protection of the liberties*, and *disposal of all the property* of the freemen of the Union—for thus stands the new Constitution. Should it be said, that not *the slaves* but their *masters* are to send a representative, the answer is plain—If the *slaves* have a *right* to be represented, they are *on a footing* with *freemen, three* of *whom* can then have no more than an equal right of representation with *three slaves*, and these when qualified by property, may elect or be elected representatives, *which is not the case*: But if they have not a right to be represented, their masters can have no right derived from their slaves, for *these* cannot transfer to others what they have not themselves. Mr. Locke, in treating of political or civil societies, chap. 7, sect. 85, says, that men "being in the state of slavery, not capable of any property, cannot, in that state, be considered as any part of civil society, the chief end whereof, is the preservation of property." If slaves, then, are no part of civil society, there can be no more reason in admitting them, than there would be in admitting the *beasts* of the field, or *trees* of the forest, to be classed with *free electors*. What covenant are the freemen of Massachusetts about to ratify? A covenant that will degrade them to the *level of slaves*, and give to the States who have as many blacks as whites, *eight* representatives, *for the same number of freemen* as will enable this State to elect *five*—Is this an *equal*, a *safe*, or a *righteous* plan government? Indeed it is not. But if to encrease these objections, it should be urged, "that representation being regulated by the same rule as taxation, and taxation being regulated by a rule intended to ascertain the relative property of the States, representation will then be regulated by the principle of property." This *answer* would be the only one that could be made, for representation, according to the new Constitution is to be regulated, either by *numbers* or *property*.

Let us now inquire of those who take this ground, what right they have to put a construction on the constitution, which is repugnant to the express terms of the Constitution itself? This provides, "that representatives shall be apportioned among the several States, *according to their respective numbers*." Not a word of *property* is mentioned, but the word "numbers" is repeatedly expressed—Admitting however that property was intended by the Constitution as the rule of representation, does this *mend the matter*? It will be but a short time, after the adoption of the new Constitution, before the State *legislatures*, and *establishments in general* will be so *burthensome* and *useless* as to make the people desirous of being rid of them, for they will not be able to support them. The *State appointment* of Representatives will then cease, *but the principle of representation according to property*, will undoubtedly be retained, and before *it is established* it is necessary to consider whether it is a just *one*, for if *once* it is *adopted* it will *not be easily altered*— According to this principle, a man worth £50,000 is to have as many votes for representatives in the new Congress, as *one thousand men*, worth £50 each: And *sixty such nabobs* may send *two representatives*, while *sixty thousand* freemen having £50 *each* can only send the same number. Does not this establish in the representative branch of the new Congress, a principle of aristocracy, with a vengeance? The Constitution of the several States, admit of no such principle, neither can any freeman with safety thus surrender, not only the intire disposition of their property, but also, the controul of their liberties and lives to a few opulent citizens. Should it be said that the rule of federal taxation, being advantageous to the State, it should be content with the same rule for representation. The answer is plain, the rule gives no advantage, but is supposed to be advantageous to Massachusetts, and to be an accommodation very beneficial to the southern States; But admitting this State will be benefited by the rule, is it disposed to sell its birthright, the right of an equal representation in the federal councils *for so small a consideration*? Would this State give up that right to any State that would pay our whole proportion of *direct* and *indirect taxes*? Shall we relinquish some of the most essential rights of government, which are our only security for every thing dear to us, to avoid our proportion of the publick expense? Shall we give up all we have, for a small part of it? This if agreed to, would be no great evidence of our wisdom or foresight. But it is not probable, in the opinion of some of the ablest advocates for the new system, that *direct taxes* will ever be levied on the States, and if not, the provision for levying such taxes will be *nugatory*; We shall receive no kind of benefit from it, and shall have committed ourselves to the mercy of the states having slaves, *without any consideration whatever*. Indeed, should direct taxes be necessary, shall we not by increasing the representation of those States, put it in their power to prevent the levying such taxes, and thus defeat our own purpose? Certainly we shall, and having given up a substantial and *essential* right, shall in lieu of it, have a mere *visionary advantage*. Upon the whole then, it must be evident, that we might as well have committed ourselves to the parliament of Great Britain, under the idea of a *virtual representation* as in this manner resign ourselves to the federal government.

FROM

Speeches of Melancton Smith in the New York Ratifying Convention

The speaker was a prominent merchant operating in both New York City and Poughkeepsie. He had been a member of New York's first Provincial Congress, a delegate in the Continental Congress, and sheriff of Dutchess County.

June 21, 1788

. . . To determine whether the number of representatives proposed by this Constitution is sufficient, it is proper to examine the qualifications which this house ought to possess, in order to exercise their powers discreetly for the happiness of the people. The idea that naturally suggests itself to our minds, when we speak of representatives is, that they resemble those they represent; they should be a true picture of the people; possess the knowledge of their circumstances and their wants; sympathize in all their distresses, and be disposed to seek their true interests. The knowledge necessary for the representatives of a free people, not only comprehends extensive political and commercial information, such as is acquired by men of refined education, who have leisure to attain to high degrees of improvement, but it should also comprehend that kind of acquaintance with the common concerns and occupations of the people, which men of the middling class of life are in general much better competent to, than those of a superior class. To understand the true commercial interests of a country, not only requires just ideas of the general commerce of the world, but also, and principally, a knowledge of the productions of your own country and their value, what your soil is capable of producing[,] the nature of your manufactures, and the capacity of the country to increase both. To exercise the power of laying taxes, duties and excises with discretion, requires something more than an acquaintance with the abstruse parts of the system of finance. It calls for a knowledge of the circumstances and ability of the people in general, a discernment how the burdens imposed will bear upon the different classes.

From these observations results this conclusion that the number of representatives should be so large, as that while it embraces men of the first class, it should admit those of the middling class of life. I am convinced that this Government is so constituted, that the representatives will generally be composed of the first class in the community, which I shall distinguish by the name of the natural aristocracy of the country. I do not mean to give offence by using this term. I am sensible this idea is treated by many gentlemen as chimerical. I shall be asked what is meant by the natural aristocracy—and told that no such distinction of classes of men exists among us. It is true it is our singular felicity that we have no legal or hereditary distinctions of this kind; but still there are real differences: Every society naturally divides itself into classes. The author of nature has bestowed on some greater capacities than on others—birth, education, talents and wealth, create distinctions among men as visible and of as much influence as titles, stars and garters. In every society, men of this class will command a superior degree of respect—and if the government is so constituted as to admit but few to exercise the powers of it, it will, according to the natural course of things, be in their hands. Men in the middling class, who are qualified as representatives, will not be so anxious to be chosen as those of the first. When the number is so small the office will be highly elevated and distinguished—the stile in which the members live will probably be high—circumstances of this kind, will render the place of a representative not a desirable one to sensible, substantial men, who have been used to walk in the plain and frugal paths of life.

Besides, the influence of the great will generally enable them to succeed in elections—it will be difficult to combine a district of country containing 30 or 40,000 inhabitants, frame your election laws as you please, in any one character; unless it be in one of conspicuous, military, popular, civil or legal talents. The great easily form associations; the poor and middling class form them with difficulty. If the elections be by plurality, as probably will be the case in this state, it is almost certain, none but the great will be chosen—for they easily unite their interest—The common people will divide, and their divisions will be promoted by the others. There will be scarcely a chance of their uniting, in any other but some great man, unless in some popular demagogue, who will probably be destitute of principle. A substantial yeoman of sense and discernment, will hardly ever be chosen. From these remarks it appears that the government will fall into the hands of the few and the great. This will be a government of oppression. I do not mean to declaim against the great, and charge them indiscriminately with want of principle and honesty.—The same passions and prejudices govern all men. The circumstances in which men are placed in a great measure give a cast to the human character. Those in middling circumstances, have less temptation—they are inclined by habit and the company with whom they associate, to set bounds to their passions and appetites—if this is not sufficient, the want of means to gratify them will be a restraint—they are obliged to employ their time in their respective callings—hence the substantial yeomanry of the country are more temperate, of better morals and less ambition than the great. The latter do not feel for the poor and middling class; the reasons are obvious—they are not obliged to use the pains and labour to procure property as the other.—They feel not the inconveniences arising from the payment of small sums. The great consider themselves above the common people—entitled to more respect—do not associate with them—they fancy themselves to have a right of pre-eminence in every thing. In short, they possess the same feelings, and are under the influence of the same motives, as an hereditary nobility. I know the idea that such a distinction exists in this country is ridiculed by some—But I am not the less apprehensive of danger from their influence on this account—Such distinctions exist all the world over—have been taken notice of by all writers on free government—and are founded in the nature of things. It has been the principal care of free governments to guard against the encroachments of the great. Common observation and experience prove the existence of such distinctions. Will any one say, that there does not exist in this country the pride of family, of wealth, of talents; and that they do not command influence and respect among the common people? Congress, in their address to the inhabitants of the province of Quebec, in 1775, state this distinction in the following forcible words quoted from the Marquis Beccaria. "In every human society, there is an essay continually tending to confer on one part the height of power and happiness, and to reduce the other to the extreme of weakness and misery. The intent of good laws is to oppose this effort, and to diffuse their influence universally and equally." We ought to guard against the government being placed in the hands of this class— They cannot have that sympathy with their constituents which is necessary to connect them closely to their interest: Being in the habit of profuse living, they will be profuse in the public expences. They find no difficulty in paying their taxes, and therefore do not feel public burthens: Besides if they govern, they will enjoy the emoluments of the government. The middling class, from their frugal habits, and feeling themselves the public burdens, will be careful how they increase them.

But I may be asked, would you exclude the first class in the community, from any share in legislation? I answer by no means— they would be more dangerous out of power than in it—they would be factious—discontented and constantly disturbing the government—it would also be unjust—they have their liberties to protect as well as others—and the largest share of property. But my idea is, that the Constitution should be so framed as to admit this class, together with a sufficient number of the middling class to controul them. You will then combine the abilities and honesty of the community—a proper degree of information, and a disposition to pursue the public good. A representative body, composed principally of respectable yeomanry is the best possible security to liberty.—When the interest of this part of the community is pursued, the public good is pursued; because the body of every nation consists of this class. And because the interest of both the rich and the poor are involved in that of the middling class. No burden can be laid on the poor, but what will sensibly affect the middling class. Any law rendering property insecure, would be injurious to them.—When therefore this class in society pursue their own interest, they promote that of the public, for it is involved in it. . . .

Wednesday, June 25

Section third was again read—when

Mr. *Smith* resumed his argument as follows. The amendment embraces two objects: First, that the senators shall be eligible for only six years in any term of twelve years; Second, that they shall be subject to the recall of the legislatures of their several states. It is proper that we take up these points separately. I concur with the honorable gentleman,* that there is a necessity for giving this branch a greater stability than the house of representatives. I think his reasons are conclusive on this point. But, Sir, it does not follow from this position that the senators ought to hold their places during life. Declaring them ineligible during a certain term after six years, is far from rendering them less stable than is necessary. We think the amendment will place the senate in a proper medium between a fluctuating and a perpetual body. As the clause now stands, there is no doubt that the senators will hold their office perpetually; and in this situation, they must of necessity lose their dependence and attachment to the people. It is certainly inconsistent with the established principles of republicanism, that the senate should be a fixed and unchangeable body of men. There should be then some constitutional provision against this evil. A rotation I consider as the best possible mode of affecting a remedy. The amendment will not only have a tendency to defeat any plots, which may be formed against the liberty and authority of the state governments, but will be the best means to extinguish the factions which often prevail, and which are sometimes so fatal in legislative bodies. This appears to me an important consideration. We have generally found, that perpetual bodies have either combined in some scheme of usurpation, or have been torn and distracted with cabals—Both have been the source of misfortunes to the state. Most people acquainted with history will acknowledge these facts. Our Congress would have been a fine field for party spirit to act in—That body would undoubtedly have suffered all the evils of faction, had it not been secured by the rotation established by the articles of the confederation. I think a rotation in the government is a very important and truly republican institu-

* The member to whom Smith is replying in this speech is George Livingston, the mover of this amendment. (Editor)

tion. All good republicans, I presume to say, will treat it with respect.

It is a circumstance strongly in favor of rotation, that it will have a tendency to diffuse a more general spirit of emulation, and to bring forward into the office the genius and abilities of the continent—The ambition of gaining the qualifications necessary to govern, will be in some proportion to the chance of success. If the office is to be perpetually confined to a few, other men of equal talents and virtue, but not possessed of so extensive an influence, may be discouraged from aspiring to it. The more perfectly we are versed in the political science, the more firmly will the happy principles of republicanism be supported. The true policy of constitutions will be to increase the information of the country, and disseminate the knowledge of government as universally as possible. If this be done, we shall have, in any dangerous emergency, a numerous body of enlightened citizens, ready for the call of their country. As the constitution now is, you only give an opportunity to two men to be acquainted with the public affairs. It is a maxim with me, that every man employed in a high office by the people, should from time to time return to them, that he may be in a situation to satisfy them with respect to his conduct and the measures of administration. If I recollect right, it was observed by an honorable member from New York, that this amendment would be an infringement of the natural rights of the people. I humbly conceive, if the gentleman reflects maturely on the nature of his argument, he will acknowledge its weakness. What is government itself, but a restraint upon the natural rights of the people? What constitution was ever devised, that did not operate as a restraint on their original liberties? What is the whole system of qualifications, which take place in all free governments, but a restraint? Why is a certain age made necessary? Why a certain term of citizenship? This constitution itself, Sir, has restraints innumerable.—The amendment, it is true, may exclude two of the best men: but it can rarely happen, that the state will sustain any material loss by this. I hope and believe that we shall always have more than two men, who are capable of discharging the duty of a senator. But if it should so happen that the state possessed only two capable men, it will be necessary that they should return home, from time to time, to inspect and regulate our domestic affairs. I do not conceive the state can suffer any inconvenience. The argument indeed might have some weight were the representation very large: But as the power is to be exercised upon only two men, the apprehensions of the gentlemen are entirely without foundation.

With respect to the second part of the amendment, I would observe that as the senators are the representatives of the state legislatures, it is reasonable and proper that they should be under their control. When a state sends an agent commissioned to transact any business, or perform any service, it certainly ought to have a power to recall him. These are plain principles, and so far as they apply to the case under examination, they ought to be adopted by us. Form this government as you please, you must at all events lodge in it very important powers: These powers must be in the hands of a few men, so situated as to produce a small degree of responsibility. These circumstances ought to put us upon our guard; and the inconvenience of this necessary delegation of power should be corrected, by providing some suitable checks.

Against this part of the amendment a great deal of argument has been used, and with considerable plausibility. It is said if the amendment takes place, the senators will hold their office only during the pleasure of the state legislatures, and consequently will not possess the necessary firmness and stability. I conceive, Sir, there is a fallacy in this argument, founded upon the suspicion that the legislature of a state will possess the qualities of a mob, and be incapable of any regular conduct. I know that the impulses of the multitude are inconsistent with systematic government. The people are frequently incompetent to deliberate discussion, and subject to errors and imprudencies. Is this the complexion of the state legislatures? I presume it is not. I presume that they are never actuated by blind impulses—that they rarely do things hastily and without consideration. [The state legislatures were select bodies of men, chosen for their superior wisdom, and so organized as to be capable of calm and regular conduct.*] My apprehension is, that the power of recall would not be exercised as often as it ought. It is highly improbable that a man, in whom the state has confided, and who has an established influence, will be recalled, unless his conduct has been notoriously wicked.—The arguments of the gentleman therefore, do not apply in this case. It is further observed, that it would be improper to give the legislatures this power, because the local interests and prejudices of the states ought

* Smith added this comment.

not to be admitted into the general government; and that if the senator is rendered too independent of his constituents, he will sacrifice the interests of the Union to the policy of his state. Sir, the senate has been generally held up by all parties as a safe guard to the rights of the several states. In this view, the closest connection between them has been considered as necessary. But now it seems we speak a different language—We now look upon the least attachment to their states as dangerous—We are now for separating them, and rendering them entirely independent, that we may root out the last vestige of state sovereignty.

An honorable gentleman from New-York observed yesterday, that the states would always maintain their importance and authority, on account of their superior influence over the people. To prove this influence, he mentioned the aggregate number of the state representatives throughout the continent. But I ask him, how long the people will retain their confidence for two thousand representatives, who shall meet once in a year to make laws for regulating the heighth of your fences and the repairing of your roads? Will they not by and by be saying,—Here, we are paying a great number of men for doing nothing: We had better give up all the civil business of our state with its powers to congress, who are sitting all the year round: We had better get rid of the useless burthen. That matters will come to this at last, I have no more doubt than I have of my existence. The state governments, without object or authority, will soon dwindle into insignificance, and be despised by the people themselves. I am, sir, at a loss to know how the state legislatures will spend their time. Will they make laws to regulate agriculture? I imagine this will be best regulated by the sagacity and industry of those who practise it. Another reason offered by the gentleman is, that the states will have a greater number of officers than the general government. I doubt this. Let us make a comparison. In the first place, the federal government must have a compleat set of judicial officers of different ranks throughout the continent: Then, a numerous train of executive officers, in all the branches of the revenue, both internal and external, and all the civil and military departments. Add to this, their salaries will probably be larger and better secured than those of any state officers. If these numerous offices are not at once established, they are in the power of congress, and will all in time be created. Very few offices will be objects of ambition in the states. They will have no establishments at all to correspond with some of those I have mentioned—In other branches, they will have the same as congress. But I ask, what will be their comparative influence and importance? I will leave it, sir, to any man of candour, to determine whether there will not probably be more lucrative and honorable places in the gift of congress than in the disposal of the states all together. But the whole reasoning of the gentleman rests upon the principle that the states will be able to check the general government, by exciting the people to opposition: It only goes to prove, that the state officers will have such an influence over the people, as to impell them to hostility and rebellion. This kind of check, I contend, would be a pernicious one; and certainly ought to be prevented. Checks in government ought to act silently, and without public commotion. I think that the harmony of the two powers should by all means be maintained: If it be not, the operation of government will be baneful—One or the other of the parties must finally be destroyed in the conflict. The constitutional line between the authority of each should be so obvious, as to leave no room for jealous apprehensions or violent contests.

It is further said, that the operation of local interests should be counteracted; for which purpose, the senate should be rendered permanent. I conceive that the true interest of every state is the interest of the whole; and that if we should have a well regulated government, this idea will prevail. We shall indeed have few local interests to pursue, under the new constitution: because it limits the claims of the states by so close a line, that on their part there can be little dispute, and little worth disputing about. But, sir, I conceive that partial interests will grow continually weaker, because there are not those fundamental differences between the real interests of the several states, which will long prevent their coming together and becoming uniform.

Another argument advanced by the gentleman is, that our amendment would be the means of producing factions among the electors: That aspiring men would misrepresent the conduct of a faithful senator; and by intrigue, procure a recall, upon false grounds, in order to make room for themselves. But, sir, men who are ambitious for places will rarely be disposed to render those places unstable. A truly ambitious man will never do this, unless he is mad. It is not to be supposed that a state will recall a man once in twenty years, to make way for another. Dangers of this kind are very remote: I think they ought not to be brought seriously into view.

More than one of the gentlemen have ridiculed my apprehensions of corruption. How, say they, are the people to be corrupted? By their own money? Sir, in many countries, the people pay money to corrupt themselves: why should it not happen in this? Certainly, the congress will be as liable to corruption as other bodies of men. Have they not the same frailties, and the same temptations? With respect to the corruption arising from the disposal of offices, the gentlemen have treated the argument as insignificant. But let any one make a calculation, and see whether there will not be good offices enough, to dispose of to every man who goes there, who will then freely resign his seat: for, can any one suppose, that a member of congress would not go out and relinquish his four dollars a day, for two or three thousand pounds a year? It is here objected that no man can hold an office created during the time he is in Congress—But it will be easy for a man of influence, who has in his eye a favorite office previously created and already filled, to say to his friend, who holds it—Here—I will procure you another place of more emolument, provided you will relinquish yours in favor of me. The constitution appears to be a restraint, when in fact it is none at all. I presume, sir, there is not a government in the world in which there is greater scope for influence and corruption in the disposal of offices. Sir, I will not declaim, and say all men are dishonest; but I think that, in forming a constitution, if we presume this, we shall be on the safest side. This extreme is certainly less dangerous than the other. It is wise to multiply checks to a greater degree than the present state of things requires. It is said that corruption has never taken place under the old government—I believe, gentlemen hazard this assertion without proofs. That it has taken place in some degree is very probable. Many millions of money have been put into the hands of government, which have never yet been accounted for: The accounts are not yet settled, and Heaven only knows when they will be.

I have frequently observed a restraint upon the state governments, which Congress never can be under, construct that body as you please. It is a truth, capable of demonstration, that the nearer the representative is to his constituent, the more attached and dependent he will be—In the states, the elections are frequent, and the representatives numerous: They transact business in the midst of their constituents, and every man may be called upon to account for his conduct. In this state the council of appointment are elected for one year.—The proposed constitution establishes a council of appointment who will be perpetual—Is there any comparison between the two governments in point of security? It is said that the governor of this state is always eligible: But this is not in point. The governor of this state is limited in his powers—Indeed his authority is small and insignificant, compared to that of the senate of the United States.

Friday, June 27

. . . Sir, I contemplate the abolition of the state constitutions as an event fatal to the liberties of America. These liberties will not be violently wrested from the people; they will be undermined and gradually consumed. On subjects of this kind we cannot be too critical. The investigation is difficult, because we have no examples to serve as guides. The world has never seen such a government over such a country. If we consult authorities in this matter, they will declare the impracticability of governing a free people, on such an extensive plan. In a country, where a portion of the people live more than twelve hundred miles from the center, I think that one body cannot possibly legislate for the whole. Can the legislature frame a system of taxation that will operate with uniform advantages? Can they carry any system into execution? Will it not give occasion for an innumerable swarm of officers, to infest our country and consume our substance? People will be subject to impositions, which they cannot support, and of which their complaints can never reach the government.

Another idea is in my mind, which I think conclusive against a simple government for the United States. It is not possible to collect a set of representatives, who are acquainted with all parts of the continent. Can you find men in Georgia who are acquainted with the situation of New Hampshire? who know what taxes will best suit the inhabitants; and how much they are able to bear? Can the best men make laws for a people of whom they are entirely ignorant? Sir, we have no reason to hold our state governments in contempt, or to suppose them incapable of acting wisely. I believe they have operated more beneficially than most people expected, who considered that those governments were erected in a time of war and confusion, when they were very liable to errors in their structure. It will be a matter of astonishment to all unprejudiced men hereafter, who shall reflect upon our situation, to observe to what a great degree good government has prevailed. It is true some bad laws have been passed in most of the states; but they arose more from the difficulty of the times, than from any want of honesty or wisdom. Perhaps there never was a government, which in the course of ten years did not do something to be repented of. As for Rhode-Island, I do not mean to justify her—She deserves to be condemned—If there were in the world but one example of political depravity, it would be her's: And no nation ever merited or suffered a more genuine infamy, than a wicked administration has attached to her character. Massachusetts also has been guilty of errors: and has lately been distracted by an internal convulsion. Great-Britain, notwithstanding her boasted constitution, has been a perpetual scene of revolutions and civil war—Her parliaments have been abolished; her kings have been banished and murdered. I assert that the majority of the governments in the union have operated better than any body had reason to expect: and that nothing but experience and habit is wanting, to give the state laws all the stability and wisdom necessary to make them respectable. If these things be true, I think we ought not to exchange our condition, with a hazard of losing our state constitutions. We all agree that a general government is necessary: But it ought not to go so far, as to destroy the authority of the members. We shall be unwise, to make a new experiment in so important a matter, without some known and sure grounds to go upon. The state constitutions should be the guardians of our domestic rights and interests; and should be both the support and the check of the federal government. The want of the means of raising a general revenue has been the principal cause of our difficulties. I believe no man will doubt that if our present Congress had money enough, there would be few complaints of their weakness. Requisitions have perhaps been too much condemned. What has been their actual operation[?] Let us attend to experience, and see if they are such poor, unproductive things, as is commonly supposed. If I calculate right, the requisitions for the ten years past, have amounted to thirty-six millions of dollars; of which twenty-four millions, or two thirds, have been actually paid. Does not this fact warrant a conclusion that some reliance is to be placed on this mode? Besides, will any gentleman say that the states have generally been able to collect more than two thirds of their taxes from the people? The delinquency of some states has arisen from the fluctuations of paper money, &c. Indeed it is my decided opinion, that no government in the difficult circumstances, which we have passed thro', will be able to realize more than two thirds of the taxes it imposes. I might suggest two other considerations which have weight with me—There has probably been more money called for, than was actually wanted, on the expectation of delinquencies; and it is equally probable, that in a short course of time the increasing ability of the country will render requisitions a much more efficient mode of raising a revenue. The war left the people under very great burthens, and oppressed with both public and private debts. They are now fast emerging from their difficulties. Many individuals without doubt still feel great inconveniences; but they will find a gradual remedy. Sir, has any country which has suffered distresses like ours, exhibited within a few years, more striking marks of improvement and prosperity? How its population has grown; How its agriculture, commerce and manufactures have been extended and improved! How many forests have been cut down; How many wastes have been cleared and cultivated; How many additions have been made to the extent and beauty of our towns and cities! I think our advancement has been rapid. In a few years, it is to be hoped, that we shall be relieved from our embarrassments; and unless new, calamities come upon us, shall be flourishing and happy. Some difficulties will ever occur in the collection of taxes by any mode whatever. Some states will pay more; some less. If New-York lays a tax, will not one county or district furnish more, another less than its proportion? The same will happen to the United States, as happens in New-York, and in every other country.—Let them impose a duty equal and uniform—those districts, where there is plenty of money, will pay punctually: Those, in which money is scarce, will be in some measure delinquent. The idea that Congress ought to have unlimited powers, is entirely novel; I never heard it, till the meeting of this convention. The general government once called on the states, to invest them with the command of funds adequate to the exigencies of the union: but they did not ask to command all the resources of the states—They did not wish to have a controul over all the property of the people. If we now give them this controul, we may as well give up the state governments with it. I have no notion of setting the two powers at variance; nor would I give a farthing for a government, which could not command a farthing. On the whole, it appears to me probable, that unless some certain, specific source of revenue is reserved to the states, their governments, with their independency will be totally annihilated.

FROM

Speeches of Patrick Henry in the Virginia Ratifying Convention

Patrick Henry was undoubtedly the most nationally prominent opponent of the Constitution, though he had rarely left Virginia—of which he served as first Governor upon Independence. He was celebrated as author of the Virginia resolutions against the Stamp Act and was prominent in the First Continental Congress.

June 4, 1788

. . . This proposal of altering our Federal Government is of a most alarming nature: Make the best of this new Government—say it is composed by any thing but inspiration—you ought to be extremely cautious, watchful, jealous of your liberty; for instead of securing your rights you may lose them forever. If a wrong step be now made, the Republic may be lost forever. If this new Government will not come up to the expectation of the people, and they should be disappointed—their liberty will be lost, and tyranny must and will arise. I repeat it again, and I beg Gentlemen to consider, that a wrong step made now will plunge us in misery, and our Republic will be lost. It will be necessary for this Convention to have a faithful historical detail of the facts, that preceded the session of the Federal Convention, and the reasons that actuated its members in proposing an entire alteration of Government—and demonstrate the dangers that awaited us: If they were of such awful magnitude, as to warrant a proposal so extremely perilous at this, I must assert, that this Convention has an absolute right to a thorough discovery of every circumstance relative to this great event. And here I would make this enquiry of those worthy characters who composed a part of the late Federal Convention. I am sure they were fully impressed with the necessity of forming a great consolidated Government, instead of a confederation. That this is a consolidated Government is demonstrably clear, and the danger of such a Government, is, to my mind, very striking. I have the highest veneration of those Gentlemen,—but, Sir, give me leave to demand, what right had they to say, *We, the People.* My political curiosity, exclusive of my anxious solicitude for the public welfare, leads me to ask who authorised them to speak the language of, *We, the People*, instead of *We, the States*? States are the characteristics, and the soul of a confederation. If the States be not the agents of this compact, it must be one great consolidated National Government of the people of all the States. I have the highest respect for those Gentlemen of the people of all the States. I have the highest respect for those Gentlemen who formed the Convention, and were some of them not here, I would express some testimonial of my esteem for them. America had on a former occasion put the utmost confidence in them: A confidence which was well placed: And I am sure, Sir, I would give up any thing to them; I would chearfully confide in them as my Representatives. But, Sir, on this great occasion, I would demand the cause of their conduct.—Even from that illustrious man, who saved us by his valor, I would have a reason for his conduct—that liberty which he has given us by his valor, tells me to ask this reason,—and sure I am, were he here, he would give us that reason: But there are other Gentlemen here, who can give us this information. The people gave them no power to use their name. That they exceeded their power is perfectly clear. It is not mere curiosity that actuates me—I wish to hear the real actual existing danger, which should lead us to take those steps so dangerous in my conception. Disorders have arisen in other parts of America, but here, Sir, no dangers, no insurrection of tumult, has happened—every thing has been calm and tranquil. But notwithstanding this, we are wandering on the great ocean of human affairs. I see no landmark to guide us. We are running we know not whither. Difference in opinion has gone to a degree of inflammatory resentment in different parts of the country—which has been occasioned by this perilous innovation. The Federal Convention ought to have amended the old system—for this purpose they were solely delegated: The object of their mission extended to no other consideration. You must therefore forgive the solicitation of one unworthy member, to know what danger could have arisen under the present confederation, and what are the causes of this proposal to change our Government.

June 5, 1788

Mr. Chairman—I am much obliged to the very worthy Gentleman [Henry Lee] for his encomium. I wish I was possessed of talents, or possessed of any thing, that might enable me to elucidate this great subject. I am not free from suspicion: I am apt to entertain doubts: I rose yesterday to ask a question, which arose in my mind. When I asked the question, I thought the meaning of my interrogation was obvious: The fate of this question and America may depend on this: Have they said, we the States? Have they made a proposal of a compact between States? If they had, this would be a confederation: It is otherwise most clearly a consolidated government. The question turns, Sir, on that poor little thing—the expression, *We, the people*, instead of the States of America. I need not take much pains to show, that the principles of this system, are extremely pernicious, impolitic, and dangerous. Is this a Monarchy, like England—a compact between Prince and people; with checks on the former, to secure the liberty of the latter? Is this a Confederacy, like Holland—an association of a number of independent States, each of which retain its individual sovereignty? It is not a democracy, wherein the people retain all their rights securely. Had these principles been adhered to, we should not have been brought to this alarming transition, from a Confederacy to a consolidated Government. We have no detail of those great considerations which, in my opinion, ought to have abounded before we should recur to a government of this kind. Here is a revolution as radical as that which separated us from Great Britain. It is as radical, if in this transition our rights and privileges are endangered, and the sovereignty of the States be relinquished: And cannot we plainly see, that this is actually the case? The rights of conscience, trial by jury, liberty of the press, all your immunities and franchises, all pretensions to human rights and privileges, are rendered insecure, if not lost, by this change so loudly talked of by some, and inconsiderately by others. Is this same relinquishment of rights worthy of freemen? Is it worthy of that manly fortitude that ought to characterize republicans? It is said eight States have adopted this plan. I declare that if twelve States and an half had adopted it, I would with manly firmness, and in spite of an erring world, reject it. You are not to inquire how your trade may be increased, nor how you are to become a great and powerful people, but how your liberties can be secured; for liberty ought to be the direct end of your Government. Having premised these things, I shall, with the aid of my judgment and information, which I confess are not extensive, go into the discussion of this system more minutely. Is it necessary for your liberty, that you should abandon those great rights by the adoption of this system? Is the relinquishment of the trial by jury, and the liberty of the press, necessary for your liberty? Will the abandonment of your most sacred rights tend to the security of your liberty? Liberty the greatest of all earthly blessings—give us that precious jewel, and you may take every thing else: But I am fearful I have lived long enough to become an old fashioned fellow: Perhaps an invincible attachment to the dearest rights of man, may, in these refined enlightened days, be deemed *old fashioned:* If so, I am contented to be so: I say, the time has been, when every pore of my heart beat for American liberty, and which, I believe, had a counterpart in the breast of every true American: But suspicions have gone forth—suspicions of my integrity—publicly reported that my professions are not real—23 years ago was I supposed a traitor to my country; I was then said to be a bane of sedition, because I supported the rights of my country: I may be thought suspicious when I say our privileges and rights are in danger: But, Sir, a number of the people of this country are weak enough to think these things are too true: I am happy to find that the Honorable Gentleman on the other side, declares they are groundless: But, Sir, suspicion is a virtue, as long as its object is the preservation of the public good, and as long as it stays within proper bounds: Should it fall on me, I am contented: Conscious rectitude is a powerful consolation: I trust, there are many who think my professions for the public good to be real. Let your suspicion look to both sides: There are many on the other side, who, possibly may have been persuaded of the necessity of these measures, which I conceive to be dangerous to your liberty. Guard with jealous attention the public liberty. Suspect every one who approaches that jewel. Unfortunately, nothing will preserve it, but downright force: Whenever you give up that force, you are inevitably ruined. I am answered by Gentlemen, that though I might speak of terrors, yet the fact was, that we were surrounded by none of the dangers I apprehended. I conceive this new Government to be one of those dangers: It has produced those horrors, which distress many of our best citizens. We are come hither to preserve the poor Commonwealth of Virginia, if it can be possibly done: Something must be done to preserve your liberty and mine: The Confederation; this same despised Government, merits, in my opinion, the highest encomium: It carried us through a long and dangerous war: It rendered us victorious in that bloody conflict with a powerful nation: It has secured us a territory greater than any European Monarch possesses: And shall a Government which has been thus strong and vigorous, be accused of imbecility and abandoned for want of energy? Consider what you are about to do before you part with this Government. Take longer time in reckoning things: Revolutions like this have happened in almost every country in Europe: Similar examples are to be found in ancient Greece and ancient Rome: Instances of the people loosing their liberty by their own carelessness and the ambition of a few. . . .

What, Sir, is the genius of democracy? Let me read that clause of the Bill of Rights of Virginia, which relates to this: 3d cl. "That Government is or ought to be instituted for the common benefit, protection, and security of the people, nation, or community: Of all the various modes and forms of Government, that is best which is capable of producing the greatest degree of happiness and safety, and is most effectually secured against the danger of mal-administration, and *that whenever any Government shall be found inadequate, or contrary to these purposes, a majority of the community hath, an undubitable, unalienable and indefeasible right to reform, alter, or abolish it, in such manner as shall be judged most conducive to the public weal.*" This, Sir, is the language of democracy; that a majority of the community have a right to alter their Government when found to be oppressive: But how different is the genius of your new Constitution from this? How different from the sentiments of freemen, that a contemptible minority can prevent the good of the majority? If then Gentlemen standing on this ground, are come to that point, that they are willing to bind themselves and their posterity to be oppressed, I am amazed and inexpressibly astonished. If this be the opinion of the majority, I must submit; but to me, Sir, it appears perilous and destructive: I cannot help thinking so: Perhaps it may be the result of my age; these may be feelings natural to a man of my years, when the American spirit has left him, and his mental powers, like the members of the body, are decayed. If, Sir, amendments are left to the twentieth or the tenth part of the people of America, your liberty is gone forever. We have heard that there is a great deal of bribery practiced in the House of Commons in England; and that many of the members raised themselves to preferments, by selling the rights of the people. But, Sir, the tenth part of that body cannot continue oppressions on the rest of the people. English liberty is in this case, on a firmer foundation than American liberty. It will be easily contrived to procure the opposition of one tenth of the people to any alteration, however judicious. The Honorable Gentleman who presides, told us, that to prevent abuses in our Government, we will assemble in Convention, recall our delegated powers, and punish our servants for abusing the trust reposed in them. Oh, Sir, we should have fine times indeed, if to punish tyrants, it were only sufficient to assemble the people. Your arms wherewith you could defend yourselves, are gone; and have no longer a aristocratical; no longer democratical spirit. Did you ever read of any revolution in any nation, brought about by the punishment of those in power, inflicted by those who had no power at all? You read of a riot act in a country which is called one of the freest in the world, where a few neighbours cannot assemble without the risk of being shot by a hired soldiery, the engines of despotism. We may see such an act in America. A standing army we shall have also, to execute the execrable commands of tyranny: And how are you to punish them? Will you order them to be punished? Who shall obey these orders? Will your Mace-bearer be a match for a disciplined regiment? In what situation are we to be? The clause before you gives a power of direct taxation, unbounded and unlimitted: Exclusive power of Legislation in all cases whatsoever, for ten miles square; and over all places purchased for the erection of forts, magazines, arsenals, dock-yards, &c. What resistance could be made? The attempt would be madness. You will find all the strength of this country in the hands of your enemies: Those garrisons will naturally be the strongest places in the country. Your militia is given up to Congress also in another part of this plan: They will therefore act as they think proper: All power will be in their own possession: You cannot force them to receive their punishment: Of what service would militia be to you, when most probably you will not have a single musket in the State; for as arms are to be provided by Congress, they may or may not furnish them. Let me here call your attention to that part which gives the Congress power, "To provide for organizing, arming, and disciplining the militia, and for governing such a part of them as may be employed in the service of the United States, reserving to the States respectively, the appointment of the officers, and the authority of training the militia, according to the discipline prescribed by Congress." By this, Sir, you see that their controul over our last and best defence, is unlimitted. If they neglect or refuse to discipline or arm our militia, they will be useless: The States can do neither, this power being exclusively given to Congress: The power of appointing officers over men not disciplined or armed, is ridiculous: So that this pretended little remains of power left to the States, may, at the pleasure of Congress, be rendered nugatory. Our situation will be deplorable indeed: Nor can we ever expect to get this government amended, since I have already shewn, that a very small minority may prevent it; and that small minority interested in the continuance of the oppression: Will the oppressor let go the oppressed? Was there ever an instance? Can the annals of mankind exhibit one single example, where rulers overcharged with power, willingly let go the oppressed, though solicited and requested most earnestly? The application for amendments will therefore be fruitless. Sometimes the oppressed have got loose by one of those bloody struggles that desolate a country. A willing relinquishment of power is one of those things which human nature never was, nor ever will be capable of: The Honorable Gentleman's observations respecting the people's right of being the agents in the formation of this Government, are not accurate in my humble conception. The distinction between a National Government and a Confederacy is not sufficiently discerned. Had the delegates who were sent to Philadelphia a power to propose a Consolidated Government instead of a Confederacy? Were they not deputed by States, and not by the people? The assent of the people in their collective capacity is not necessary to the formation of a Federal Government. The people have no right to enter into leagues, alliances, or confederations: They are not the proper agents for this purpose: States and sovereign powers are the only proper agents for this kind of Government: Shew me an instance where the people have exercised this business: Has it not always gone through the Legislatures? I refer you to the treaties with France, Holland, and other nations: How were they made? Were they not made by the States? Are the people therefore in their aggregate capacity, the proper persons to form a Confederacy? This, therefore, ought to depend on the consent of the Legislatures; the people having never sent delegates to make any proposition of changing the Government. Yet I must say, at the same time, that it was made on grounds the most pure, and perhaps I might have been brought to consent to it so far as to the change of Government; but there is one thing in it which I never would acquiesce in. I mean the changing it into a Consolidated Government; which is so abhorent to my mind. The Honorable Gentleman then went on to the figure we make with foreign nations; the contemptible one we make in France and Holland; which, according to the system of my notes, he attributes to the present feeble Government. An opinion has gone forth, we find, that we are a contemptible people: The time has been when we were thought otherwise: Under this same despised Government, we commanded the respect of all Europe: Wherefore are we now reckoned otherwise? The American spirit has fled from hence: It has gone to regions, where it has never been expected: It has gone to the people of France in search of a splendid Government—a strong energetic Government. Shall we imitate the example of those nations who have gone from a simple to a splendid Government. Are those nations more worthy of our imitation? What can make an adequate satisfaction to them for the loss they suffered in attaining such a Government for the loss of their liberty? If we admit this Consolidated Government it will be because we like a great splendid one. Some way or other we must be a great and mighty empire; we must have an army, and a navy, and a number of things: When the American spirit was in its youth, the language of America was different: Liberty, Sir, was then the primary object. We are descended from a people whose Government was founded on liberty: Our glorious forefathers of Great-Britain, made liberty the foundation of every thing. That country is become a great, mighty, and splendid nation; not because their Government is strong and energetic; but, Sir, because liberty is its direct end and foundation: We drew the spirit of liberty from our British ancestors; by that spirit we have triumphed over every difficulty: But now, Sir, the American spirit, assisted by the ropes and chains of consolidation, is about to convert this country to a powerful and mighty empire: If you make the citizens of this country agree to become the subjects of one great consolidated empire of America, your Government will not have sufficient energy to keep them together: Such a Government is incompatible with the genius of republicanism: There will be no checks, no real balances, in this Government: What can avail your specious imaginary balances, your rope-dancing, chain-rattling, ridiculous ideal checks and contrivances? But, Sir, we are not feared by foreigners: we do not make nations tremble: Would this, Sir, constitute happiness, or secure liberty? I trust, Sir, our political hemisphere will ever direct their operations to the security of those objects. Consider our situation, Sir: Go to the poor man, ask him what he does; he will inform you, that he enjoys the fruits of his labour, under his own fig-tree, with his wife and children around him, in peace and security. Go to every other member of the society, you will find the same tranquil ease and content; you will find no alarms or disturbances: Why then tell us of dangers to terrify us into an adoption of this new Government? and yet who knows the dangers that this new system may produce; they are out of the sight of the common people: They cannot foresee latent consequences; I dread the operation of it on the middling and lower class of people: It is for them I fear the adoption of this system. I fear I tire the patience of the Committee, but I beg to be indulged with a few more observations: When I thus profess myself an advocate for the liberty of the people, I shall be told, I am a designing man, that I am to be a great man, that I am to be a demagogue; and many similar illiberal insinuations will be thrown out; but, Sir, conscious rectitude, out-weighs these things with me: I see great jeopardy in this new Government. I see none from our present one: I hope some Gentleman or other will bring forth, in full array, those dangers, if there be any, that we may see and touch them. . . .

This Constitution is said to have beautiful features; but when I come to examine these features, Sir, they appear to me horridly frightful: Among other deformities, it has an awful squinting; it squints towards monarchy: And does not this raise indignation in the breast of every American? Your President may easily become King: Your Senate is so imperfectly constructed that your dearest rights may be sacrificed by what may be a small minority; and a very small minority may continue forever unchangeably this Government, although horridly defective: Where are your checks in this Government? Your strong holds will be in the hands of your enemies: It is on a supposition that our American Governors shall be honest, that all the good qualities of this Government are founded: But its defective, and imperfect construction, puts it in their power to perpetrate the worst of mischiefs, should they be bad men: And, Sir, would not all the world, from the Eastern to the Western hemisphere, blame our distracted folly in resting our rights upon the contingency of our rulers being good or bad. Shew me that age and country where the rights and liberties of the people were placed on the sole chance of their rulers being good men, without a consequent loss of liberty? I say that the loss of that dearest privilege has ever followed with absolute certainty, every such mad attempt. If your American chief, be a man of ambition, and abilities, how easy is it for him to render himself absolute: The army is in his hands, and, if he be a man of address, it will be attached to him; and it will be the subject of long meditation with him to seize the first auspicious moment to accomplish his design; and, Sir, will the American spirit solely relieve you when this happens? I would rather infinitely, and I am sure most of this Convention are of the same opinion, have a King, Lords, and Commons, than a Government so replete with such insupportable evils. If we make a King, we may prescribe the rules by which he shall rule his people, and interpose such checks as shall prevent him from infringing them: But the President, in the field, at the head of his army, can prescribe the terms on which he shall reign master, so far that it will puzzle any American ever to get his neck from under the galling yoke. I cannot with patience, think of this idea. If ever he violates the laws, one of two things will happen: He shall come to the head of his army to carry every thing before him; or, he will give bail, or do what Mr. Chief Justice will order him. If he be guilty, will not the recollection of his crimes teach him to make one bold push for the American throne? Will not the immense difference between being master of every thing, and being ignominiously tried and punished, powerfully excite him to make this bold push? But, Sir, where is the existing force to punish him? Can he not at the head of his army beat down every opposition? Away with your President, we shall have a King: The army will salute him Monarch; your militia will leave you and assist in making him King, and fight against you: And what have you to oppose this force? What will then become of you and your rights? Will not absolute despotism ensue? [Here Mr. Henry strongly and pathetically expatiated on the probability of the President's enslaving America and the horrible consequences that must result.] . . .

George Mason
Objections to the Proposed Federal Constitution

Mason, a great land and slave owner in the Northern Neck of Virginia, had drafted the state's constitution in 1776 and was a member of the Constitutional Convention in 1787. His part in the debates there did not give much indication of his forthcoming dissent, but he refused to sign the Constitution.

This essay is reproduced for the sake of brevity. He spoke at considerable length in the Virginia ratifying convention.

. . . There is no declaration of rights: and the laws of the general government being paramount to the laws and constitutions of the several states, the declarations of rights, in the separate states, are no security. Nor are the people secured even in the enjoyment of the benefit of the common law, which stands here upon no other foundation than its having been adopted by the respective acts forming the constitutions of the several states.

In the House of Representatives there is not the substance, but the shadow only of representation; which can never produce proper information in the legislature, or inspire confidence in the people.—The laws will, therefore, be generally made by men little concerned in, and unacquainted with their effects and consequences.*

The Senate have the power of altering all money-bills, and of

* This objection has been in some degree lessened, by an amendment, often before refused, and at last made by an erasure, after the engrossment upon parchment, of the word forty, and inserting thirty, in the third clause of the second section of the first article.

originating appropriations of money, and the salaries of the officers of their appointment, in conjunction with the President of the United States—Although they are not the representatives of the people, or amenable to them. These, with their other great powers, (viz. their powers in the appointment of ambassadors, and all public officers, in making treaties, and in trying all impeachments) their influence upon, and connection with, the supreme executive from these causes, their duration of office, and their being a constant existing body, almost continually sitting, joined with their being one complete branch of the legislature, will destroy any balance in the government, and enable them to accomplish what usurpations they please, upon the rights and liberties of the people.

The judiciary of the United States is so constructed and extended, as to absorb and destroy the judiciaries of the several states; thereby rendering laws as tedious, intricate, and expensive, and justice as unattainable by a great part of the community, as in England; and enabling the rich to oppress and ruin the poor.

The President of the United States has no constitutional council (a thing unknown in any safe and regular government.) he will therefore be unsupported by proper information and advice; and will generally be directed by minions and favorites—or he will become a tool to the Senate—or a council of state will grow out of the principal officers of the great departments—the worst and most dangerous of all ingredients for such a council, in a free country; for they may be induced to join in any dangerous or oppressive measures, to shelter themselves, and prevent an inquiry into their own misconduct in office. Whereas, had a constitutional council been formed (as was proposed) of six members, viz., two from the eastern, two from the middle, and two from the southern states, to be appointed by vote of the states in the House of Representatives, with the same duration and rotation of office as the Senate, the executive would always have had safe and proper information and advice; the president of such a council might have acted as Vice-President of the United States, *pro tempore*, upon any vacancy or disability of the chief magistrate; and long continued sessions of the Senate, would in a great measure have been prevented. From this fatal defect of a constitutional council, has arisen the improper power of the Senate, in the appointment of the public officers, and the alarming dependence and connexion between that branch of the legislature and the supreme executive. Hence, also, sprung that unnecessary officer, the Vice-President, who, for want of other employment, is made President of the Senate; thereby dangerously blending the executive and legislative powers; besides always giving to some one of the states an unnecessary and unjust pre-eminence over the others.

The President of the United States has the unrestrained power of granting pardon for treason; which may be sometimes exercised to screen from punishment those whom he had secretly instigated to commit the crime, and thereby prevent a discovery of his own guilt. By declaring all treaties supreme laws of the land, the executive and the Senate have, in many cases, an exclusive power of legislation, which might have been avoided, by proper distinctions with respect to treaties, and requiring the assent of the House of Representatives, where it could be done with safety.

By requiring only a majority to make all commercial and navigation laws, the five southern states (whose produce and circumstances are totally different from those of the eight northern and eastern states) will be ruined: for such rigid and premature regulations may be made, as will enable the merchants of the northern and eastern states not only to demand an exorbitant freight, but to monopolize the purchase of the commodities, at their own price, for many years, to the great injury of the landed interest, and the impoverishment of the people: and the danger is the greater, as the gain on one side will be in proportion to the loss on the other. Whereas, requiring two-thirds of the members present in both houses, would have produced mutual moderation, promoted the general interest, and removed an insuperable objection to the adoption of the government.

Under their own construction of the general clause at the end of the enumerated powers, the Congress may grant monopolies in trade and commerce, constitute new crimes, inflict unusual and severe punishments, and extend their power as far as they shall think proper; so that the state legislatures have no security for the powers now presumed to remain to them; or the people for their rights. There is no declaration of any kind for preserving the liberty of the press, the trial by jury in civil cases, nor against the danger of standing armies in time of peace.

The state legislatures are restrained from laying export duties on their own produce—the general legislature is restrained from prohibiting the further importation of slaves for twenty odd years, though such importations render the United States weaker, more vulnerable, and less capable of defence. Both the general legislature, and the state legislatures are expressly prohibited making *ex post facto* laws, though there never was, nor can be, a legislature, but must and will make such laws, when necessity and the public safety require them, which will hereafter be a breach of all the constitutions in the union, and afford precedents for other innovations.

This government will commence in a moderate aristocracy; it is at present impossible to foresee whether it will, in its operation, produce a monarchy, or a corrupt oppressive aristocracy; it will most probably vibrate some years between the two, and then terminate in the one or the other.

THE FEDERALIST

The Federalist

Publius: John Jay, Alexander Hamilton, and James Madison

No. 1

ALEXANDER HAMILTON

October 27, 1787

To the People of the State of New York.

After an unequivocal experience of the inefficacy of the subsisting Fœderal Government, you are called upon to deliberate on a new Constitution for the United States of America. The subject speaks its own importance; comprehending in its consequences, nothing less than the existence of the UNION, the safety and welfare of the parts of which it is composed, the fate of an empire, in many respects, the most interesting in the world. It has been frequently remarked, that it seems to have been reserved to the people of this country, by their conduct and example, to decide the important question, whether societies of men are really capable or not, of establishing good government from reflection and choice, or whether they are forever destined to depend, for their political constitutions, on accident and force. If there be any truth in the remark, the crisis, at which we are arrived, may with propriety be regarded as the æra in which that decision is to be made; and a wrong election of the part we shall act, may, in this view, deserve to be considered as the general misfortune of mankind.

This idea will add the inducements of philanthropy to those of

From *The Independent Journal*, October 27, 1787. This essay appeared on October 30 in both *The New-York Packet* and *The Daily Advertiser*.

patriotism to heighten the solicitude, which all considerate and good men must feel for the event. Happy will it be if our choice should be directed by a judicious estimate of our true interests, unperplexed and unbiassed by considerations not connected with the public good. But this is a thing more ardently to be wished, than seriously to be expected. The plan offered to our deliberations, affects too many particular interests, innovates upon too many local institutions, not to involve in its discussion a variety of objects foreign to its merits, and of views, passions and prejudices little favourable to the discovery of truth.

Among the most formidable of the obstacles which the new Constitution will have to encounter, may readily be distinguished the obvious interest of a certain class of men in every State to resist all changes which may hazard a diminution of the power, emolument and consequence of the offices they hold under the State-establishments—and the perverted ambition of another class of men, who will either hope to aggrandise themselves by the confusions of their country, or will flatter themselves with fairer prospects of elevation from the subdivision of the empire into several partial confederacies, than from its union under one government.

It is not, however, my design to dwell upon observations of this nature. I am well aware that it would be disingenuous to resolve indiscriminately the opposition of any set of men (merely because their situations might subject them to suspicion) into interested or ambitious views: Candour will oblige us to admit, that even such men may be actuated by upright intentions; and it cannot be doubted that much of the opposition which has made its appearance, or may hereafter make its appearance, will spring from sources, blameless at least, if not respectable, the honest errors of minds led astray by preconceived jealousies and fears. So numerous indeed and so powerful are the causes, which serve to give a false bias to the judgment, that we upon many occasions, see wise and good men on the wrong as well as on the right side of questions, of the first magnitude to society. This circumstance, if duly attended to, would furnish a lesson of moderation to those, who are ever so much persuaded of their being in the right, in any controversy. And a further reason for caution, in this respect, might be drawn from the reflection, that we are not always sure, that those who advocate the truth are influenced by purer principles than their antagonists. Ambition, avarice, personal animosity, party opposition, and many other motives, not more laudable than these, are apt to operate as well upon those who support as upon those who oppose the right side of a question. Were there not even these inducements to moderation, nothing could be more illjudged than that intolerant spirit, which has, at all times, characterised political parties. For, in politics as in religion, it is equally absurd to aim at making proselytes by fire and sword. Heresies in either can rarely be cured by persecution.

And yet however just these sentiments will be allowed to be, we have already sufficient indications, that it will happen in this as in all former cases of great national discussion. A torrent of angry and malignant passions will be let loose. To judge from the conduct of the opposite parties, we shall be led to conclude, that they will mutually hope to evince the justness of their opinions, and to increase the number of their converts by the loudness of their declamations, and by the bitterness of their invectives. An enlightened zeal for the energy and efficiency of government will be stigmatized, as the off-spring of a temper fond of despotic power and hostile to the principles of liberty. An overscrupulous jealousy of danger to the rights of the people, which is more commonly the fault of the head than of the heart, will be represented as mere pretence and artifice; the bait for popularity at the expence of public good. It will be forgotten, on the one hand, that jealousy is the usual concomitant of violent love, and that the noble enthusiasm of liberty is too apt to be infected with a spirit of narrow and illiberal distrust. On the other hand, it will be equally forgotten, that the vigour of government is essential to the security of liberty; that, in the contemplation of a sound and well informed judgment, their interest can never be separated; and that a dangerous ambition more often lurks behind the specious mask of zeal for the rights of the people, than under the forbidding appearance of zeal for the firmness and efficiency of government. History will teach us, that the former has been found a much more certain road to the introduction of despotism, than the latter, and that of those men who have overturned the liberties of republics the greatest number have begun their carreer, by paying an obsequious court to the people, commencing Demagogues and ending Tyrants.

In the course of the preceeding observations I have had an eye, my Fellow Citizens, to putting you upon your guard against all attempts, from whatever quarter, to influence your decision in a matter of the utmost moment to your welfare by any impressions other than those which may result from the evidence of truth. You will, no doubt, at the same time, have collected from the general scope of them that they proceed from a source not unfriendly to the New Constitution. Yes, my Countrymen, I own to you, that, after having given it an attentive consideration, I am clearly of opinion, it is your interest to adopt it. I am convinced, that this is the safest course for your liberty, your dignity, and your happiness. I effect not reserves, which I do not feel. I will not amuse you with an appearance of deliberation, when I have decided. I frankly acknowledge to you my convictions, and I will freely lay before you the reasons on which they are founded. The consciousness of good intentions disdains ambiguity. I shall not however multiply professions on this head. My motives must remain in the depository of my own breast: My arguments will be open to all, and may be judged of by all. They shall at least be offered in a spirit, which will not disgrace the cause of truth.

I propose in a series of papers to discuss the following interesting particulars—*The utility of the* UNION *to your political prosperity—The insufficiency of the present Confederation to preserve that Union—The necessity of a government at least equally energetic with the one proposed to the attainment of this object—The conformity of the proposed constitution to the true principles of republican government—Its analogy to your own state constitution*—and lastly, *The additional security, which its adoption will afford to the preservation of that species of government, to liberty and to property*. . . .

Publius.

No. 2

JOHN JAY

October 31, 1787

To the People of the State of New York.

When the people of America reflect that they are now called upon to decide a question, which, in its consequences, must prove one of the most important, that ever engaged their attention, the pro-

From *The Independent Journal*, October 31, 1787. This essay appeared on November 1 in *The Daily Advertiser* and on November 2 in *The New-York Packet.*

priety of their taking a very comprehensive, as well as a very serious view of it, will be evident.

Nothing is more certain than the indispensable necessity of Government, and it is equally undeniable, that whenever and however it is instituted, the people must cede to it some of their natural rights, in order to vest it with requisite powers. It is well worthy of consideration therefore, whether it would conduce more to the interest of the people of America, that they should, to all general purposes, be one nation, under one fœderal Government, than that they should divide themselves into separate confederacies, and give to the head of each, the same kind of powers which they are advised to place in one national Government.

It has until lately been a received and uncontradicted opinion, that the prosperity of the people of America depended on their continuing firmly united, and the wishes, prayers, and efforts of our best and wisest Citizens have been constantly directed to that object. But Politicians now appear, who insist that this opinion is erroneous, and that instead of looking for safety and happiness in union, we ought to seek it in a division of the States into distinct confederacies or sovereignties. However extraordinary this new doctrine may appear, it nevertheless has its advocates; and certain characters who were much opposed to it formerly, are at present of the number. Whatever may be the arguments or inducements, which have wrought this change in the sentiments and declarations of these Gentlemen, it certainly would not be wise in the people at large to adopt these new political tenets without being fully convinced that they are founded in truth and sound Policy.

It has often given me pleasure to observe, that Independent America was not composed of detached and distant territories, but that one connected, fertile, wide spreading country was the portion of our western sons of liberty. Providence has in a particular manner blessed it with a variety of soils and productions, and watered it with innumerable streams, for the delight and accomodation of its inhabitants. A succession of navigable waters forms a kind of chain round its borders, as if to bind it together; while the most noble rivers in the world, running at convenient distances, present them with highways for the easy communication of friendly aids, and the mutual transportation and exchange of their various commodities.

With equal pleasure I have as often taken notice, that Providence has been pleased to give this one connected country, to one united people, a people descended from the same ancestors, speaking the same language, professing the same religion, attached to the same principles of government, very similar in their manners and customs, and who, by their joint counsels, arms and efforts, fighting side by side throughout a long and bloody war, have nobly established their general Liberty and Independence.

This country and this people seem to have been made for each other, and it appears as if it was the design of Providence, that an inheritance so proper and convenient for a band of brethren, united to each other by the strongest ties, should never be split into a number of unsocial, jealous and alien sovereignties.

Similar sentiments have hitherto prevailed among all orders and denominations of men among us. To all general purposes we have uniformly been one people—each individual citizen every where enjoying the same national rights, privileges, and protection. As a nation we have made peace and war—as a nation we have vanquished our common enemies—as a nation we have formed alliances and made treaties, and entered into various compacts and conventions with foreign States.

A strong sense of the value and blessings of Union induced the people, at a very early period, to institute a Fœderal Government to preserve and perpetuate it. They formed it almost as soon as they had a political existence; nay at a time, when their habitations were in flames, when many of their Citizens were bleeding, and when the progress of hostility and desolation left little room for those calm and mature enquiries and reflections, which must ever precede the formation of a wise and well balanced government for a free people. It is not to be wondered at that a Government instituted in times so inauspicious, should on experiment be found greatly deficient and inadequate to the purpose it was intended to answer.

This intelligent people perceived and regretted these defects. Still continuing no less attached to union, than enamoured of liberty, they observed the danger, which immediately threatened the former and more remotely the latter; and being persuaded that ample security for both, could only be found in a national Government more wisely framed, they, as with one voice, convened the late Convention at Philadelphia, to take that important subject under consideration.

This Convention, composed of men, who possessed the confidence of the people, and many of whom had become highly distinguished by their patriotism, virtue and wisdom, in times which tried the minds and hearts of men, undertook the arduous task. In the mild season of peace, with minds unoccupied by other subjects, they passed many months in cool uninterrupted and daily consultations: and finally, without having been awed by power, or influenced by any passions except love for their Country, they presented and recommended to the people the plan produced by their joint and very unanimous counsels.

Admit, for so is the fact, that this plan is only *recommended*, not imposed, yet let it be remembered, that it is neither recommended to *blind* approbation, nor to *blind* reprobation; but to that sedate and candid consideration, which the magnitude and importance of the subject demand, and which it certainly ought to receive. But this, (as was remarked in the foregoing number of this Paper,) is more to be wished than expected that it may be so considered and examined. Experience on a former occasion teaches us not to be too sanguine in such hopes. It is not yet forgotten, that well grounded apprehensions of imminent danger induced the people of America to form the Memorable Congress of 1774. That Body recommended certain measures to their Constituents, and the event proved their wisdom; yet it is fresh in our memories how soon the Press began to teem with Pamphlets and weekly Papers against those very measures. Not only many of the Officers of Government who obeyed the dictates of personal interest, but others from a mistaken estimate of consequences, or the undue influence of former attachments, or whose ambition aimed at objects which did not correspond with the public good, were indefatigable in their endeavours to persuade the people to reject the advice of the Patriotic Congress. Many indeed were deceived and deluded, but the great majority of the people reasoned and decided judiciously; and happy they are in reflecting that they did so.

They considered that the Congress was composed of many wise and experienced men. That being convened from different parts of the country, they brought with them and communicated to each other a variety of useful information. That in the course of the time they passed together in enquiring into and discussing the true interests of their country, they must have acquired very accurate knowledge on that head. That they were individually interested in the public liberty and prosperity, and therefore that it was not less their inclination, than their duty, to recommend only such measures, as after the most mature deliberation they really thought prudent and adviseable.

These and similar considerations then induced the people to rely greatly on the judgment and integrity of the Congress; and they took their advice, notwithstanding the various arts and endeavours used to deter and disuade them from it. But if the people at large had reason to confide in the men of that Congress, few of whom had then been fully tried or generally known, still greater reason have they now to respect the judgment and advice of the Convention, for it is well known that some of the most distinguished members of that Congress, who have been since tried and justly approved for patriotism and abilities, and who have grown old in acquiring political information, were also members of this Convention and carried into it their accumulated knowledge and experience.

It is worthy of remark that not only the first, but every succeeding Congress, as well as the late Convention, have invariably joined with the people in thinking that the prosperity of America depended on its Union. To preserve and perpetuate it, was the great object of the people in forming that Convention, and it is also the great object of the plan which the Convention has advised them to adopt. With what propriety therefore, or for what good purposes, are attempts at this particular period, made by some men, to depreciate the importance of the Union? or why is it suggested that three or four confederacies would be better than one? I am persuaded in my own mind, that the people have always thought right on this subject, and that their universal and uniform attachment to the cause of the Union, rests on great and weighty reasons, which I shall endeavour to develope and explain in some ensuing papers. They who promote the idea of substituting a number of distinct confederacies in the room of the plan of the Convention, seem clearly to foresee that the rejection of it would put the continuance of the Union in the utmost jeopardy. That certainly would be the case, and I sincerely wish that it may be as clearly foreseen by every good Citizen, that whenever the dissolution of the Union arrives, America will have reason to exclaim in the words of the Poet, "FAREWELL, A LONG FAREWELL, TO ALL MY GREATNESS."

Publius.

No. 3

JOHN JAY

Examines external relations, defense, and the enforcement of treaty provisions.

No. 4

JOHN JAY

Draws attention to international economic rivalries.

No. 5

JOHN JAY

Points out dangers of rivalries between separate American confederacies if the Constitution is not ratified and the Confederation breaks up.

No. 6

ALEXANDER HAMILTON

November 14, 1787

To the People of the State of New York.

The three last numbers of this Paper have been dedicated to an enumeration of the dangers to which we should be exposed, in a state of disunion, from the arms and arts of foreign nations. I shall now proceed to delineate dangers of a different, and perhaps, still more alarming kind, those which will in all probability flow from dissentions between the States themselves, and from domestic factions and convulsions. These have been already in some instances slightly anticipated, but they deserve a more particular and more full investigation.

A man must be far gone in Utopian speculations who can se-

From *The Independent Journal*, November 14, 1787. This essay appeared on November 15 in *The Daily Advertiser* and on November 16 in *The New-York Packet.*

riously doubt, that if these States should either be wholly disunited, or only united in partial confederacies, the subdivisions into which they might be thrown would have frequent and violent contests with each other. To presume a want of motives for such contests, as an argument against their existence, would be to forget that men are ambitious, vindictive and rapacious. To look for a continuation of harmony between a number of independent unconnected sovereignties, situated in the same neighbourhood, would be to disregard the uniform course of human events, and to set at defiance the accumulated experience of ages.

The causes of hostility among nations are innumerable. There are some which have a general and almost constant operation upon the collective bodies of society: Of this description are the love of power or the desire of preeminence and dominion—the jealousy of power, or the desire of equality and safety. There are others which have a more circumscribed, though an equally operative influence, within their spheres: Such are the rivalships and competitions of commerce between commercial nations. And there are others, not less numerous than either of the former, which take their origin intirely in private passions; in the attachments, enmities, interests, hopes and fears of leading individuals in the communities of which they are members. Men of this class, whether the favourites of a king or of a people, have in too many instances abused the confidence they possessed; and assuming the pretext of some public motive, have not scrupled to sacrifice the national tranquility to personal advantage, or personal gratification.

The celebrated Pericles, in compliance with the resentments of a prostitute,* at the expence of much of the blood and treasure of his countrymen, attacked, vanquished and destroyed, the city of the *Samnians*. The same man, stimulated by private pique against the *Megarensians*,† another nation of Greece, or to avoid a prosecution with which he was threatened as an accomplice in a supposed theft of the statuary *Phidias*,‡ or to get rid of the accusations prepared to be brought against him for dissipating the funds of the State in the purchase of popularity,§ or from a combination of all these causes, was the primitive author of that famous and

* Aspasia, vide Plutarch's life of Pericles. (Publius)

† Idem. (Publius)

‡ Idem. Phidias was supposed to have stolen some public gold with the connivance of Pericles for the embelishment of the statue of Minerva. (Publius)

§ Idem. (Publius)

fatal war, distinguished in the Grecian annals by the name of the *Pelopponesian* war; which, after various vicissitudes, intermissions and renewals, terminated in the ruin of the Athenian commonwealth.

The ambitious Cardinal, who was Prime Minister to Henry VIIIth. permitting his vanity to aspire to the Tripple-Crown,* entertained hopes of succeeding in the acquisition of that splendid prize by the influence of the Emperor Charles Vth. To secure the favour and interest of this enterprising and powerful Monarch, he precipitated England into a war with France, contrary to the plainest dictates of Policy, and at the hazard of the safety and independence, as well of the Kingdom over which he presided by his councils, as of Europe in general. For if there ever was a Sovereign who bid fair to realise the project of universal monarchy it was the Emperor Charles Vth, of whose intrigues Wolsey was at once the instrument and the dupe.

The influence which the bigottry of one female,† the petulancies of another,‡ and the cabals of a third,§ had in the co[n]temporary policy, ferments and pacifications of a considerable part of Europe are topics that have been too often descanted upon not to be generally known.

To multiply examples of the agency of personal considerations in the production of great national events, either foreign or domestic, according to their direction would be an unnecessary waste of time. Those who have but a superficial acquaintance with the sources from which they are to be drawn will themselves recollect a variety of instances; and those who have a tolerable knowledge of human nature will not stand in need of such lights, to form their opinion either of the reality or extent of that agency. Perhaps however a reference, tending to illustrate the general principle, may with propriety be made to a case which has lately happened among ourselves. If SHAYS had not been a *desperate debtor* it is much to be doubted whether Massachusetts would have been plunged into a civil war.

But notwithstanding the concurring testimony of experience, in this particular, there are still to be found visionary, or designing

* Worn by the Popes.
† Madame De Maintenon.
‡ Dutchess of Marlborough.
§ Madame De Pompadoure.

men, who stand ready to advocate the paradox of perpetual peace between the States, though dismembered and alienated from each other. The genius of republics (say they) is pacific; the spirit of commerce has a tendency to soften the manners of men and to extinguish those inflammable humours which have so often kindled into wars. Commercial republics, like ours, will never be disposed to waste themselves in ruinous contentions with each other. They will be governed by mutual interest, and will cultivate a spirit of mutual amity and concord.

Is it not (we may ask these projectors in politics) the true interest of all nations to cultivate the same benevolent and philosophic spirit? If this be their true interest, have they in fact pursued it? Has it not, on the contrary, invariably been found, that momentary passions and immediate interests have a more active and imperious controul over human conduct than general or remote considerations of policy, utility or justice? Have republics in practice been less addicted to war than monarchies? Are not the former administered by *men* as well as the latter? Are there not aversions, predilections, rivalships and desires of unjust acquisition that affect nations as well as kings? Are not popular assemblies frequently subject to the impulses of rage, resentment, jealousy, avarice, and of other irregular and violent propensities? Is it not well known that their determinations are often governed by a few individuals, in whom they place confidence, and are of course liable to be tinctured by the passions and views of those individuals? Has commerce hitherto done any thing more than change the objects of war? Is not the love of wealth as domineering and enterprising a passion as that of power or glory? Have there not been as many wars founded upon commercial motives, since that has become the prevailing system of nations, as were before occasioned by the cupidity of territory or dominion? Has not the spirit of commerce in many instances administered new incentives to the appetite both for the one and for the other? Let experience the least fallible guide of human opinions be appealed to for an answer to these inquiries.

Sparta, Athens, Rome and Carthage were all Republics; two of them, Athens and Carthage, of the commercial kind. Yet were they as often engaged in wars, offensive and defensive, as the neighbouring Monarchies of the same times. Sparta was little better than a well regulated camp; and Rome was never sated of carnage and conquest.

Carthage, though a commercial Republic, was the aggressor in the very war that ended in her destruction. Hannibal had carried her arms into the heart of Italy and to the gates of Rome, before Scipio, in turn, gave him an overthrow in the territories of Carthage and made a conquest of the Commonwealth.

Venice in latter times figured more than once in wars of ambition; 'till becoming an object of terror to the other Italian States, Pope Julius the Second found means to accomplish that formidable league,* which gave a deadly blow to the power and pride of this haughty Republic.

The Provinces of Holland, 'till they were overwhelmed in debts and taxes, took a leading and conspicuous part in the wars of Europe. They had furious contests with England for the dominion of the sea; and were among the most persevering and most implacable of the opponents of Lewis XIV.

In the government of Britain the representatives of the people compose one branch of the national legislature. Commerce has been for ages the predominant pursuit of that country. Few nations, nevertheless, have been more frequently engaged in war; and the wars, in which that kingdom has been engaged, have in numerous instances proceeded from the people.

There have been, if I may so express it, almost as many popular as royal wars. The cries of the nation and the importunities of their representatives have, upon various occasions, dragged their monarchs into war, or continued them in it contrary to their inclinations, and, sometimes, contrary to the real interests of the State. In that memorable struggle for superiority, between the rival Houses of *Austria* and *Bourbon* which so long kept Europe in a flame, it is well known that the antipathies of the English against the French, seconding the ambition, or rather the avarice of a favourite leader,† protracted the war beyond the limits marked out by sound policy and for a considerable time in opposition to the views of the Court.

The wars of these two last mentioned nations have in a great measure grown out of commercial considerations—The desire of supplanting and the fear of being supplanted either in particular

---

* The League of Cambray, comprehending the Emperor, the King of France, the King of Arragon, and most of the Italian Princes and States.

†The Duke of Marlborough.

branches of traffic or in the general advantages of trade and navigation; and sometimes even the more culpable desire of sharing in the commerce of other nations, without their consent.

The last war but two between Britain and Spain sprang from the attempts of the English merchants, to prosecute an illicit trade with the Spanish main. These unjustifiable practices on their part produced severities on the part of the Spaniards, towards the subjects of Great Britain, which were not more justifiable; because they exceeded the bounds of a just retaliation, and were chargeable with inhumanity and cruelty. Many of the English who were taken on the Spanish coasts were sent to dig in the mines of Potosi; and by the usual progress of a spirit of resentment, the innocent were after a while confounded with the guilty in indiscriminate punishment. The complaints of the merchants kindled a violent flame throughout the nation, which soon after broke out in the house of commons, and was communicated from that body to the ministry. Letters of reprisal were granted and a war ensued, which in its consequences overthrew all the alliances that but twenty years before had been formed, with sanguine expectations of the most beneficial fruits.

From this summary of what has taken place in other countries, whose situations have borne the nearest resemblance to our own, what reason can we have to confide in those reveries, which would seduce us into an expectation of peace and cordiality between the members of the present confederacy, in a state of separation? Have we not already seen enough of the fallacy and extravagance of those idle theories which have amused us with promises of an exemption from the imperfections, weaknesses and evils incident to society in every shape? Is it not time to awake from the deceitful dream of a golden age, and to adopt as a practical maxim for the direction of our political conduct, that we, as well as the other inhabitants of the globe, are yet remote from the happy empire of perfect wisdom and perfect virtue?

Let the point of extreme depression to which our national dignity and credit have sunk—let the inconveniences felt every where from a lax and ill administration of government—let the revolt of a part of the State of North-Carolina—the late menacing disturbances in Pennsylvania and the actual insurrections and rebellions in Massachusetts declare!

So far is the general sense of mankind from corresponding with the tenets of those, who endeavour to lull asleep our apprehensions of discord and hostility between the States, in the event of disunion, that it has from long observation of the progress of society become a sort of axiom in politics, that vicinity, or nearness of situation, constitutes nations natural enemies. An intelligent writer expresses himself on this subject to this effect—"NEIGHBOURING NATIONS (says he) are naturally ENEMIES of each other, unless their common weakness forces them to league in a CONFEDERATE REPUBLIC, and their constitution prevents the differences that neighbourhood occasions, extinguishing that secret jealousy, which disposes all States to aggrandise themselves at the expence of their neighbours."* This passage, at the same time points out the EVIL and suggests the REMEDY.

Publius.

No. 7

ALEXANDER HAMILTON

Deals with disputes among states.

No. 8

ALEXANDER HAMILTON

On dangers of standing armies in America, which will become a feature of American life if new confederations are formed.

No. 9

ALEXANDER HAMILTON

November 21, 1787

. . . The utility of a confederacy, as well to suppress faction and to guard the internal tranquillity of States, as to increase their external force and security, is in reality not a new idea. It has been practiced upon in different countries and ages, and has received the sanction of the most applauded writers, on the subjects of politics. The opponents of the PLAN proposed have with great assiduity cited and circulated the observations of Montesquieu on the necessity of a contracted territory for a republican government.

From *The Independent Journal*, November 21, 1787.

* Vide Principes des Negotiations par L'Abbe de Mably.

But they seem not to have been apprised of the sentiments of that great man expressed in another part of his work, nor to have adverted to the consequences of the principle to which they subscribe, with such ready acquiescence.

When Montesquieu recommends a small extent for republics, the standards he had in view were of dimensions, far short of the limits of almost every one of these States. Neither Virginia, Massachusetts, Pennsylvania, New-York, North-Carolina, nor Georgia, can by any means be compared with the models, from which he reasoned and to which the terms of his description apply. If we therefore take his ideas on this point, as the criterion of truth, we shall be driven to the alternative, either of taking refuge at once in the arms of monarchy, or of spliting ourselves into an infinity of little jealous, clashing, tumultuous commonwealths, the wretched nurseries of unceasing discord and the miserable objects of universal pity or contempt. Some of the writers, who have come forward on the other side of the question, seem to have been aware of the dilemma; and have even been bold enough to hint at the division of the larger States, as a desirable thing. Such an infatuated policy, such a desperate expedient, might, by the multiplication of petty offices, answer the views of men, who possess not qualifications to extend their influence beyond the narrow circles of personal intrigue, but it could never promote the greatness or happiness of the people of America.

Referring the examination of the principle itself to another place, as has been already mentioned, it will be sufficient to remark here, that in the sense of the author who has been most emphatically quoted upon the occasion, it would only dictate a reduction of the SIZE of the more considerable MEMBERS of the Union; but would not militate against their being all comprehended in one Confederate Government. And this is the true question, in the discussion of which we are at present interested.

So far are the suggestions of Montesquieu from standing in opposition to a general Union of the States, that he explicitly treats of a CONFEDERATE REPUBLIC as the expedient for extending the sphere of popular government and reconciling the advantages of monarchy with those of republicanism.

"It is very probable (says he★) that mankind would have been obliged, at length, to live constantly under the government of a

---

★ *Spirit of Laws*, Vol. I. Book IX. Chap. I.

SINGLE PERSON, had they not contrived a kind of constitution, that has all the internal advantages of a republican, together with the external force of a monarchial government. I mean a CONFEDERATE REPUBLIC.

"This form of Government is a Convention, by which several smaller *States* agree to become members of a larger *one*, which they intend to form. It is a kind of assemblage of societies, that constitute a new one, capable of encreasing by means of new associations, till they arrive to such a degree of power as to be able to provide for the security of the united body.

"A republic of this kind, able to withstand an external force, may support itself without any internal corruption. The form of this society prevents all manner of inconveniencies.

"If a single member should attempt to usurp the supreme authority, he could not be supposed to have an equal authority and credit, in all the confederate states. Were he to have too great influence over one, this would alarm the rest. Were he to subdue a part, that which would still remain free might oppose him with forces, independent of those which he had usurped, and overpower him before he could be settled in his usurpation.

"Should a popular insurrection happen, in one of the confederate States, the others are able to quell it. Should abuses creep into one part, they are reformed by those that remain sound. The State may be destroyed on one side, and not on the other; the confederacy may be dissolved, and the confederates preserve their sovereignty.

"As this government is composed of small republics it enjoys the internal happiness of each, and with respect to its external situation it is possessed, by means of the association of all the advantages of large monarchies."

I have thought it proper to quote at length these interesting passages, because they contain a luminous abrigement of the principal arguments in favour of the Union, and must effectually remove the false impressions, which a misapplication of other parts of the work was calculated to produce. They have at the same time an intimate connection with the more immediate design of this Paper; which is to illustrate the tendency of the Union to repress domestic faction and insurrection. . . .

No. 10

JAMES MADISON

November 22, 1787

To the People of the State of New York.

Among the numerous advantages promised by a well constructed Union, none deserves to be more accurately developed than its tendency to break and control the violence of faction. The friend of popular governments, never finds himself so much alarmed for their character and fate, as when he contemplates their propensity to this dangerous vice. He will not fail therefore to set a due value on any plan which, without violating the principles to which he is attached, provides a proper cure for it. The instability, injustice and confusion introduced into the public councils, have in truth been the mortal diseases under which popular governments have every where perished; as they continue to be the favorite and fruitful topics from which the adversaries to liberty derive their most specious declamations. The valuable improvements made by the American Constitutions on the popular models, both ancient and modern, cannot certainly be too much admired; but it would be an unwarrantable partiality, to contend that they have as effectually obviated the danger on this side as was wished and expected. Complaints are every where heard from our most considerate and virtuous citizens, equally the friends of public and private faith, and of public and personal liberty; that our governments are too unstable; that the public good is disregarded in the conflicts of rival parties; and that measures are too often decided, not according to the rules of justice, and the rights of the minor party; but by the superior force of an interested and over-bearing majority. However anxiously we may wish that these complaints had no foundation, the evidence of known facts will not permit us to deny that they are in some degree true. It will be found indeed, on a candid review of our situation, that some of the distresses under which we labor, have been erroneously charged on the operation of our governments; but it will be found, at the same time, that other causes will not alone account for many of our heaviest mis-

---

From *The Daily Advertiser*, November 22, 1787. This essay appeared in *The New-York Packet* on November 23 and in *The Independent Journal* on November 24.

fortunes; and particularly, for that prevailing and increasing distrust of public engagements, and alarm for private rights, which are echoed from one end of the continent to the other. These must be chiefly, if not wholly, effects of the unsteadiness and injustice, with which a factious spirit has tainted our public administrations.

By a faction I understand a number of citizens, whether amounting to a majority or minority of the whole, who are united and actuated by some common impulse of passion, or of interest, adverse to the rights of other citizens, or to the permanent and aggregate interests of the community.

There are two methods of curing the mischiefs of faction: the one, by removing its causes; the other, by controling its effects.

There are again two methods of removing the causes of faction: the one by destroying the liberty which is essential to its existence; the other, by giving to every citizen the same opinions, the same passions, and the same interests.

It could never be more truly said than of the first remedy, that it is worse than the disease. Liberty is to faction, what air is to fire, an aliment without which it instantly expires. But it could not be a less folly to abolish liberty, which is essential to political life, because it nourishes faction, than it would be to wish the annihilation of air, which is essential to animal life, because it imparts to fire its destructive agency.

The second expedient is as impracticable, as the first would be unwise. As long as the reason of man continues fallible, and he is at liberty to exercise it, different opinions will be formed. As long as the connection subsists between his reason and his self-love, his opinions and his passions will have a reciprocal influence on each other; and the former will be objects to which the latter will attach themselves. The diversity in the faculties of men from which the rights of property originate, is not less an insuperable obstacle to a uniformity of interests. The protection of these faculties is the first object of Government. From the protection of different and unequal faculties of acquiring property, the possession of different degrees and kinds of property immediately results: and from the influence of these on the sentiments and views of the respective proprietors, ensues a division of the society into different interests and parties.

The latent causes of faction are thus sown in the nature of man; and we see them every where brought into different degrees of activity, according to the different circumstances of civil society.

A zeal for different opinions concerning religion, concerning Government and many other points, as well of speculation as of practice; an attachment to different leaders ambitiously contending for pre-eminence and power; or to persons of other descriptions whose fortunes have been interesting to the human passions, have in turn divided mankind into parties, inflamed them with mutual animosity, and rendered them much more disposed to vex and oppress each other, than to co-operate for their common good. So strong is this propensity of mankind to fall into mutual animosities, that where no substantial occasion presents itself, the most frivolous and fanciful distinctions have been sufficient to kindle their unfriendly passions, and excite their most violent conflicts. But the most common and durable source of factions, has been the various and unequal distribution of property. Those who hold, and those who are without property, have ever formed distinct interests in society. Those who are creditors, and those who are debtors, fall under a like discrimination. A landed interest, a manufacturing interest, a mercantile interest, a monied interest, with many lesser interests, grow up of necessity in civilized nations, and divide them into different classes, actuated by different sentiments and views. The regulation of these various and interfering interests forms the principal task of modern Legislation, and involves the spirit of party and faction in the necessary and ordinary operations of Government.

No man is allowed to be a judge in his own cause; because his interest would certainly bias his judgment, and, not improbably, corrupt his integrity. With equal, nay with greater reason, a body of men, are unfit to be both judges and parties, at the same time; yet, what are many of the most important acts of legislation, but so many judicial determinations, not indeed concerning the rights of single persons, but concerning the rights of large bodies of citizens; and what are the different classes of legislators, but advocates and parties to the causes which they determine? Is a law proposed concerning private debts? It is a question to which the creditors are parties on one side, and the debtors on the other. Justice ought to hold the balance between them. Yet the parties are and must be themselves the judges; and the most numerous party, or, in other words, the most powerful faction must be expected to prevail. Shall domestic manufactures be encouraged, and in what degree, by restrictions on foreign manufactures? are questions which would be differently decided by the landed and the manufacturing classes; and probably by neither, with a sole regard to justice and the public good. The apportionment of taxes on the various descriptions of property, is an act which seems to require the most exact impartiality; yet, there is perhaps no legislative act in which greater opportunity and temptation are given to a predominant party, to trample on the rules of justice. Every shilling with which they over-burden the inferior number, is a shilling saved to their own pockets.

It is in vain to say, that enlightened statesmen will be able to adjust these clashing interests, and render them all subservient to the public good. Enlightened statesmen will not always be at the helm: Nor, in many cases, can such an adjustment be made at all, without taking into view indirect and remote considerations, which will rarely prevail over the immediate interest which one party may find in disregarding the rights of another, or the good of the whole.

The inference to which we are brought is, that the *causes* of faction cannot be removed; and that relief is only to be sought in the means of controling its *effects*.

If a faction consists of less than a majority, relief is supplied by the republican principle, which enables the majority to defeat its sinister views by regular vote: It may clog the administration, it may convulse the society; but it will be unable to execute and mask its violence under the forms of the Constitution.

When a majority is included in a faction, the form of popular government on the other hand enables it to sacrifice to its ruling passion or interest, both the public good and the rights of other citizens. To secure the public good, and private rights, against the danger of such a faction, and at the same time to preserve the spirit and the form of popular government, is then the great object to which our enquiries are directed: Let me add that it is the great desideratum, by which alone this form of government can be rescued from the opprobrium under which it has so long labored, and be recommended to the esteem and adoption of mankind.

By what means is this object attainable? Evidently by one of two only. Either the existence of the same passion or interest in a majority at the same time, must be prevented; or the majority, having such co-existent passion or interest, must be rendered, by their number and local situation, unable to concert and carry into effect schemes of oppression. If the impulse and the opportunity be suffered to coincide, we well know that neither moral nor religious motives can be relied on as an adequate control. They are not found to be such on the injustice and violence of individuals, and lose their efficacy in proportion to the number combined together; that is, in proportion as their efficacy becomes needful.

From this view of the subject, it may be concluded, that a pure Democracy, by which I mean, a Society, consisting of a small number of citizens, who assemble and administer the Government in person, can admit of no cure for the mischiefs of faction. A common passion or interest will, in almost every case, be felt by a majority of the whole; a communication and concert results from the form of Government itself; and there is nothing to check the inducements to sacrifice the weaker party, or an obnoxious individual. Hence it is, that such Democracies have ever been spectacles of turbulence and contention; have ever been found incompatible with personal security, or the rights of property; and have in general been as short in their lives, as they have been violent in their deaths. Theoretic politicians, who have patronized this species of Government, have erroneously supposed, that by reducing mankind to a perfect equality in their political rights, they would, at the same time, be perfectly equalized and assimilated in their possessions, their opinions, and their passions.

A Republic, by which I mean a Government in which the scheme of representation takes place, opens a different prospect, and promises the cure for which we are seeking. Let us examine the points in which it varies from pure Democracy, and we shall comprehend both the nature of the cure, and the efficacy which it must derive from the Union.

The two great points of difference between a Democracy and a Republic are, first, the delegation of the Government, in the latter, to a small number of citizens elected by the rest: secondly, the greater number of citizens, and greater sphere of country, over which the latter may be extended.

The effect of the first difference is, on the one hand to refine and enlarge the public views, by passing them through the medium of a chosen body of citizens, whose wisdom may best discern the true interest of their country, and whose patriotism and love of justice, will be least likely to sacrifice it to temporary or partial considerations. Under such a regulation, it may well happen that the public voice pronounced by the representatives of the people, will be more consonant to the public good, than if pronounced by the people themselves convened for the purpose. On the other hand, the effect may be inverted. Men of factious tempers, of local prejudices, or of sinister designs, may by intrigue, by corruption or by other means, first obtain the suffrages, and then betray the interests of the people. The question resulting is, whether small or extensive Republics are most favorable to the election of proper guardians of the public weal: and it is clearly decided in favor of the latter by two obvious considerations.

In the first place it is to be remarked that however small the Republic may be, the Representatives must be raised to a certain number, in order to guard against the cabals of a few; and that however large it may be, they must be limited to a certain number, in order to guard against the confusion of a multitude. Hence the number of Representatives in the two cases, not being in proportion to that of the Constituents, and being proportionally greatest in the small Republic, it follows, that if the proportion of fit characters, be not less, in the large than in the small Republic, the former will present a greater option, and consequently a greater probability of a fit choice.

In the next place, as each Representative will be chosen by a greater number of citizens in the large than in the small Republic, it will be more difficult for unworthy candidates to practise with success the vicious arts, by which elections are too often carried; and the suffrages of the people being more free, will be more likely to centre on men who possess the most attractive merit, and the most diffusive and established characters.

It must be confessed, that in this, as in most other cases, there is a mean, on both sides of which inconveniencies will be found to lie. By enlarging too much the number of electors, you render the representative too little acquainted with all their local circumstances and lesser interests; as by reducing it too much, you render him unduly attached to these, and too little fit to comprehend and pursue great and national objects. The Federal Constitution forms a happy combination in this respect; the great and aggregate interests being referred to the national, the local and particular, to the state legislatures.

The other point of difference is, the greater number of citizens and extent of territory which may be brought within the compass of Republican, than of Democratic Government; and it is this circumstance principally which renders factious combinations less to be dreaded in the former, than in the latter. The smaller the society, the fewer probably will be the distinct parties and interests composing it; the fewer the distinct parties and interest, the more frequently will a majority be found of the same party; and the smaller the number of individuals composing a majority, and the smaller the compass within which they are placed, the more easily will they concert and execute their plans of oppression. Extend the sphere, and you take in a greater variety of parties and interests; you make it less probable that a majority of the whole will have a common motive to invade the rights of other citizens; or if such a common motive exists, it will be more difficult for all who feel it to discover their own strength, and to act in unison with each other. Besides other impediments, it may be remarked, that where there is a consciousness of unjust or dishonorable purposes, communication is always checked by distrust, in proportion to the number whose concurrence is necessary.

Hence it clearly appears, that the same advantage, which a Republic has over a Democracy, in controling the effects of faction, is enjoyed by a large over a small Republic—is enjoyed by the Union over the States composing it. Does this advantage consist in the substitution of Representatives, whose enlightened views and virtuous sentiments render them superior to local prejudices, and to schemes of injustice? It will not be denied, that the Representation of the Union will be most likely to possess these requisite endowments. Does it consist in the greater security afforded by a greater variety of parties, against the event of any one party being able to outnumber and oppress the rest? In an equal degree does the encreased variety of parties, comprised within the Union, encrease this security. Does it, in fine, consist in the greater obstacles opposed to the concert and accomplishment of the secret wishes of an unjust and interested majority? Here, again, the extent of the Union gives it the most palpable advantage.

The influence of factious leaders may kindle a flame within their particular States, but will be unable to spread a general conflagration through the other States: a religious sect, may degenerate into a political faction in a part of the Confederacy; but the variety of sects dispersed over the entire face of it, must secure the national Councils against any danger from that source: a rage for paper money, for an abolition of debts, for an equal division of property, or for any other improper or wicked project, will be less apt to pervade the whole body of the Union, than a particular member of it; in the same proportion as such a malady is more likely to taint a particular county or district, than an entire State.

In the extent and proper structure of the Union, therefore, we behold a Republican remedy for the diseases most incident to Republican Government. And according to the degree of pleasure and pride, we feel in being Republicans, ought to be our zeal in cherishing the spirit, and supporting the character of Federalists.

Publius.

No. 11

ALEXANDER HAMILTON

November 24, 1787

To the People of the State of New York.

The importance of the Union, in a commercial light, is one of those points, about which there is least room to entertain a difference of opinion, and which has in fact commanded the most general assent of men, who have any acquaintance with the subject. This applies as well to our intercourse with foreign countries, as with each other.

There are appearances to authorise a supposition, that the adventurous spirit, which distinguishes the commercial character of America, has already excited uneasy sensations in several of the maritime powers of Europe. They seem to be apprehensive of our too great interference in that carrying trade, which is the support of their navigation and the foundation of their naval strength. Those of them, which have colonies in America, look forward, to what this country is capable of becoming, with painful solicitude. They foresee the dangers, that may threaten their American dominions from the neighbourhood of States, which have all the dispositions, and would possess all the means, requisite to the creation of a powerful marine. Impressions of this kind will naturally indicate the policy of fostering divisions among us, and of depriving us as far as possible of an ACTIVE COMMERCE in our own bottoms. This would answer the threefold purpose of preventing our interference in their navigation of monopolising the profits of our trade, and of clipping the wings, by which we might soar to

---

From *The Independent Journal*, November 24, 1787. This essay appeared on November 27 in *The New-York Packet*. It was begun in *The Daily Advertiser* on November 27, and concluded on November 28.

a dangerous greatness. Did not prudence forbid the detail, it would not be difficult to trace by facts the workings of this policy to the cabinets of Ministers.

If we continue united, we may counteract a policy so unfriendly to our prosperity in a variety of ways. By prohibitory regulations, extending at the same time throughout the States, we may oblige foreign countries to bid against each other, for the privileges of our markets. This assertion will not appear chimerical to those who are able to appreciate the importance of the markets of three millions of people—increasing in rapid progression, for the most part exclusively addicted to agriculture, and likely from local circumstances to remain so—to any manufacturing nation; and the immense difference there would be to the trade and navigation of such a nation, between a direct communication in its own ships, and an indirect conveyance of its products and returns, to and from America, in the ships of another country. Suppose, for instance, we had a government in America, capable of excluding Great-Britain (with whom we have at present no treaty of commerce) from all our ports, what would be the probable operation of this step upon her politics? Would it not enable us to negotiate with the fairest prospect of success for commercial privileges of the most valuable and extensive kind in the dominions of that kingdom? When these questions have been asked, upon other occasions, they have received a plausible but not a solid or satisfactory answer. It has been said, that prohibitions on our part would produce no change in the system of Britain; because she could prosecute her trade with us, through the medium of the Dutch, who would be her immediate customers and paymasters for those articles which were wanted for the supply of our markets. But would not her navigation be materially injured, by the loss of the important advantage of being her own carrier in that trade? Would not the principal part of its profits be intercepted by the Dutch, as a compensation for their agency and risk? Would not the mere circumstance of freight occasion a considerable deduction? Would not so circuitous an intercourse facilitate the competitions of other nations, by enhancing the price of British commodities in our markets, and by transferring to other hands the management of this interesting branch of the British commerce?

A mature consideration of the objects, suggested by these questions, will justify a belief, that the real disadvantages to Britain, from such a state of things, conspiring with the prepossessions of a great part of the nation in favour of the American trade, and with the importunities of the West-India islands, would produce a relaxation in her present system, and would let us into the enjoyment of privileges in the markets of those islands and elsewhere, from which our trade would derive the most substantial benefits. Such a point gained from the British government, and which could not be expected without an equivalent in exemptions and immunities in our markets, would be likely to have a correspondent effect on the conduct of other nations, who would not be inclined to see themselves, altogether supplanted in our trade.

A further resource for influencing the conduct of European nations towards us, in this respect would arise from the establishment of a fœderal navy. There can be no doubt, that the continuance of the Union, under an efficient government, would put it in our power, at a period not very distant, to create a navy, which, if it could not vie with those of the great maritime powers, would at least be of respectable weight, if thrown into the scale of either of two contending parties. This would be more particularly the case in relation to operations in the West-Indies. A few ships of the line sent opportunely to the reinforcement of either side, would often be sufficient to decide the fate of a campaign, on the event of which interests of the greatest magnitude were suspended. Our position is in this respect a very commanding one. And if to this consideration we add that of the usefulness of supplies from this country, in the prosecution of military operations in the West-Indies, it will readily be perceived, that a situation so favourable would enable us to bargain with great advantage for commercial privileges. A price would be set not only upon our friendship, but upon our neutrality. By a steady adherance to the Union we may hope ere long to become the Arbiter of Europe in America; and to be able to incline the ballance of European competitions in this part of the world as our interest may dictate.

But in the reverse of this elegible situation we shall discover, that the rivalships of the parts would make them checks upon each other, and would frustrate all the tempting advantages, which nature has kindly placed within our reach. In a state so insignificant, our commerce would be a prey to the wanton inter-meddlings of all nations at war with each other; who, having nothing to fear from us, would with little scruple or remorse supply their wants by depredations on our property, as often as it fell in their way. The rights of neutrality will only be respected, when they are defended by an adequate power. A nation, despicable by its weakness, forfeits even the privilege of being neutral.

Under a vigorous national government, the natural strength and resources of the country, directed to a common interest, would baffle all the combinations of European jealousy to restrain our growth. This situation would even take away the motive to such combinations, by inducing an impracticability of success. An active commerce, an extensive navigation, and a flourishing marine would then be the inevitable offspring of moral and physical necessity. We might defy the little arts of little politicians to controul, or vary, the irresistible and unchangeable course of nature.

But in a state of disunion these combinations might exist, and might operate with success. It would be in the power of the maritime nations, availing themselves of our universal impotence, to prescribe the conditions of our political existence; and as they have a common interest in being our carriers, and still more in preventing our being theirs, they would in all probability combine to embarrass our navigation in such a manner, as would in effect destroy it, and confine us to a PASSIVE COMMERCE. We should thus be compelled to content ourselves with the first price of our commodities, and to see the profits of our trade snatched from us to enrich our enemies and persecutors. That unequalled spirit of enterprise, which signalises the genius of the American Merchants and Navigators, and which is in itself an inexhaustible mine of national wealth, would be stifled and lost; and poverty and disgrace would overspread a country, which with wisdom might make herself the admiration and envy of the world.

There are rights of great moment to the trade of America, which are rights of the Union. I allude to the fisheries, to the navigation of the Western lakes and to that of the Mississippi. The dissolution of the confederacy would give room for delicate questions, concerning the future existence of these rights; which the interest of more powerful partners would hardly fail to solve to our disadvantage. The disposition of Spain with regard to the Mississippi needs no comment. France and Britain are concerned with us in the fisheries; and view them as of the utmost moment to their navigation. They, of course, would hardly remain long indifferent to that decided mastery of which experience has shewn us to be possessed in this valuable branch of traffic; and by which we are able to undersell those nations in their own markets. What more natural, than that they should be disposed to exclude, from the lists, such dangerous competitors?

This branch of trade ought not to be considered as a partial benefit. All the navigating States may in different degrees advantageously participate in it and under circumstances of a greater extension of mercantile capital would not be unlikely to do it. As a nursery of seamen it now is, or when time shall have more nearly assimilated the principles of navigation in the several States, will become an universal resource. To the establishment of a navy it must be indispensible.

To this great national object a NAVY, Union will contribute in various ways. Every institution will grow and flourish in proportion to the quantity and extent of the means concentered towards its formation and support. A navy of the United States, as it would embrace the resources of all, is an object far less remote than a navy of any single State, or partial confederacy, which would only embrace the resources of a part. It happens indeed that different portions of confederated America possess each some peculiar advantage for this essential etablishment. The more Southern States furnish in greater abundance certain kinds of naval stores—tar, pitch and turpentine. Their wood for the construction of ships is also of a more solid and lasting texture. The difference in the duration of the ships of which the navy might be composed, if chiefly constructed of Southern wood would be of signal importance either in the view of naval strength or of national œconomy. Some of the Southern and of the middle States yield a greater plenty of iron and of better quality. Seamen must chiefly be drawn from the Northern hive. The necessity of naval protection to external or maritime commerce, does not require a particular elucidation, no more than the conduciveness of that species of commerce to the prosperity of a navy. They, by a kind of reaction, mutually beneficial, promote each other.

An unrestrained intercourse between the States themselves will advance the trade of each, by an interchange of their respective productions, not only for the supply of reciprocal wants at home, but for exportation to foreign markets. The veins of commerce in every part will be replenished, and will acquire additional motion and vigour from a free circulation of the commodities of every part. Commercial enterprise will have much greater scope, from the diversity in the productions of different States. When the staple of one fails, from a bad harvest or unproductive crop, it can call to its aid the staple of another. The variety not less than the value of products for exportation, contributes to the activity of foreign commerce. It can be conducted upon much better terms, with a large number of materials of a given value, than with a small number of materials of the same value; arising from the competitions of trade and from the fluctuations of markets. Particular articles may be in great demand, at certain periods, and unsaleable at others; but if there be a variety of articles it can scarcely happen that they should all be at one time in the latter predicament; and on this account the operations of the merchant would be less liable to any considerable obstruction, or stagnation. The speculative trader will at once perceive the force of these observations; and will acknowledge that the aggregate ballance of commerce of the United States would bid fair to be much more favorable, than that of the thirteen States, without union, or with partial unions.

It may perhaps be replied to this, that whether the States are united, or disunited, there would still be an intimate intercourse between them which would answer the same ends: But this intercourse would be fettered, interrupted and narrowed by a multiplicity of causes; which in the course of these Papers have been amply detailed. An unity of commercial, as well as political interests, can only result from an unity of government.

There are other points of view, in which this subject might be placed, of a striking and animating kind. But they would lead us too far into the regions of futurity, and would involve topics not proper for a Newspaper discussion. I shall briefly observe, that our situation invites, and our interests prompt us, to aim at an ascendant in the system of American affairs. The world may politically, as well as geographically, be divided into four parts, each having a distinct set of interests. Unhappily for the other three, Europe by her arms and by her negociations, by force and by fraud, has, in different degrees, extended her dominion over them all. Africa, Asia, and America have successively felt her domination. The superiority, she has long maintained, has tempted her to plume herself as the Mistress of the World, and to consider the rest of mankind as created for her benefit. Men admired as profound philosophers have, in direct terms, attributed to her inhabitants a physical superiority; and have gravely asserted that all animals, and with them the human species, degenerate in America—that even dogs cease to bark after having breathed a while in our atmosphere.* Facts have too long supported these arrogant pretensions of the European. It belongs to us to vindicate the honor of the human race, and to teach that assuming brother moderation. Union will enable us to do it. Disunion will add another victim to his triumphs. Let Americans disdain to be the instruments of European greatness! Let the thirteen States, bound together in a strict and indissoluble union, concur in erecting one great American system, superior to the controul of all trans-atlantic force or influence, and able to dictate the terms of the connection between the old and the new world!

Publius.

No. 12

ALEXANDER HAMILTON

Land values rise when commerce flourishes—which will happen under the Constitution.

No. 13

ALEXANDER HAMILTON

On the disadvantages of several confederations.

No. 14

JAMES MADISON

On effects of geography on the republic. Representation invented in Europe, applied in America to extended republic.

No. 15

ALEXANDER HAMILTON

Men need government. Sovereign power is impatient of control.

---

* *Recherches philosophiques sur les Américains.*

No. 16

ALEXANDER HAMILTON

On relations between states and federal government. First mention of judiciary: federal review of state legislation.

No. 17

ALEXANDER HAMILTON

December 5, 1787

To the People of the State of New York.

An objection of a nature different from that which has been stated and answered, in my last address, may perhaps be likewise urged against the principle of legislation for the individual citizens of America. It may be said, that it would tend to render the government of the Union too powerful, and to enable it to absorb in itself those residuary authorities, which it might be judged proper to leave with the States for local purposes. Allowing the utmost latitude to the love of power, which any reasonable man can require, I confess I am at a loss to discover what temptation the persons entrusted with the administration of the general government could ever feel to divest the States of the authorities of that description. The regulation of the mere domestic police of a State appears to me to hold out slender allurements to ambition. Commerce, finance, negociation and war seem to comprehend all the objects, which have charms for minds governed by that passion; and all the powers necessary to these objects ought in the first instance to be lodged in the national depository. The administration of private justice between the citizens of the same State, the supervision of agriculture and of other concerns of a similar nature, all those things in short which are proper to be provided for by local legislation, can never be desirable cares of a general jurisdiction. It is therefore improbable that there should exist a disposition in the Fœderal councils to usurp the powers with which they are connected; because the attempt to exercise those powers would be as troublesome as it would be nugatory; and the possession of

From *The Independent Journal*, December 5, 1787. This essay appeared on December 7 in both *The New-York Packet* and *The Daily Advertiser*.

them, for that reason, would contribute nothing to the dignity, to the importance, or to the splendour of the national government.

But let it be admitted for argument sake, that mere wantonness and lust of domination would be sufficient to beget that disposition, still it may be safely affirmed, that the sense of the constituent body of the national representatives, or in other words of the people of the several States would controul the indulgence of so extravagant an appetite. It will always be far more easy for the State governments to encroach upon the national authorities, than for the national government to encroach upon the State authorities. The proof of this proposition turns upon the greater degree of influence, which the State governments, if they administer their affairs with uprightness and prudence, will generally possess over the people; a circumstance which at the same time teaches us, that there is an inherent and intrinsic weakness in all Fœderal Constitutions; and that too much pains cannot be taken in their organization, to give them all the force which is compatible with the principles of liberty.

The superiority of influence in favour of the particular governments would result partly from the diffusive construction of the national government; but chiefly from the nature of the objects to which the attention of the State administrations would be directed.

It is a known fact in human nature that its affections are commonly weak in proportion to the distance or diffusiveness of the object. Upon the same principle that a man is more attached to his family than to his neighbourhood, to his neighbourhood than to the community at large, the people of each State would be apt to feel a stronger byass towards their local governments than towards the government of the Union; unless the force of that principle should be destroyed by a much better administration of the latter.

This strong propensity of the human heart would find powerful auxiliaries in the objects of State regulation.

The variety of more minute interests, which will necessarily fall under the superintendence of the local administrations, and which will form so many rivulets of influence running through every part of the society, cannot be particularised without involving a detail too tedious and uninteresting to compensate for the instruction it might afford.

There is one transcendent advantage belonging to the province of the State governments which alone suffices to place the matter in a clear and satisfactory light. I mean the ordinary administration of criminal and civil justice. This of all others is the most powerful, most universal and most attractive source of popular obedience and attachment. It is that, which—being the immediate and visible guardian of life and property—having its benefits and its terrors in constant activity before the public eye—regulating all those personal interests and familiar concerns to which the sensibility of individuals is more immediately awake—contributes more than any other circumstance to impressing upon the minds of the people affection, esteem and reverence towards the government. This great cement of society which will diffuse itself almost wholly through the channels of the particular governments, independent of all other causes of influence, would ensure them so decided an empire over their respective citizens, as to render them at all times a complete counterpoise and not unfrequently dangerous rivals to the power of the Union.

The operations of the national government on the other hand falling less immediately under the observation of the mass of the citizens the benefits derived from it will chiefly be perceived and attended to by speculative men. Relating to more general interests, they will be less apt to come home to the feelings of the people; and, in proportion, less likely to inspire a habitual sense of obligation and an active sentiment of attachment.

The reasoning on this head has been abundantly exemplified by the experience of all Fœderal constitutions, with which we are acquainted, and of all others, which have borne the least analogy to them.

Though the ancient feudal systems were not strictly speaking confederacies, yet they partook of the nature of that species of association. There was a common head, a chieftain, or sovereign, whose authority extended over the whole nation; and a number of subordinate vassals; or feudatories, who had large portions of land allotted to them and numerous trains of *inferior* vassals or retainers, who occupied and cultivated that land upon the tenure of fealty or obedience to the persons of whom they held it. Each principal vassal was a kind of sovereign within his particular demesnes. The consequences of this situation were a continual opposition to the authority of the sovereign, and frequent wars between the great barons, or chief feudatories themselves. The power of the head of the nation was commonly too weak either to preserve the public peace or to protect the people against the oppressions of their immediate lords. This period of European affairs is emphatically stiled by historians the times of feudal anarchy. . . .

Nos. 18, 19, 20

JAMES MADISON WITH ALEXANDER HAMILTON

Consider the histories of leagues in the ancient and European worlds, and discuss the weaknesses of the Netherlands.

No. 21

ALEXANDER HAMILTON

Criticizes the weakness of the Confederation.

No. 22

ALEXANDER HAMILTON

December 14, 1787

. . . A circumstance, which crowns the defects of the confederation, remains yet to be mentioned—the want of a judiciary power. Laws are a dead letter without courts to expound and define their true meaning and operation. The treaties of the United States to have any force at all, must be considered as part of the law of the land. Their true import as far as respects individuals, must, like all other laws, be ascertained by judicial determinations. To produce uniformity in these determinations, they ought to be submitted in the last resort, to one SUPREME TRIBUNAL. And this tribunal ought to be instituted under the same authority which forms the treaties themselves. These ingredients are both indispensable. If there is in each State, a court of final jurisdiction, there may be as many different final determinations on the same point, as there are courts. There are endless diversities in the opinions of men. We often see not only different courts, but the Judges of the same court differing from each other. To avoid the confusion which would unavoidably result from the contradictory decisions of a number of independent

---

From *The New-York Packet*, December 14, 1787. Also in *The Independent Journal*, December 15, and *The Daily Advertiser*, December 17 and 18.

judicatories, all nations have found it necessary to establish one court paramount to the rest—possessing a general superintendance, and authorised to settle and declare in the last resort, an uniform rule of civil justice.

This is the more necessary where the frame of the government is so compounded, that the laws of the whole are in danger of being contravened by the laws of the parts. In this case if the particular tribunals are invested with a right of ultimate jurisdiction, besides the contradictions to be expected from difference of opinion, there will be much to fear from the bias of local views and prejudices, and from the interference of local regulations. As often as such an interference was to happen, there would be reason to apprehend, that the provisions of the particular laws might be preferred to those of the general laws; for nothing is more natural to men in office, than to look with peculiar deference towards that authority to which they owe their official existence.

The treaties of the United States, under the present constitution, are liable to the infractions of thirteen different Legislatures, and as many different courts of final jurisdiction, acting under the authority of those Legislatures. The faith, the reputation, the peace of the whole union, are thus continually at the mercy of the prejudices, the passions, and the interests of every member of which it is composed. Is it possible that foreign nations can either respect or confide in such a government? Is it possible that the People of America will longer consent to trust their honor, their happiness, their safety, on so precarious a foundation? . . .

No. 23

ALEXANDER HAMILTON

Essential powers not to be limited; means ought to be apportioned to end in view.

No. 24
ALEXANDER HAMILTON
December 19, 1787

. . . If we mean to be a commercial people or even to be secure on our Atlantic side, we must endeavour as soon as possible to have a navy. To this purpose there must be dock-yards and arsenals, and, for the defence of these, fortifications and probably garrisons. When a nation has become so powerful by sea, that it can protect its dock-yards by its fleets, this supersedes the necessity of garrisons for that purpose; but where naval establishments are in their infancy, moderate garrisons will in all likelihood be found an indispensible security against descents for the destruction of the arsenals and dock-yards, and sometimes of the fleet itself.

Publius.

From *The Independent Journal*, December 19, 1787.

Nos. 25, 26
ALEXANDER HAMILTON

On the need for an American army.

No. 27
ALEXANDER HAMILTON
December 25, 1787

To the People of the State of New York.

It has been urged in different shapes that a constitution of the kind proposed by the Convention, cannot operate without the aid of a military force to execute its laws. This however, like most other things that have been alledged on that side, rests on more general assertion; unsupported by any precise or intelligible designation of the reasons upon which it is founded. As far as I have been able

From *The New-York Packet*, December 25, 1787. This essay appeared on the same day in *The New-York Journal*, and on December 26 in *The Independent Journal* and *The Daily Advertiser*.

to divine the latent meaning of the objectors, it seems to originate in a pre-supposition that the people will be disinclined to the exercise of fœderal authority in any matter of an internal nature. Waving any exception that might be taken to the inaccuracy or inexplicitness of the distinction between internal and external, let us enquire what ground there is to presuppose that disinclination in the people? Unless we presume, at the same time, that the powers of the General Government will be worse administered than those of the State governments, there seems to be no room for the presumption of ill-will, disaffection or opposition in the people. I believe it may be laid down as a general rule, that their confidence in and obedience to a government, will commonly be proportioned to the goodness or badness of its administration. It must be admitted that there are exceptions to this rule; but these exceptions depend so entirely on accidental causes, that they cannot be considered as having any relation to the intrinsic merits or demerits of a constitution. These can only be judged of by general principles and maxims.

Various reasons have been suggested in the course of these papers, to induce a probability that the General Government will be better administered than the particular governments: The principal of which reasons are that the extension of the spheres of election will present a greater option, or latitude of choice to the people, that through the medium of the State Legislatures, which are select bodies of men, and who are to appoint the members of the national Senate,—there is reason to expect that this branch will generally be composed with peculiar care and judgment: That these circumstances promise greater knowledge and more extensive information in the national councils: And that they will be less apt to be tainted by the spirit of faction, and more out of the reach of those occasional ill humors or temporary prejudices and propensities, which in smaller societies frequently contaminate the public councils, beget injustice and oppression of a part of the community, and engender schemes, which though they gratify a momentary inclination or desire, terminate in general distress, dissatisfaction and disgust. Several additional reasons of considerable force, to fortify that probability, will occur when we come to survey with a more critic[al] eye, the interior structure of the edifice, which we are invited to erect. It will be sufficient here to remark, that until satisfactory reasons can be assigned to justify an opinion, that the fœderal government is likely to be administered in such a manner as to render it odious or contemptible to the people, there can be no reasonable foundation for the supposition, that the laws of the Union will meet with any greater obstruction from them, or will stand in need of any other methods to enforce their execution, than the laws of the particular members.

The hope of impunity is a strong incitement to sedition—the dread of punishment—a proportionately strong discouragement to it. Will not the government of the Union, which, if possessed of a due degree of power, can call to its aid the collective resources of the whole confederacy, be more likely to repress the *former* sentiment, and to inspire the *latter*, than that of a single State, which can only command the resources within itself? A turbulent faction in a State may easily suppose itself able to contend with the friends to the government in that State; but it can hardly be so infatuated as to imagine itself a match for the combined efforts of the Union. If this reflection be just, there is less danger of resistance from irregular combinations of individuals, to the authority of the confederacy, than to that of a single member.

I will in this place hazard an observation which will not be the less just, because to some it may appear new; which is, that the more the operations of the national authority are intermingled in the ordinary exercise of government; the more the citizens are accustomed to meet with it in the common occurrences of their political life; the more it is familiarised to their sight and to their feelings; the further it enters into those objects which touch the most sensible cords, and put in motion the most active springs of the human heart; the greater will be the probability that it will conciliate the respect and attachment of the community. Man is very much a creature of habit. A thing that rarely strikes his senses will generally have but little influence upon his mind. A government continually at a distance and out of sight, can hardly be expected to interest the sensations of the people. The inference is, that the authority of the Union, and the affections of the citizens towards it, will be strengthened rather than weakened by its extension to what are called matters of internal concern; and will have less occasion to recur to force in proportion to the familiarity and comprehensiveness of its agency. The more it circulates through those channels and currents, in which the passions of mankind naturally flow, the less will it require the aid of the violent and perilous expedients of compulsion.

One thing at all events, must be evident, that a government like the one proposed, would bid much fairer to avoid the necessity of using force, than that species of league contended for by most of its opponents; the authority of which should only operate upon the States in their political or collective capacities. It has been shewn, that in such a confederacy, there can be no sanction for the laws but force; that frequent delinquencies in the members, are the natural offspring of the very frame of the government; and that as often as these happen they can only be redressed, if at all, by war and violence.

The plan reported by the Convention, by extending the authority of the fœderal head to the individual citizens of the several States, will enable the government to employ the ordinary magistracy of each in the execution of its laws. It is easy to perceive that this will tend to destroy, in the common apprehension, all distinction between the sources from which they might proceed; and will give the Fœderal Government the same advantage for securing a due obedience to its authority, which is enjoyed by the government of each State; in addition to the influence on public opinion, which will result from the important consideration of its having power to call to its assistance and support the resources of the whole Union. It merits particular attention in this place, that the laws of the confederacy, as to the *enumerated* and *legitimate* objects of its jurisdiction, will become the SUPREME LAW of the land; to the observance of which, all officers legislative, executive and judicial in each State, will be bound by the sanctity of an oath. Thus the Legislatures, Courts and Magistrates of the respective members will be incorporated into the operations of the national government, *as far as its just and constitutional authority extends;* and will be rendered auxiliary to the enforcement of its laws. Any man, who will pursue by his own reflections the consequences of this situation, will perceive that there is good ground to calculate upon a regular and peaceable execution of the laws of the Union; if its powers are administered with a common share of prudence. If we will arbitrarily suppose the contrary, we may deduce any inferences we please from the supposition; for it is certainly possible, by an injudicious exercise of the authorities of the best government, that ever was or ever can be instituted, to provoke and precipitate the people into the wildest excesses. But though the adversaries of the proposed constitution should presume that the national rulers would be insensible to the motives of public good, or to the obligations of duty; I would still ask them, how the interests of ambition, or the views of encroachment, can be promoted by such a conduct?

Publius.

No. 28

ALEXANDER HAMILTON

The state needs force.

No. 29

ALEXANDER HAMILTON

Rebuts Anti-Federalist charges that the federal government will abuse its power to call out state militias.

No. 30

ALEXANDER HAMILTON

December 28, 1787

To the People of the State of New York.

It has been already observed, that the Fœderal Government ought to possess the power of providing for the support of the national forces; in which proposition was intended to be included the expence of raising troops, of building and equiping fleets, and all other expences in any wise connected with military arrangements and operations. But these are not the only objects to which the jurisdiction of the Union, in respect to revenue, must necessarily be empowered to extend—It must embrace a provision for the support of the national civil list—for the payment of the national debts contracted, or that may be contracted—and in general for all those matters which will call for disbursements out of the national treasury. The conclusion is, that there must be interwoven

From *The New-York Packet*, December 28, 1787. This essay appeared on December 29 in *The Independent Journal* and *The Daily Advertiser*, and was begun on January 2, 1788, and concluded on January 4 in *The New-York Journal*.

in the frame of the government, a general power of taxation in one shape or another.

Money is with propriety considered as the vital principle of the body politic; as that which sustains its life and motion, and enables it to perform its most essential functions. A complete power therefore to procure a regular and adequate supply of it, as far as the resources of the community will permit, may be regarded as an indispensable ingredient in every constitution. From a deficiency in this particular, one of two evils must ensue; either the people must be subjected to continual plunder as a substitute for a more eligible mode of supplying the public wants, or the government must sink into a fatal atrophy, and in a short course of time perish.

In the Ottoman or Turkish empire, the sovereign, though in other respects absolute master of the lives and fortunes of his subjects, has no right to impose a new tax. The consequence is, that he permits the Bashaws or Governors of provinces to pillage the people without mercy; and in turn squeezes out of them the sums of which he stands in need to satisfy his own exigencies and those of the State. In America, from a like cause, the government of the Union has gradually dwindled into a state of decay, approaching nearly to annihilation. Who can doubt that the happiness of the people in both countries would be promoted by competent authorities in the proper hands, to provide the revenues which the necessities of the public might require?

The present confederation, feeble as it is, intended to repose in the United States, an unlimited power of providing for the pecuniary wants of the Union. But proceeding upon an erroneous principle, it has been done in such a manner as entirely to have frustrated the intention. Congress by the articles which compose that compact (as has been already stated) are authorised to ascertain and call for any sums of money necessary, in their judgment, to the service of the United States; and their requisitions, if conformable to the rule of apportionment, are in every constitutional sense obligatory upon the States. These have no right to question the propriety of the demand—no discretion beyond that of devising the ways and means of furnishing the sums demanded. But though this be strictly and truly the case; though the assumption of such a right be an infringement of the articles of Union; though it may seldom or never have been avowedly claimed; yet in practice it has been constantly exercised; and would continue to be so, as long as the revenues of the confederacy should remain dependant on the intermediate agency of its members. What the consequences of this system have been, is within the knowledge of every man, the least conversant in our public affairs, and has been amply unfolded in different parts of these inquiries. It is this which has chiefly contributed to reduce us to a situation which affords ample cause, both of mortification to ourselves, and of triumph to our enemies.

What remedy can there be for this situation but, in a change of the system, which has produced it? In a change of the fallacious and delusive system of quotas and requisitions? What substitute can there be imagined for this *ignis fatuus* in finance, but that of permitting the national government to raise its own revenues by the ordinary methods of taxation, authorised in every well ordered constitution of civil government? Ingenious men may declaim with plausibility on any subject; but no human ingenuity can point out any other expedient to rescue us from the inconveniences and embarrassments, naturally resulting from defective supplies of the public treasury.

The more intelligent adversaries of the new constitution admit the force of this reasoning; but they qualify their admission by a distinction between what they call *internal* and *external* taxation. The former they would reserve to the State governments; the latter, which they explain into commercial imposts, or rather duties on imported articles, they declare themselves willing to concede to the Fœderal Head. This distinction, however, would violate that fundamental maxim of good sense and sound policy, which dictates that every POWER ought to be proportionate to its OBJECT; and would still leave the General Government in a kind of tutelage to the State governments, inconsistent with every idea of vigor or efficiency. Who can pretend that commercial imposts are or would be alone equal to the present and future exigencies of the Union? Taking into the account the existing debt, foreign and domestic, upon any plan of extinguishment, which a man moderately impressed with the importance of public justice and public credit could approve, in addition to the establishments, which all parties will acknowledge to be necessary, we could not reasonably flatter ourselves, that this resource alone, upon the most improved scale, would even suffice for its present necessities. Its future necessities admit not of calculation or limitation; and upon the principle, more than once adverted to, the power of making provision for them as they arise, ought to be equally unconfined. I believe it may be regarded as a position, warranted by the history of mankind, that *in the usual progress of things, the necessities of a nation in every stage of its existence will be found at least equal to its resources.*

To say that deficiencies may be provided for by requisitions upon the States, is on the one hand, to acknowledge that this system cannot be depended upon; and on the other hand, to depend upon it for every thing beyond a certain limit. Those who have carefully attended to its vices and deformities as they have been exhibited by experience, or delineated in the course of these papers, must feel an invincible repugnancy to trusting the national interests, in any degree, to its operation. Its inevitable tendency, whenever it is brought into activity, must be to enfeeble the Union and sow the seeds of discord and contention between the Fœderal Head and its members, and between the members themselves. Can it be expected that the deficiencies would be better supplied in this mode, than the total wants of the Union have heretofore been supplied, in the same mode? It ought to be recollected, that if less will be required from the States, they will have proportionately less means to answer the demand. If the opinions of those who contend for the distinction which has been mentioned, were to be received as evidence of truth, one would be led to conclude that there was some known point in the œconomy of national affairs, at which it would be safe to stop, and say, thus far the ends of public happiness will be promoted by supplying the wants of government, and all beyond this is unworthy of our care or anxiety. How is it possible that a government half supplied and always necessitous, can fulfil the purposes of its institution—can provide for the security of—advance the prosperity—or support the reputation of the commonwealth? How can it ever possess either energy or stability, dignity or credit, confidence at home or respectability abroad? How can its administration be any thing else than a succession of expedients temporising, impotent, disgraceful? How will it be able to avoid a frequent sacrifice of its engagements to immediate necessity? How can it undertake or execute any liberal or enlarged plans of public good?

Let us attend to what would be the effects of this situation in the very first war in which we should happen to be engaged. We will presume for argument sake, that the revenue arising from the impost-duties answer the purposes of a provision for the public debt, and of a peace establishment for the Union. Thus circumstanced, a war breaks out. What would be the probable conduct of the government in such an emergency? Taught by experience that proper dependence could not be placed on the success of requisitions: unable by its own authority to lay hold of fresh resources, and urged by considerations of national danger, would it not be driven to the expedient of diverting the funds already appropriated from their proper objects to the defence of the State? It is not easy to see how a step of this kind could be avoided; and if it should be taken, it is evident that it would prove the destruction of public credit at the very moment that it was become essential to the public safety. To imagine that at such a crisis credit might be dispensed with, would be the extreme of infatuation. In the modern system of war, nations the most wealthy are obliged to have recourse to large loans. A country so little opulent as ours, must feel this necessity in a much stronger degree. But who would lend to a government that prefaced its overtures for borrowing, by an act which demonstrated that no reliance could be placed on the steadiness of its measures for paying? The loans it might be able to procure, would be as limited in their extent as burthensome in their conditions. They would be made upon the same principles that usurers commonly lend to bankrupt and fraudulent debtors; with a sparing hand, and at enormous premiums.

It may perhaps be imagined, that from the scantiness of the resources of the country, the necessity of diverting the established funds in the case supposed, would exist; though the national government should possess an unrestrained power of taxation. But two considerations will serve to quiet all apprehension on this head; one is, that we are sure the resources of the community in their full extent, will be brought into activity for the benefit of the Union; the other is, that whatever deficiencies there may be, can without difficulty be supplied by loans.

The power of creating new funds upon new objects of taxation by its own authority, would enable the national government to borrow, as far as its necessities might require. Foreigners as well as the citizens of America, could then reasonably repose confidence in its engagements; but to depend upon a government, that must itself depend upon thirteen other governments for the means of fulfilling its contracts, when once its situation is clearly understood, would require a degree of credulity, not often to be met with in the pecuniary transactions of mankind, and little reconcileable with the usual sharp-sightedness of avarice.

Reflections of this kind, may have trifling weight with men, who hope to see realized in America, the halcyon scenes of the poetic or fabulous age; but to those who believe we are likely to experience a common portion of the vicissitudes and calamities, which have fallen to the lot of other nations, they must appear entitled to serious attention. Such men must behold the actual situation of their country with painful solicitude, and deprecate the evils which ambition or revenge might, with too much facility, inflict upon it.

No. 31

ALEXANDER HAMILTON

Answers Anti-Federalist fears of possible federal usurpation.

No. 32

ALEXANDER HAMILTON

January 2, 1788

To the People of the State of New York.

Although I am of opinion that there would be no real danger of the consequences, which seem to be apprehended to the State Governments, from a power in the Union to controul them in the levies of money; because I am persuaded that the sense of the people, the extreme hazard of provoking the resentments of the State Governments, and a conviction of the utility and necessity of local administrations, for local purposes, would be a complete barrier against the oppressive use of such a power: Yet I am willing here to allow in its full extent the justness of the reasoning, which requires that the individual States should possess an independent and uncontrolable authority to raise their own revenues for the supply of their own wants. And making this concession I affirm that (with the sole exception of duties on imports and exports) they would under the plan of the Convention retain that authority in the most absolute and unqualified sense; and that an attempt

From *The Independent Journal*, January 2, 1788. This essay also appeared on January 3 in *The Daily Advertiser*, on January 4 in *The New-York Packet*, and on January 8 in *The New-York Journal*.

on the part of the national Government to abridge them in the exercise of it would be a violent assumption of power unwarranted by any article or clause of its Constitution.

An intire consolidation of the States into one complete national sovereignty would imply an intire subordination of the parts; and whatever powers might remain in them would be altogether dependent on the general will. But as the plan of the Convention aims only at a partial Union or consolidation, the State Governments would clearly retain all the rights of sovereignty which they before had and which were not by that act *exclusively* delegated to the United States. This exclusive delegation or rather this alienation of State sovereignty would only exist in three cases; where the Constitution in express terms granted an exclusive authority to the Union; where it granted in one instance an authority to the Union and in another prohibited the States from exercising the like authority; and where it granted an authority to the Union, to which a similar authority in the States would be absolutely and totally *contradictory* and *repugnant*. I use these terms to distinguish this last case from another which might appear to resemble it; but which would in fact be essentially different; I mean where the exercise of a concurrent jurisdiction might be productive of occasional interferences in the *policy* of any branch of administration, but would not imply any direct contradiction or repugnancy in point of constitutional authority. These three cases of exclusive jurisdiction in the Fœderal Government may be exemplified by the following instances: The last clause but one in the 8th. section of the 1st. article provides expressly that Congress shall exercise *"exclusive legislation"* over the district to be appropriated as the seat of government. This answers to the first case. The first clause of the same section impowers Congress *"to lay and collect taxes, duties, imposts and excises"* and the 2d. clause of the 10th. section of the same article declares that *"no State shall* without the consent of Congress, *lay any imposts or duties on imports or exports* except for the purpose of executing its inspection laws." Hence would result an exclusive power in the Union to lay duties on imports and exports with the particular exception mentioned; but this power is abriged by another clause which declares that no tax or duty shall be laid on articles exported from any State; in consequence of which qualification it now only extends to the *duties on imports*. This answers to the second case. The third will be found in that clause, which declares that Congress shall have power "to establish an UNIFORM RULE of naturalization throughout the United States." This must necessarily be exclusive; because if each State had power to prescribe a DISTINCT RULE there could be no UNIFORM RULE.

A case which may perhaps be thought to resemble the latter, but which is in fact widely different, affects the question immediately under consideration. I mean the power of imposing taxes on all articles other than exports and imports. This, I contend, is manifestly a concurrent and coequal authority in the United States and in the individual States. There is plainly no expression in the granting clause which makes that power *exclusive* in the Union. There is no independent clause or sentence which prohibits the States from exercising it. So far is this from being the case, that a plain and conclusive argument to the contrary is to be deduced from the restraint laid upon the States in relation to duties on imports and exports. This restriction implies an admission, that if it were not inserted the States would possess the power it excludes, and it implies a further admission, that as to all other taxes the authority of the States remains undiminished. In any other view it would be both unnecessary and dangerous; it would be unnecessary because if the grant to the Union of the power of laying such duties implied the exclusion of the States, or even their subordination in this particular there could be no need of such a restriction; it would be dangerous because the introduction of it leads directly to the conclusion which has been mentioned and which if the reasoning of the objectors be just, could not have been intended; I mean that the States in all cases to which the restriction did not apply would have a concurrent power of taxation with the Union. The restriction in question amounts to what lawyers call a NEGATIVE PREGNANT; that is a *negation* of one thing and an *affirmance* of another; a negation of the authority of the States to impose taxes on imports and exports, and an affirmance of their authority to impose them on all other articles. It would be mere sophistry to argue that it was meant to exclude them *absolutely* from the imposition of taxes of the former kind, and to leave them at liberty to lay others *subject to the controul* of the national Legislature. The restraining or prohibitory clause only says, that they shall not *without the consent of Congress* lay such duties; and if we are to understand this in the sense last mentioned, the Constitution would then be made to introduce a formal provision for the sake of a very absurd conclusion; which is that the States *with the consent* of the national Legislature might tax imports and exports; and that they might tax every other article *unless controuled* by the same body. If this was the intention why not leave it in the first instance to what is alleged to be the natural operation of the original clause conferring a general power of taxation upon the Union? It is evident that this could not have been the intention and that it will not bear a construction of the kind.

As to a supposition of repugnancy between the power of taxation in the States and in the Union, it cannot be supported in that sense which would be requisite to work an exclusion of the States. It is indeed possible that a tax might be laid on a particular article by a State which might render it *inexpedient* that thus a further tax should be laid on the same article by the Union; but it would not imply a constitutional inability to impose a further tax. The quantity of the imposition, the expediency or inexpediency of an increase on either side, would be mutually questions of prudence; but there would be involved no direct contradiction of power. The particular policy of the national and of the State systems of finance might now and then not exactly coincide, and might require reciprocal forbearances. It is not however a mere possibility of inconvenience in the exercise of powers, but an immediate constitutional repugnancy, that can by implication alienate and extinguish a pre-existing right of sovereignty.

The necessity of a concurrent jurisdiction in certain cases results from the division of the sovereign power; and the rule that all authorities of which the States are not explicitly divested in favour of the Union remain with them in full vigour, is not only a theoretical consequence of that division, but is clearly admitted by the whole tenor of the instrument which contains the articles of the proposed constitution. We there find that notwithstanding the affirmative grants of general authorities, there has been the most pointed care in those cases where it was deemed improper that the like authorities should reside in the States, to insert negative clauses prohibiting the exercise of them by the States. The tenth section of the first article consists altogether of such provisions. This circumstance is a clear indication of the sense of the Convention, and furnishes a rule of interpretation out of the body of the act which justifies the position I have advanced, and refutes every hypothesis to the contrary.

Publius.

No. 33

ALEXANDER HAMILTON

January 2, 1788

The residue of the argument against the provisions in the constitution, in respect to taxation, is ingrafted upon the following clauses; the last clause of the eighth section of the first article of the plan under consideration, authorises the national legislature "to make all laws which shall be *necessary* and *proper*, for carrying into execution *the powers* by that Constitution vested in the government of the United States, or in any department or officer thereof"; and the second clause of the sixth article declares, that "the Constitution and the Laws of the United States made *in pursuance thereof*, and the treaties made by their authority shall be the *supreme law* of the land; any thing in the constitution or laws of any State to the contrary notwithstanding."

These two clauses have been the sources of much virulent invective and petulant declamation against the proposed constitution, they have been held up to the people, in all the exaggerated colours of misrepresentation, as the pernicious engines by which their local governments were to be destroyed and their liberties exterminated—as the hideous monster whose devouring jaws would spare neither sex nor age, nor high nor low, nor sacred nor profane; and yet strange as it may appear, after all this clamour, to those who may not have happened to contemplate them in the same light, it may be affirmed with perfect confidence, that the constitutional operation of the intended government would be precisely the same, if these clauses were entirely obliterated, as if they were repeated in every article. They are only declaratory of a truth, which would have resulted by necessary and unavoidable implication from the very act of constituting a Fœderal Government, and vesting it with certain specified powers. This is so clear a proposition, that moderation itself can scarcely listen to the railings which have been so copiously vented against this part of the plan, without emotions that disturb its equanimity.

What is a power, but the ability or faculty of doing a thing? What is the ability to do a thing but the power of employing the

---

From *The Independent Journal*, January 2, 1788. This essay appeared on January 3 in *The Daily Advertiser*, on January 4 in *The New-York Packet*, and on January 8 in *The New-York Journal*.

means necessary to its execution? What is a LEGISLATIVE power but a power of making LAWS? What are the *means* to execute a LEGISLATIVE power but LAWS? What is the power of laying and collecting taxes but a *legislative power*, or a power of *making laws*, to lay and collect taxes? What are the proper means of executing such a power but *necessary* and *proper* laws?

This simple train of enquiry furnishes us at once with a test by which to judge of the true nature of the clause complained of. It conducts us to this palpable truth, that a power to lay and collect taxes must be a power to pass all laws *necessary* and *proper* for the execution of that power; and what does the unfortunate and calumniated provision in question do more than declare the same truth; to wit, that the national legislature to whom the power of laying and collecting taxes had been previously given, might in the execution of that power pass all laws *necessary* and *proper* to carry it into effect? I have applied these observations thus particularly to the power of taxation, because it is the immediate subject under consideration, and because it is the most important of the authorities proposed to be conferred upon the Union. But the same process will lead to the same result in relation to all other powers declared in the constitution. And it is *expressly* to execute these powers, that the sweeping clause, as it has been affectedly called, authorises the national legislature to pass all *necessary* and *proper* laws. If there is any thing exceptionable, it must be sought for in the specific powers, upon which this general declaration is predicated. The declaration itself, though it may be chargeable with tautology or redundancy, is at least perfectly harmless.

But SUSPICION may ask why then was it introduced? The answer is, that it could only have been done for greater caution, and to guard against all cavilling refinements in those who might hereafter feel a disposition to curtail and evade the legitimate authorities of the Union. The Convention probably foresaw what it has been a principal aim of these papers to inculcate that the danger which most threatens our political welfare, is, that the State Governments will finally sap the foundations of the Union; and might therefore think it necessary, in so cardinal a point, to leave nothing to construction. Whatever may have been the inducement to it, the wisdom of the precaution is evident from the cry which has been raised against it; as that very cry betrays a disposition to question the great and essential truth which it is manifestly the object of that provision to declare.

But it may be again asked, who is to judge of the *necessity* and *propriety* of the laws to be passed for executing the powers of the Union? I answer first that this question arises as well and as fully upon the simple grant of those powers, as upon the declaratory clause: And I answer in the second place, that the national government, like every other, must judge in the first instance of the proper exercise of its powers; and its constituents in the last. If the Fœderal Government should overpass the just bounds of its authority, and make a tyrannical use of its powers; the people whose creature it is must appeal to the standard they have formed, and take such measures to redress the injury done to the constitution, as the exigency may suggest and prudence justify. The propriety of a law in a constitutional light, must always be determined by the nature of the powers upon which it is founded. Suppose by some forced constructions of its authority (which indeed cannot easily be imagined) the Fœderal Legislature should attempt to vary the law of descent in any State; would it not be evident that in making such an attempt it had exceeded its jurisdiction and infringed upon that of the State? Suppose again that upon the pretence of an interference with its revenues, it should undertake to abrogate a land tax imposed by the authority of a State, would it not be equally evident that this was an invasion of that concurrent jurisdiction in respect to this species of tax which its constitution plainly supposes to exist in the State governments? If there ever should be a doubt on this head the credit of it will be intirely due to those reasoners, who, in the imprudent zeal of their animosity to the plan of the Convention, have laboured to invelope it in a cloud calculated to obscure the plainest and simplest truths.

But it is said, that the laws of the Union are to be the *supreme law* of the land. But what inference can be drawn from this or what would they amount to, if they were not to be supreme? It is evident they would amount to nothing. A LAW by the very meaning of the term includes supremacy. It is a rule which those to whom it is prescribed are bound to observe. This results from every political association. If individuals enter into a state of society the laws of that society must be the supreme regulator of their conduct. If a number of political societies enter into a larger political society, the laws which the latter may enact, pursuant to the powers entrusted to it by its constitution, must necessarily be supreme over those societies, and the individuals of whom they are composed. It would otherwise be a mere treaty, dependent on the good faith of the parties, and not a government; which is only another word for POLITICAL POWER AND SUPREMACY. But it will not follow from this doctrine that acts of the larger society which are *not pursuant* to its constitutional powers but which are invasions of the residuary authorities of the smaller societies will become the supreme law of the land. These will be merely acts of usurpation and will deserve to be treated as such. Hence we perceive that the clause which declares the supremacy of the laws of the Union, like the one we have just before considered, only declares a truth, which flows immediately and necessarily from the institution of a Fœderal Government. It will not, I presume, have escaped observation that it *expressly* confines this supremacy to laws made *pursuant to the Constitution*; which I mention merely as an instance of caution in the Convention; since that limitation would have been to be understood though it had not been expressed.

Though a law therefore for laying a tax for the use of the United States would be supreme in its nature, and could not legally be opposed or controuled; yet a law for abrogating or preventing the collection of a tax laid by the authority of a State (unless upon imports and exports) would not be the supreme law of the land, but an usurpation of power not granted by the constitution. As far as an improper accumulation of taxes on the same object might tend to render the collection difficult or precarious, this would be a mutual inconvenience not arising from a superiority or defect of power on either side, but from an injudicious exercise of power by one or the other, in a manner equally disadvantageous to both. It is to be hoped and presumed however that mutual interest would dictate a concert in this respect which would avoid any material inconvenience. The inference from the whole is—that the individual States would, under the proposed constitution, retain an independent and uncontroulable authority to raise revenue to any extent of which they may stand in need by every kind of taxation except duties on imports and exports. It will be shewn in the next paper that this CONCURRENT JURISDICTION in the article of taxation was the only admissible substitute for an intire subordination, in respect to this branch of power, of the State authority to that of the Union.

Publius.

No. 34

ALEXANDER HAMILTON

January 5, 1788

To the People of the State of New York.

I flatter myself it has been clearly shewn in my last number, that the particular States, under the proposed Constitution, would have CO-EQUAL authority with the Union in the article of revenue, except as to duties on imports. As this leaves open to the States far the greatest part of the resources of the community, there can be no color for the assertion, that they would not possess means, as abundant as could be desired, for the supply of their own wants, independent of all external control. That the field is sufficiently wide, will more fully appear, when we come to advert to the inconsiderable share of the public expences, for which, it will fall to the lot of the State Governments to provide.

To argue upon abstract principles, that this co-ordinate authority cannot exist, is to set up supposition and theory, against fact and reality. However proper such reasonings might be, to show that a thing *ought not to exist*, they are wholly to be rejected, when they are made use of to prove that it does not exist, contrary to the evidence of the fact itself. It is well known, that in the Roman Republic, the Legislative authority in the last resort, resided for ages in two different political bodies; not as branches of the same Legislature, but as distinct and independent Legislatures, in each of which an opposite interest prevailed; in one, the Patrician—in the other, the Plebeian. Many arguments might have been adduced to prove the unfitness of two such seemingly contradictory authorities, each having power to *annul* or *repeal* the acts of the other. But a man would have been regarded as frantic, who should have attempted at Rome, to disprove their existence. It will readily be understood, that I allude to the COMITIA CENTURIATA, *and* COMITIA TRIBUTA. The former, in which the people voted by Centuries, was so arranged as to give a superiority to the Patrician interest: in the latter, in which numbers prevailed, the Plebeian interest had an entire predominancy. And yet these

---

From *The Independent Journal*, January 5, 1788. This essay appeared on the same day in both *The New-York Packet* and *The Daily Advertiser* and on January 8 in *The New-York Journal*.

two Legislatures co-existed for ages, and the Roman Republic attained to the utmost height of human greatness.

In the case particularly under consideration, there is no such contradiction as appears in the example cited, there is no power on either side to annul the acts of the other. And in practice, there is little reason to apprehend any inconvenience; because, in a short course of time, the wants of the States will naturally reduce themselves within a *a very narrow compass*; and in the interim, the United States will, in all probability, find it convenient to abstain wholly from those objects, to which the particular States would be inclined to resort.

To form a more precise judgment of the true merits of this question, it will be well to advert to the proportion between the objects that will require a Federal provision in respect to revenue; and those which will require a State provision. We shall discover that the former are altogether unlimited; and, that the latter are circumscribed within very moderate bounds. In pursuing this enquiry, we must bear in mind, that we are not to confine our view to the present period, but to look forward to remote futurity. Constitutions of civil Government are not to be framed upon a calculation of existing exigencies; but upon a combination of these, with the probable exigencies of ages, according to the natural and tried course of human affairs. Nothing therefore can be more fallacious, than to infer the extent of any power, proper to be lodged in the National Government, from an estimate of its immediate necessities. There ought to be a CAPACITY to provide for future contingencies, as they may happen; and, as these are illimitable in their nature, it is impossible safely to limit that capacity. It is true, perhaps, that a computation might be made, with sufficient accuracy to answer the purpose of the quantity of revenue, requisite to discharge the subsisting engagements of the Union, and to maintain those establishments, which for some time to come, would suffice in time of peace. But would it be wise, or would it not rather be the extreme of folly, to stop at this point, and to leave the Government entrusted with the care of the National defence, in a state of absolute incapacity to provide for the protection of the community, against future invasions of the public peace, by foreign war, or domestic convulsions? If, on the contrary, we ought to exceed this point, where can we stop, short of an indefinite power of providing for emergencies as they might arise? Though it is easy to assert, in general terms, the possibility of forming a rational judgment of a due provision against probable dangers; yet we may safely challenge those who make the assertion, to bring forward their data, and may affirm, that they would be found as vague and uncertain, as any that could be produced to establish the probable duration of the world. Observations, confined to the mere prospects of internal attacks, can deserve no weight, though even these will admit of no satisfactory calculation: But if we mean to be a commercial people, it must form a part of our policy, to be able one day to defend that commerce. The support of a navy, and of naval wars must baffle all the efforts of political arithmetic admitting that we ought to try the novel and absurd experiment in politics, of tying up the hands of Government from offensive war, founded upon reasons of state: Yet, certainly we ought not to disable it from guarding the community against the ambition or enmity of other Nations. A cloud has been for some time hanging over the European world. If it should break forth into a storm, who can insure us, that in its progress, a part of its fury would not be spent upon us? No reasonable man would hastily pronounce that we are entirely out of its reach. Or if the combustible materials that now seem to be collecting, should be dissipated without coming to maturity; or, if a flame should be kindled, without extending to us, what security can we have, that our tranquility will long remain undisturbed from some other cause, or from some other quarter? Let us recollect, that peace or war, will not always be left to our option; that however moderate or unambitious we may be, we cannot count upon the moderation, or hope to extinguish the ambition of others. Who could have imagined, at the conclusion of the last war, that France and Britain, wearied and exhausted as they both were, would so soon have looked with so hostile an aspect upon each other? To judge from the history of mankind, we shall be compelled to conclude, that the fiery and destructive passions of war, reign in the human breast, with much more powerful sway, than the mild and beneficent sentiments of peace; and, that to model our political systems upon speculations of lasting tranquility, is to calculate on the weaker springs of the human character.

What are the chief sources of expence in every Government? What has occasioned that enormous accumulation of debts with which several of the European Nations are oppressed? The answer, plainly is, wars and rebellions—the support of those institutions which are necessary to guard the body politic, against these two most mortal diseases of society. The expences arising from those institutions, which are relative to the mere domestic police of a State—to the support of its Legislative, Executive and Judicial departments, with their different appendages, and to the internal encouragement of agriculture and manufactures, (which will comprehend almost all the objects of State expenditure) are insignificant, in comparison with those which relate to the National defence.

In the kingdom of Great-Britain, where all the ostentatious apparatus of Monarchy is to be provided for, not above a fifteenth part of the annual income of the nation is appropriated to the class of expences last mentioned; the other fourteen fifteenths are absorbed in the payment of the interest of debts, contracted for carrying on the wars in which that country has been engaged, and in the maintenance of fleets and armies. If on the one hand it should be observed, that the expences incurred in the prosecution of the ambitious enterprizes and vain-glorious pursuits of a Monarchy, are not a proper standard by which to judge of those which might be necessary in a republic; it ought on the other hand to be remarked, that there should be as great a disproportion, between the profusion and extravagance of a wealthy kingdom in its domestic administration, and the frugality and œconomy, which, in that particular, become the modest simplicity of republican Government. If we balance a proper deduction from one side against that which it is supposed ought to be made from the other, the proportion may still be considered as holding good.

But let us advert to the large debt which we have ourselves contracted in a single war, and let us only calculate on a common share of the events which disturb the peace of nations, and we shall instantly perceive without the aid of any elaborate illustration, that there must always be an immense disproportion between the objects of Federal and State expenditures. It is true that several of the States separately are incumbered with considerable debts, which are an excrescence of the late war. But when these are discharged, the only call for revenue of any consequence, which the State Governments will continue to experience, will be for the mere support of their respective civil lists; to which, if we add all contingencies, the total amount in every State, ought not to exceed two hundred thousand pounds.

In framing a Government for posterity as well as ourselves, we ought in those provisions which are designed to be permanent, to calculate not on temporary, but on permanent causes of expence. If this principle be a just one, our attention would be directed to a provision in favor of the State Governments for an annual sum of about 200,000 pounds; while the exigencies of the Union could be susceptible of no limits, even in imagination. In this view of the subject by what logic can it be maintained, that the local Governments ought to command in perpetuity, an EXCLUSIVE source of revenue for any sum beyond the extent of 200,000 pounds? To extend its power further in *exclusion* of the authority of the Union, would be to take the resources of the community out of those hands which stood in need of them for the public welfare, in order to put them in other hands, which could have no just or proper occasion for them.

Suppose then the Convention had been inclined to proceed upon the principle of a repartition of the objects of revenue between the Union and its members, in *proportion* to their comparative necessities; what particular fund could have been selected for the use of the States, that would not either have been too much or too little; too little for their present, and too much for their future wants. As to the line of separation between external and internal taxes, this would leave to the States at a rough computation, the command of two thirds of the resources of the community, to defray from a tenth to a twentieth part of its expences, and to the Union, one third of the resources of the community, to defray from nine tenths to nineteen twentieths of its expences. If we desert this boundary, and content ourselves with leaving to the States an exclusive power of taxing houses and lands, there would still be a great disproportion between the *means* and the *end*; the possession of one third of the resources of the community, to supply at most one tenth of its wants. If any fund could have been selected and appropriated equal to and not greater than the object, it would have been inadequate to the discharge of the existing debts of the particular States, and would have left them dependent on the Union for a provision for this purpose.

The preceeding train of observations will justify the position which has been elsewhere laid down, that, "A CONCURRENT JURISDICTION in the article of taxation, was the only admissible substitute for an entire subordination, in respect to this branch of power, of the State authority to that of the Union." Any separation of the objects of revenue, that could have been fallen upon, would have amounted to a sacrifice of the great INTERESTS of the Union to the POWER of the individual States. The Convention thought the concurrent jurisdiction preferable to that subordination; and it is evident that it has at least the merit of reconciling an indefinite constitutional power of taxation in the Federal Government, with an adequate and independent power in the States to provide for their own necessities. There remain a few other lights, in which this important subject of taxation will claim a further consideration.

Publius.

No. 35

ALEXANDER HAMILTON

January 5, 1788

To the People of the State of New York.

Before we proceed to examine any other objections to an indefinite power of taxation in the Union, I shall make one general remark; which is, that if the jurisdiction of the national government in the article of revenue should be restricted to particular objects, it would naturally occasion an undue proportion of the public burthens to fall upon those objects. Two evils would spring from this source, the oppression of particular branches of industry, and an unequal distribution of the taxes, as well among the several States as among the citizens of the same State.

Suppose, as has been contended for, the fœderal power of taxation were to be confined to duties on imports, it is evident that the government, for want of being able to command other resources, would frequently be tempted to extend these duties to an injurious excess. There are persons who imagine that this can never be carried to too great a length; since the higher they are, the more it is alleged they will tend to discourage an extravagant consumption, to produce a favourable balance of trade, and to promote domestic manufactures. But all extremes are pernicious in various ways. Exorbitant duties on imported articles would beget a general spirit of smuggling; which is always prejudicial to the

---

From *The Independent Journal*, January 5, 1788. This essay appeared on January 7 in *The Daily Advertiser*, on January 8 in *The New-York Packet*, and on January 9 in *The New-York Journal*.

fair trader, and eventually to the revenue itself: They tend to render other classes of the community tributary in an improper degree to the manufacturing classes to whom they give a premature monopoly of the markets: They sometimes force industry out of its more natural channels into others in which it flows with less advantage. And in the last place they oppress the merchant, who is often obliged to pay them himself without any retribution from the consumer. When the demand is equal to the quantity of goods at market, the consumer generally pays the duty; but when the markets happen to be overstocked, a great proportion falls upon the merchant, and sometimes not only exhausts his profits, but breaks in upon his capital. I am apt to think that a division of the duty between the seller and the buyer more often happens than is commonly imagined. It is not always possible to raise the price of a commodity, in exact proportion to every additional imposition laid upon it. The merchant especially, in a country of small commercial capital, is often under a necessity of keeping prices down, in order to a more expeditious sale.

The maxim that the consumer is the payer, is so much oftener true than the reverse of the proposition, that it is far more equitable the duties on imports should go into a common stock, than that they should redound to the exclusive benefit of the importing States. But it is not so generally true as to render it equitable that those duties should form the only national fund. When they are paid by the merchant, they operate as an additional tax upon the importing State; whose citizens pay their proportion of them in the character of consumers. In this view they are productive of inequality among the States; which inequality would be encreased with the encreased extent of the duties. The confinement of the national revenues to this species of imposts, would be attended with inequality, from a different cause between the manufacturing and the non-manufacturing States. The States which can go furthest towards the supply of their own wants, by their own manufactures, will not, according to their numbers or wealth, consume so great a proportion of imported articles, as those States which are not in the same favourable situation; they would not therefore in this mode alone contribute to the public treasury in a ratio to their abilities. To make them do this, it is necessary that recourse be had to excises; the proper objects of which are particular kinds of manufactures. New-York is more deeply interested in these considerations than such of her citizens as contend for limiting the power of the Union to external taxation can be aware of—New-York is an importing State, and is not likely speedily to be to any great extent a manufacturing State. She would of course suffer in a double light from restraining the jurisdiction of the Union to commercial imposts.

So far as these observations tend to inculcate a danger of the import duties being extended to an injurious extreme it may be observed, conformably to a remark made in another part of these papers, that the interest of the revenue itself would be a sufficient guard against such an extreme. I readily admit that this would be the case as long as other resources were open; but if the avenues to them were closed HOPE stimulated by necessity would beget experiments fortified by rigorous precautions and additional penalties; which for a time would have the intended effect, till there had been leisure to contrive expedients to elude these new precautions. The first success would be apt to inspire false opinions; which it might require a long course of subsequent experience to correct. Necessity, especially in politics, often occasions false hopes, false reasonings and a system of measures, correspondently erroneous. But even if this supposed excess should not be a consequence of the limitation of the fœderal power of taxation the inequalities spoken of would still ensue, though not in the same degree, from the other causes that have been noticed. Let us now return to the examination of objections—

One, which if we may judge from the frequency of its repetition seems most to be relied on, is that the house of representatives is not sufficiently numerous for the reception of all the different classes of citizens; in order to combine the interests and feelings of every part of the community, and to produce a due sympathy between the representative body and its constituents. This argument presents itself under a very specious and seducing form; and is well calculated to lay hold of the prejudices of those to whom it is addressed. But when we come to dissect it with attention it will appear to be made up of nothing but fair sounding words. The object it seems to aim at is in the first place impracticable, and in the sense in which it is contended for is unnecessary. I reserve for another place the discussion of the question which relates to the sufficiency of the representative body in respect to numbers; and shall content myself with examining here the particular use which has been made of a contrary supposition in reference to the immediate subject of our inquiries.

The idea of an actual representation of all classes of the people by persons of each class is altogether visionary. Unless it were expressly provided in the Constitution that each different occupation should send one or more members the thing would never take place in practice. Mechanics and manufacturers will always be inclined with few exceptions to give their votes to merchants in preference to persons of their own professions or trades. Those discerning citizens are well aware that the mechanic and manufacturing arts furnish the materials of mercantile enterprise and industry. Many of them indeed are immediately connected with the operations of commerce. They know that the merchant is their natural patron and friend; and they are aware that however great the confidence they may justly feel in their own good sense, their interests can be more effectually promoted by the merchant than by themselves. They are sensible that their habits in life have not been such as to give them those acquired endowments, without which in a deliberative assembly the greatest natural abilities are for the most part useless; and that the influence and weight and superior acquirements of the merchants render them more equal to a contest with any spirit which might happen to infuse itself into the public councils unfriendly to the manufacturing and trading interests. These considerations and many others that might be mentioned prove, and experience confirms it, that artisans and manufacturers will commonly be disposed to bestow their votes upon merchants and those whom they recommend. We must therefore consider merchants as the natural representatives of all these classes of the community.

With regard to the learned professions, little need be observed; they truly form no distinct interest in society; and according to their situation and talents will be indiscriminately the objects of the confidence and choice of each other and of other parts of the community.

Nothing remains but the landed interests; and this in a political view and particularly in relation to taxes I take to be perfectly united from the wealthiest landlord to the poorest tenant. No tax can be laid on land which will not affect the proprietor of millions of acres as well as the proprietor of a single acre. Every land-holder will therefore have a common interest to keep the taxes on land as low as possible; and common interest may always be reckoned upon as the surest bond of sympathy. But if we even could suppose a distinction of interest between the opulent land-holder and the middling farmer, what reason is there to conclude that the first would stand a better chance of being deputed to the national legislature than the last? If we take fact as our guide and look into our own senate and assembly we shall find that moderate proprietors of land prevail in both; nor is this less the case in the senate which consists of a smaller number than in the Assembly, which is composed of a greater number. Where the qualifications of the electors are the same, whether they have to choose a small or a large number their votes will fall upon those in whom they have most confidence; whether these happen to be men of large fortunes or of moderate property or of no property at all.

It is said to be necessary that all classes of citizens should have some of their own number in the representative body, in order that their feelings and interests may be the better understood and attended to. But we have seen that this will never happen under any arrangement that leaves the votes of the people free. Where this is the case, the representative body, with too few exceptions to have any influence on the spirit of the government, will be composed of land-holders, merchants, and men of the learned professions. But where is the danger that the interests and feelings of the different classes of citizens will not be understood or attended to by these three descriptions of men? Will not the land-holder know and feel whatever will promote or injure the interests of landed property? and will he not from his own interest in that species of property be sufficiently prone to resist every attempt to prejudice or incumber it? Will not the merchant understand and be disposed to cultivate as far as may be proper the interests of the mechanic and manufacturing arts to which his commerce is so nearly allied? Will not the man of the learned profession, who will feel a neutrality to the rivalships between the different branches of industry, be likely to prove an impartial arbiter between them, ready to promote either, so far as it shall appear to him conducive to the general interests of the society?

If we take into the account the momentary humors or dispositions which may happen to prevail in particular parts of the society, and to which a wise administration will never be inattentive, is the man whose situation leads to extensive inquiry and information less likely to be a competent judge of their nature, extent and foundation than one whose observation does not travel beyond the circle of his neighbours and acquaintances? Is it not natural that a man who is a candidate for the favour of the people and who is dependent on the suffrages of his fellow-citizens for the continuance of his public honors should take care to inform himself of their dispositions and inclinations and should be willing to allow them their proper degree of influence upon his conduct? This dependence, and the necessity of being bound himself and his posterity by the laws to which he gives his assent are the true, and they are the strong chords of sympathy between the representatives and the constituent.

There is no part of the administration of government that requires extensive information and a thorough knowledge of the principles of political economy so much as the business of taxation. The man who understands those principles best will be least likely to resort to oppressive expedients, or to sacrifice any particular class of citizens to the procurement of revenue. It might be demonstrated that the most productive system of finance will always be the least burthensome. There can be no doubt that in order to a judicious exercise of the power of taxation it is necessary that the person in whose hands it is should be acquainted with the general genius, habits and modes of thinking of the people at large and with the resources of the country. And this is all that can be reasonably meant by a knowledge of the interests and feelings of the people. In any other sense the proposition has either no meaning, or an absurd one. And in that sense let every considerate citizen judge for himself where the requisite qualification is most likely to be found.

Publius.

No. 36

ALEXANDER HAMILTON

Completes examination of powers to be conferred on federal government. Need for "energy."

No. 37

JAMES MADISON

Embarks on discussion of work of the Convention. Need for energy in government.

No. 38

JAMES MADISON

Congress has not abused the powers it already possesses. Reviews objections.

No. 39

JAMES MADISON

January 16, 1788

To the People of the State of New York.

The last paper having concluded the observations which were meant to introduce a candid survey of the plan of government reported by the Convention, we now proceed to the execution of that part of our undertaking. The first question that offers itself is, whether the general form and aspect of the government be strictly republican? It is evident that no other form would be reconcileable with the genius of the people of America; with the fundamental principles of the revolution; or with that honorable determination, which animates every votary of freedom, to rest all our political experiments on the capacity of mankind for self-government. If the plan of the Convention therefore be found to depart from the republican character, its advocates must abandon it as no longer defensible.

What then are the distinctive characters of the republican form? Were an answer to this question to be sought, not by recurring to principles, but in the application of the term by political writers, to the constitutions of different States, no satisfactory one would ever be found. Holland, in which no particle of the supreme authority is derived from the people, has passed almost universally under the denomination of a republic. The same title has been bestowed on Venice, where absolute power over the great body of the people, is exercised in the most absolute manner, by a small body of hereditary nobles. Poland, which is a mixture of aristocracy and of monarchy in their worst forms, has been dignified

---

From *The Independent Journal*, January 16, 1788. This essay appeared on the same day in *The Daily Advertiser*, on January 18 in *The New-York Packet*, and on January 30 in *The New-York Journal*.

with the same appellation. The government of England, which has one republican branch only, combined with a hereditery aristocracy and monarchy, has with equal impropriety been frequently placed on the list of republics. These examples, which are nearly as dissimilar to each other as to a genuine republic, shew the extreme inaccuracy with which the term has been used in political disquisitions.

If we resort for a criterion, to the different principles on which different forms of government are established, we may define a republic to be, or at least may bestow that name on, a government which derives all its powers directly or indirectly from the great body of the people; and is administered by persons holding their offices during pleasure, for a limited period, or during good behaviour. It is *essential* to such a government, that it be derived from the great body of the society, not from an inconsiderable proportion, or a favored class of it; otherwise a handful of tyrannical nobles, exercising their oppressions by a delegation of their powers, might aspire to the rank of republicans, and claim for their government the honorable title of republic. It is *sufficient* for such a government, that the persons administering it be appointed, either directly or indirectly, by the people; and that they hold their appointments by either of the tenures just specified; otherwise every government in the United States, as well as every other popular government that has been or can be well organized or well executed, would be degraded from the republican character. According to the Constitution of every State in the Union, some or other of the officers of government are appointed indirectly only by the people. According to most of them the chief magistrate himself is so appointed. And according to one, this mode of appointment is extended to one of the coordinate branches of the legislature. According to all the Constitutions also, the tenure of the highest offices is extended to a definite period, and in many instances, both within the legislative and executive departments, to a period of years. According to the provisions of most of the constitutions, again, as well as according to the most respectable and received opinions on the subject, the members of the judiciary department are to retain their offices by the firm tenure of good behaviour.

On comparing the Constitution planned by the Convention, with the standard here fixed, we perceive at once that it is in the most rigid sense conformable to it. The House of Representatives, like that of one branch at least of all the State Legislatures, is elected immediately by the great body of the people. The Senate, like the present Congress, and the Senate of Maryland, derives its appointment indirectly from the people. The President is indirectly derived from the choice of the people, according to the example in most of the States. Even the judges, with all other officers of the Union, will, as in the several States, be the choice, though a remote choice, of the people themselves. The duration of the appointments is equally conformable to the republican standard, and to the model of the State Constitutions. The House of Representatives is periodically elective as in all the States: and for the period of two years as in the State of South-Carolina. The Senate is elective for the period of six years; which is but one year more than the period of the Senate of Maryland; and but two more than that of the Senates of New-York and Virginia. The President is to continue in office for the period of four years; as in New-York and Delaware, the chief magistrate is elected for three years, and in South-Carolina for two years. In the other States the election is annual. In several of the States however, no constitutional provision is made for the impeachment of the Chief Magistrate. And in Delaware and Virginia, he is not impeachable till out of office. The President of the United States is impeachable at any time during his continuance in office. The tenure by which the Judges are to hold their places, is, as it unquestionably ought to be, that of good behaviour. The tenure of the ministerial offices generally will be a subject of legal regulation, conformably to the reason of the case, and the example of the State Constitutions.

Could any further proof be required of the republican complextion of this system, the most decisive one might be found in its absolute prohibition of titles of nobility, both under the Federal and the State Governments; and in its express guarantee of the republican form to each of the latter.

But it was not sufficient, say the adversaries of the proposed Constitution, for the Convention to adhere to the republican form. They ought, with equal care, to have preserved the *federal* form, which regards the union as a *confederacy* of sovereign States; instead of which, they have framed a *national* government, which regards the union as a *consolidation* of the States. And it is asked by what authority this bold and radical innovation was undertaken. The handle which has been made of this objection requires, that it should be examined with some precision.

Without enquiring into the accuracy of the distinction on which the objection is founded, it will be necessary to a just estimate of its force, first to ascertain the real character of the government in question; secondly, to enquire how far the Convention were authorised to propose such a government; and thirdly, how far the duty they owed to their country, could supply any defect of regular authority.

First. In order to ascertain the real character of the government it may be considered in relation to the foundation on which it is to be established; to the sources from which its ordinary powers are to be drawn; to the operation of those powers; to the extent of them; and to the authority by which future changes in the government are to be introduced.

On examining the first relation, it appears on one hand that the Constitution is to be founded on the assent and ratification of the people of America, given by deputies elected for the special purpose; but on the other, that this assent and ratification is to be given by the people, not as individuals composing one entire nation; but as composing the distinct and independent States to which they respectively belong. It is to be the assent and ratification of the several States, derived from the supreme authority in each State, the authority of the people themselves. The act therefore establishing the Constitution, will not be a *national* but a *federal* act.

That it will be a federal and not a national act, as these terms are understood by the objectors, the act of the people as forming so many independent States, not as forming one aggregate nation, is obvious from this single consideration that it is to result neither from the decision of a *majority* of the people of the Union, nor from that of a *majority* of the States. It must result from the *unanimous* assent of the several States that are parties to it, differing no other wise from their ordinary assent than in its being expressed, not by the legislative authority, but by that of the people themselves. Were the people regarded in this transaction as forming one nation, the will of the majority of the whole people of the United States, would bind the minority; in the same manner as the majority in each State must bind the minority; and the will of the majority must be determined either by a comparison of the individual votes; or by considering the will of a majority of the States, as evidence of the will of a majority of the people of the United States. Neither of these rules has been adopted. Each State in ratifying the Constitution, is considered as a sovereign body independent of all others, and only to be bound by its own voluntary act. In this relation then the new Constitution will, if established, be a *federal* and not a *national* Constitution.

The next relation is to the sources from which the ordinary powers of government are to be derived. The house of representatives will derive its powers from the people of America, and the people will be represented in the same proportion, and on the same principle, as they are in the Legislature of a particular State. So far the Government is *national* not *federal*. The Senate on the other hand will derive its powers from the States, as political and co-equal societies; and these will be represented on the principle of equality in the Senate, as they now are in the existing Congress. So far the government is *federal*, not *national*. The executive power will be derived from a very compound source. The immediate election of the President is to be made by the States in their political characters. The votes allotted to them, are in a compound ratio, which considers them partly as distinct and co-equal societies; partly as unequal members of the same society. The eventual election, again is to be made by that branch of the Legislature which consists of the national representatives; but in this particular act, they are to be thrown into the form of individual delegations from so many distinct and co-equal bodies politic. From this aspect of the Government, it appears to be of a mixed character presenting at least as many *federal* as *national* features.

The difference between a federal and national Government as it relates to the *operation of the Government* is supposed to consist in this, that in the former, the powers operate on the political bodies composing the confederacy, in their political capacities: In the latter, on the individual citizens, composing the nation, in their individual capacities. On trying the Constitution by this criterion, it falls under the *national*, not the *federal* character; though perhaps not so compleatly, as has been understood. In several cases and particularly in the trial of controversies to which States may be parties, they must be viewed and proceeded against in their collective and political capacities only. So far the national countenance of the Government on this side seems to be disfigured by a few federal features. But this blemish is perhaps unavoidable in any plan; and the operation of the Government on the people in their individual capacities, in its ordinary and most essential proceedings, may on the whole designate it in this relation a *national* Government.

But if the Government be national with regard to the *operation* of its powers, it changes its aspect again when we contemplate it in relation to the *extent* of its powers. The idea of a national Government involves in it, not only an authority over the individual citizens; but an indefinite supremacy over all persons and things, so far as they are objects of lawful Government. Among a people consolidated into one nation, this supremacy is compleatly vested in the national Legislature. Among communities united for particular purposes, it is vested partly in the general, and partly in the municipal Legislatures. In the former case, all local authorities are subordinate to the supreme; and may be controuled, directed or abolished by it at pleasure. In the latter the local or municipal authorities form distinct and independent portions of the supremacy, no more subject within their respective spheres to the general authority, than the general authority is subject to them, within its own sphere. In this relation then the proposed Government cannot be deemed a *national* one; since its jurisdiction extends to certain enumerated objects only, and leaves to the several States a residuary and inviolable sovereignty over all other objects. It is true that in controversies relating to the boundary between the two jurisdictions, the tribunal which is ultimately to decide, is to be established under the general Government. But this does not change the principle of the case. The decision is to be impartially made, according to the rules of the Constitution; and all the usual and most effectual precautions are taken to secure this impartiality. Some such tribunal is clearly essential to prevent an appeal to the sword, and a dissolution of the compact; and that it ought to be established under the general, rather than under the local Governments; or to speak more properly, that it could be safely established under the first alone, is a position not likely to be combated.

If we try the Constitution by its last relation, to the authority by which amendments are to be made, we find it neither wholly *national*, nor wholly *federal*. Were it wholly national, the supreme and ultimate authority would reside in the *majority* of the people of the Union; and this authority would be competent at all times, like that of a majority of every national society, to alter or abolish its established Government. Were it wholly federal on the other hand, the concurrence of each State in the Union would be essential to every alteration that would be binding on all. The mode provided by the plan of the Convention is not founded on either of these principles. In requiring more than a majority, and particularly, in computing the proportion by *States*, not by *citizens*, it departs from the *national*, and advances towards the *federal* character: In rendering the concurrence of less than the whole number of States sufficient, it loses again the *federal*, and partakes of the *national* character.

The proposed Constitution therefore is in strictness neither a national nor a federal constitution; but a composition of both. In its foundation, it is federal, not national; in the sources from which the ordinary powers of the Government are drawn, it is partly federal, and partly national: in the operation of these powers, it is national, not federal: In the extent of them again, it is federal, not national: And finally, in the authoritative mode of introducing amendments, it is neither wholly federal, nor wholly national.

Publius.

No. 40

JAMES MADISON

Defends legitimacy of the Convention.

No. 41

JAMES MADISON

January 19, 1788

To the People of the State of New York.

The Constitution proposed by the Convention may be considered under two general points of view. The FIRST relates to the sum or quantity of power which it vests in the Government, including the restraints imposed on the States. The SECOND, to the particular structure of the Government, and the distribution of this power, among its several branches.

From *The Independent Journal*, January 19, 1788. This essay appeared on January 22 in *The New-York Packet* and was begun on the same day and concluded on January 23 in *The Daily Advertiser*.

Under the first view of the subject two important questions arise,—1. Whether any part of the powers transferred to the general Government be unnecessary or improper?—2. Whether the entire mass of them be dangerous to the portion of jurisdiction left in the several States?

Is the aggregate power of the general Government greater than ought to have been vested in it? This is the first question.

It cannot have escaped those who have attended with candour to the arguments employed against the extensive powers of the Government, that the authors of them have very little considered how far these powers were necessary means of attaining a necessary end. They have chosen rather to dwell on the inconveniences which must be unavoidably blended with all political advantages; and on the possible abuses which must be incident to every power or trust of which a beneficial use can be made. This method of handling the subject cannot impose on the good sense of the people of America. It may display the subtlety of the writer; it may open a boundless field for rhetoric and declamation; it may inflame the passions of the unthinking, and may confirm the prejudices of the misthinking. But cool and candid people will at once reflect, that the purest of human blessings must have a portion of alloy in them, that the choice must always be made, if not of the lesser evil, at least of the GREATER, not the PERFECT good; and that in every political institution, a power to advance the public happiness, involves a discretion which may be misapplied and abused. They will see therefore that in all cases, where power is to be conferred, the point first to be decided is whether such a power be necessary to the public good; as the next will be, in case of an affirmative decision, to guard as effectually as possible against a perversion of the power to the public detriment.

That we may form a correct judgment on this subject, it will be proper to review the several powers conferred on the Government of the Union; and that this may be the more conveniently done, they may be reduced into different classes as they relate to the following different objects;—1. security against foreign danger—2. regulation of the intercourse with foreign nations—3. maintenance of harmony and proper intercourse among the States—4. certain miscellaneous objects of general utility—5. restraint of the States from certain injurious acts—6. provisions for giving due efficacy to all these powers.

The powers falling within the first class, are those of declaring war, and granting letters of marque; of providing armies and fleets; of regulating and calling forth the militia; of levying and borrowing money.

Security against foreign danger is one of the primitive objects of civil society. It is an avowed and essential object of the American Union. The powers requisite for attaining it, must be effectually confided to the fœderal councils.

Is the power of declaring war necessary? No man will answer this question in the negative. It would be superfluous therefore to enter into a proof of the affirmative. The existing confederation establishes this power in the most ample form.

Is the power of raising armies, and equipping fleets necessary? This is involved in the foregoing power. It is involved in the power of self-defence.

But was it necessary to give an INDEFINITE POWER of raising TROOPS, as well as providing fleets; and of maintaining both in PEACE, as well as in WAR?

The answer to these questions has been too far anticipated, in another place, to admit an extensive discussion of them in this place. The answer indeed seems to be so obvious and conclusive as scarcely to justify such a discussion in any place. With what colour of propriety could the force necessary for defence, be limited by those who cannot limit the force of offence? If a Federal Constitution could chain the ambition, or set bounds to the exertions of all other nations: then indeed might it prudently chain the discretion of its own Government, and set bounds to the exertions for its own safety.

How could a readiness for war in time of peace be safely prohibited, unless we could prohibit in like manner the preparations and establishments of every hostile nation? The means of security can only be regulated by the means and the danger of attack. They will in fact be ever determined by these rules, and by no others. It is in vain to oppose constitutional barriers to the impulse of self-preservation. It is worse than in vain; because it plants in the Constitution itself necessary usurpations of power, every precedent of which is a germ of unnecessary and multiplied repetitions. If one nation maintains constantly a disciplined army ready for the service of ambition or revenge, it obliges the most pacific nations, who may be within the reach of its enterprizes, to take corresponding precautions. The fifteenth century was the unhappy epoch of military establishments in time of peace. They were introduced by Charles VII. of France. All Europe has followed, or been forced into the example. Had the example not been followed by other nations, all Europe must long ago have worne the chains of a universal monarch. Were every nation except France now to disband its peace establishment, the same event might follow. The veteran legions of Rome were an overmatch for the undisciplined valour of all other nations, and rendered her mistress of the world.

Not less true is it, that the liberties of Rome proved the final victim to her military triumphs, and that the liberties of Europe, as far as they ever existed, have with few exceptions been the price of her military establishments. A standing force therefore is a dangerous, at the same time that it may be a necessary provision. On the smallest scale it has its inconveniences. On an extensive scale, its consequences may be fatal. On any scale, it is an object of laudable circumspection and precaution. A wise nation will combine all these considerations; and whilst it does not rashly preclude itself from any resource which may become essential to its safety, will exert all its prudence in diminishing both the necessity and the danger of resorting to one which may be inauspicious to its liberties.

The clearest marks of this prudence are stamped on the proposed Constitution. The Union itself which it cements and secures, destroys every pretext for a military establishment which could be dangerous. America, united with a handful of troops, or without a single soldier, exhibits a more forbidding posture to foreign ambition, than America disunited, with an hundred thousand veterans ready for combat. It was remarked on a former occasion, that the want of this pretext had saved the liberties of one nation in Europe. Being rendered by her insular situation and her maritime resources, impregnable to the armies of her neighbours, the rulers of Great-Britain have never been able, by real or artificial dangers, to cheat the public into an extensive peace establishment. The distance of the United States from the powerful nations of the world, gives them the same happy security. A dangerous establishment can never be necessary or plausible, so long as they continue a united people. But let it never for a moment be forgotten, that they are indebted for this advantage to their Union alone. The moment of its dissolution will be the date of a new order of things. The fears of the weaker or the ambition of the stronger States or Confederacies, will set the same example in the new, as Charles VII. did in the old world. The example will be followed here from the same motives which produced universal imitation there. Instead of deriving from our situation the precious advantage which Great-Britain has derived from hers, the face of America will be but a copy of that of the Continent of Europe. It will present liberty every where crushed between standing armies and perpetual taxes. The fortunes of disunited America will be even more disastrous than those of Europe. The sources of evil in the latter are confined to her own limits. No superior powers of another quarter of the globe intrigue among her rival nations, inflame their mutual animosities, and render them the instruments of foreign ambition, jealousy and revenge. In America, the miseries springing from her internal jealousies, contentions and wars, would form a part only of her lot. A plentiful addition of evils would have their source in that relation in which Europe stands to this quarter of the earth, and which no other quarter of the earth bears to Europe. This picture of the consequences of disunion cannot be too highly coloured, or too often exhibited. Every man who loves peace, every man who loves his country, every man who loves liberty, ought to have it ever before his eyes, that he may cherish in his heart a due attachment to the Union of America, and be able to set a due value on the means of preserving it.

Next to the effectual establishment of the Union, the best possible precaution against danger from standing armies, is a limitation of the term for which revenue may be appropriated to their support. This precaution the Constitution has prudently added. I will not repeat here the observations, which I flatter myself have placed this subject in a just and satisfactory light. But it may not be improper to take notice of an argument against this part of the Constitution, which has been drawn from the policy and practice of Great-Britain. It is said that the continuance of an army in that kingdom, requires an annual vote of the Legislature; whereas the American Constitution has lengthened this critical period to two years. This is the form in which the comparison is usually stated to the public: But is it a just form? Is it a fair comparison? Does the British Constitution restrain the Parliamentary discretion to one year? Does the American impose on the Congress appropriations for two years? On the contrary, it cannot be unknown to the authors of the fallacy themselves, that the British Constitution fixes no limit whatever to the discretion of the Legislature, and that the American ties down the Legislature to two years, as the longest admissible term.

Had the argument from the British example been truly stated, it would have stood thus: The term for which supplies may be appropriated to the army-establishment, though unlimited by the British Constitution, has nevertheless in practice been limited by parliamentary discretion, to a single year. Now if in Great-Britain, where the House of Commons is elected for seven years; where so great a proportion of the members are elected by so small a proportion of the people; where the electors are so corrupted by the Representatives, and the Representatives so corrupted by the Crown, the Representative body can possess a power to make appropriations to the army for an indefinite term, without desiring, or without daring, to extend the term beyond a single year; ought not suspicion herself to blush in pretending that the Representatives of the United States, elected FREELY, by the WHOLE BODY of the people, every SECOND YEAR, cannot be safely entrusted with a discretion over such appropriations, expressly limited to the short period of TWO YEARS?

A bad cause seldom fails to betray itself. Of this truth, the management of the opposition to the Federal Government is an unvaried exemplification. But among all the blunders which have been committed, none is more striking than the attempt to enlist on that side, the prudent jealousy entertained by the people, of standing armies. The attempt has awakened fully the public attention to that important subject; and has led to investigations which must terminate in a thorough and universal conviction, not only that the Constitution has provided the most effectual guards against danger from that quarter, but that nothing short of a Constitution fully adequate to the national defence, and the preservation of the Union, can save America from as many standing armies as it may be split into States or Confederacies; and from such a progressive augmentation of these establishments in each, as will render them as burdensome to the properties and ominous to the liberties of the people; as any establishment that can become necessary, under a united and efficient Government, must be tolerable to the former, and safe to the latter.

The palpable necessity of the power to provide and maintain a navy has protected that part of the Constitution against a spirit of censure, which has spared few other parts. It must indeed be numbered among the greatest blessings of America, that as her Union will be the only source of her maritime strength, so this will be a principal source of her security against danger from abroad. In this respect our situation bears another likeness to the insular advantage of Great-Britain. The batteries most capable of repelling foreign enterprizes on our safety, are happily such as can never be turned by a perfidious government against our liberties.

The inhabitants of the Atlantic frontier are all of them deeply interested in this provision for naval protection, and if they have hitherto been suffered to sleep quietly in their beds; if their property has remained safe against the predatory spirit of licencious adventurers; if their maritime towns have not yet been compelled to ransome themselves from the terrors of a conflagration, by yielding to the exactions of daring and sudden invaders, these instances of good fortune are not to be ascribed to the capacity of the existing government for the protection of those from whom it claims allegiance, but to causes that are fugitive and fallacious. If we except perhaps Virginia and Maryland, which are peculiarly vulnerable on their Eastern frontiers, no part of the Union ought to feel more anxiety on this subject than New-York. Her sea coast is extensive. The very important district of the state is an island. The state itself is penetrated by a large navigable river for more than fifty leagues. The great emporium of its commerce, the great reservoir of its wealth, lies every moment at the mercy of events, and may almost be regarded as a hostage, for ignominious compliances with the dictates of a foreign enemy, or even with the rapacious demands of pirates and barbarians. Should a war be the result of the precarious situation of European affairs, and all the unruly passions attending it, be let loose on the ocean, our escape from insults and depredations, not only on that element but every part of the other bordering on it, will be truly miraculous. In the present condition of America, the states more immediately exposed to these calamities, have nothing to hope from the phantom of a general government which now exists; and if their single resources were equal to the task of fortifying themselves against the danger, the object to be protected would be almost consumed by the means of protecting them.

The power of regulating and calling forth the militia has been already sufficiently vindicated and explained.

The power of levying and borrowing money, being the sinew of that which is to be exerted in the national defence, is properly thrown into the same class with it. This power also has been examined already with much attention, and has I trust been clearly shewn to be necessary both in the extent and form given to it by the constitution. I will address one additional reflection only to those who contend that the power ought to have been restrained to external taxation, by which they mean taxes on articles imported from other countries. It can not be doubted that this will always be a valuable source of revenue, that for a considerable time, it must be a principle source, that at this moment it is an essential one. But we may form very mistaken ideas on this subject, if we do not call to mind in our calculations, that the extent of revenue drawn from foreign commerce, must vary with the variations both in the extent and the kind of imports, and that these variations do not correspond with the progress of population, which must be the general measure of the publick wants. As long as agriculture continues the sole field of labour, the importation of manufactures must increase as the consumers multiply. As soon as domestic manufactures are begun by the hands not called for by agriculture, the imported manufactures will decrease as the numbers of people increase. In a more remote stage, the imports may consist in considerable part of raw materials which will be wrought into articles for exportation, and will therefore require rather the encouragement of bounties, than to be loaded with discouraging duties. A system of Government, meant for duration, ought to contemplate these revolutions, and be able to accommodate itself to them.

Some who have not denied the necessity of the power of taxation, have grounded a very fierce attack against the Constitution on the language in which it is defined. It has been urged and echoed, that the power "to lay and collect taxes, duties, imposts and excises, to pay the debts and provide for the common defence and general welfare of the United States," amounts to an unlimited commission to exercise every power which may be alledged to be necessary for the common defence or general welfare. No stronger proof could be given of the distress under which these writers labour for objections, than their stooping to such a misconstruction.

Had no other enumeration or definition of the powers of the Congress been found in the Constitution, than the general expression just cited, the authors of the objection might have had some colour for it; though it would have been difficult to find a reason for so awkward a form of describing an authority to legislate in all possible cases. A power to destroy the freedom of the press, the trial by jury or even to regulate the course of descents, or the forms of conveyances, must be very singularly expressed by the terms "to raise money for the general welfare."

But what colour can the objection have, when a specification of the objects alluded to by these general terms, immediately follows; and is not even separated by a longer pause than a semicolon. If the different parts of the same instrument ought to be so expounded as to give meaning to every part which will bear it; shall one part of the same sentence be excluded altogether from a share in the meaning; and shall the more doubtful and indefinite terms be retained in their full extent and the clear and precise expressions, be denied any signification whatsoever? For what purpose could the enumeration of particular powers be inserted, if these and all others were meant to be included in the preceding general power? Nothing is more natural or common than first to use a general phrase, and then to explain and qualify it by a recital of particulars. But the idea of an enumeration of particulars, which neither explain nor qualify the general meaning, and can have no other effect than to confound and mislead, is an absurdity which as we are reduced to the dilemma of charging either on the authors of the objection, or on the authors of the Constitution, we must take the liberty of supposing, had not its origin with the latter.

The objection here is the more extraordinary, as it appears, that the language used by the Convention is a copy from the articles of confederation. The objects of the Union among the States as described in article 3d. are, "their common defence, security of their liberties, and mutual and general welfare." The terms of article 8th. are still more identical. "All charges of war, and all other expences, that shall be incurred for the common defence or general welfare, and allowed by the United States in Congress, shall be defrayed out of a common treasury &c." A similar language again occurs in art. 9. Construe either of these articles by the rules which would justify, the construction put on the new Constitution, and they vest in the existing Congress a power to legislate in all cases whatsoever. But what would have been thought of that assembly, if attaching themselves to these general expressions, and disregarding the specifications, which ascertain and limit their import, they had exercised an unlimited power of providing for the common defence and general welfare? I appeal to the objectors themselves, whether they would in that case have employed the same reasoning in justification of Congress, as they now make use of against the Convention. How difficult it is for error to escape its own condemnation!

Publius.

No. 42

JAMES MADISON

January 22, 1788

To the People of the State of New York.

The *second* class of powers lodged in the General Government, consists of those which regulate the intercourse with foreign nations, to wit, to make treaties; to send and receive Ambassadors, other public Ministers and Consuls; to define and punish piracies and felonies committed on the high seas, and offences against the law of nations; to regulate foreign commerce, including a power to prohibit after the year 1808, the importation of slaves, and to lay an intermediate duty of ten dollars per head, as a discouragement to such importations.

This class of powers forms an obvious and essential branch of the fœderal administration. If we are to be one nation in any respect, it clearly ought to be in respect to other nations.

The powers to make treaties and to send and receive Ambassadors, speak their own propriety. Both of them are comprized in the articles of confederation; with this difference only, that the former is disembarrassed by the plan of the Convention of an exception, under which treaties might be substantially frustrated by regulations of the States; and that a power of appointing and receiving "other public Ministers and Consuls," is expressly and very properly added to the former provision concerning Ambassadors. The term Ambassador, if taken strictly, as seems to be required by the second of the articles of confederation, comprehends the highest grade only of public Ministers; and excludes the grades which the United States will be most likely to prefer where foreign embassies may be necessary. And under no latitude of construction will the term comprehend Consuls. Yet it has been

---

From *The New-York Packet,* January 22, 1788. This essay appeared on January 23 in *The Independent Journal* and on January 24 in *The Daily Advertiser.*

found expedient, and has been the practice of Congress to employ the inferior grades of public Ministers; and to send and receive Consuls. It is true that where treaties of commerce stipulate for the mutual appointment of Consuls, whose functions are connected with commerce, the admission of foreign Consuls may fall within the power of making commercial treaties; and that where no such treaties exist, the mission of American Consuls into foreign countries, may *perhaps* be covered under the authority given by the 9th article of the Confederation, to appoint all such civil officers as may be necessary for managing the general affairs of the United States. But the admission of Consuls into the United States, where no previous treaty has stipulated it, seems to have been no where provided for. A supply of the omission is one of the lesser instances in which the Convention have improved on the model before them. But the most minute provisions become important when they tend to obviate the necessity or the pretext for gradual and unobserved usurpations of power; a list of the cases in which Congress have been betrayed, or forced by the defects of the confederation into violations of their chartered authorities, would not a little surprize those who have paid no attention to the subject; and would be no inconsiderable argument in favor of the new Constitution, which seems to have provided no less studiously for the lesser, than the more obvious and striking defects of the old.

The power to define and punish piracies and felonies committed on the high seas, and offences against the law of nations, belongs with equal propriety to the general government; and is a still greater improvement on the articles of confederation. These articles contain no provision for the case of offences against the law of nations; and consequently leave it in the power of any indiscreet member to embroil the confederacy with foreign nations. The provision of the fœderal articles on the subject of piracies and felonies, extends no farther than to the establishment of courts for the trial of these offences. The definition of piracies might perhaps without inconveniency, be left to the law of nations; though a legislative definition of them, is found in most municipal codes. A definition of felonies on the high seas is evidently requisite. Felony is a term of loose signification even in the common law of England; and of various import in the statute law of that kingdom. But neither the common, nor the statute law of that or any other nation ought to be a standard for the proceedings of this, unless previously made its own by legislative adoption. The meaning of the term as defined in the codes of the several States, would be as impracticable as the former would be a dishonorable and illegitimate guide. It is not precisely the same in any two of the States; and varies in each with every revision of its criminal laws. For the sake of certainty and uniformity therefore, the power of defining felonies in this case, was in every respect necessary and proper.

The regulation of foreign commerce, having fallen within several views which have been taken of this subject, has been too fully discussed to need additional proofs here of its being properly submitted to the fœderal administration.

It were doubtless to be wished that the power of prohibiting the importation of slaves, had not been postponed until the year 1808, or rather that it had been suffered to have immediate operation. But it is not difficult to account either for this restriction on the general government, or for the manner in which the whole clause is expressed. It ought to be considered as a great point gained in favor of humanity, that a period of twenty years may terminate for ever within these States, a traffic which has so long and so loudly upbraided the barbarism of modern policy; that within that period it will receive a considerable discouragement from the fœderal Government, and may be totally abolished by a concurrence of the few States which continue the unnatural traffic, in the prohibitory example which has been given by so great a majority of the Union. Happy would it be for the unfortunate Africans, if an equal prospect lay before them, of being redeemed from the oppressions of their European brethren! Attempts have been made to pervert this clause into an objection against the Constitution, by representing it on one side as a criminal toleration of an illicit practice, and on another, as calculated to prevent voluntary and beneficial emigrations from Europe to America. I mention these misconstructions, not with a view to give them an answer, for they deserve none; but as specimens of the manner and spirit in which some have thought fit to conduct their opposition to the proposed government.

The powers included in the *third* class, are those which provide for the harmony and proper intercourse among the States.

Under this head might be included the particular restraints imposed on the authority of the States, and certain powers of the judicial department; but the former are reserved for a distinct class, and the latter will be particularly examined when we arrive at the structure and organization of the government. I shall confine myself to a cursory review of the remaining powers comprehended under this third description, to wit, to regulate commerce among the several States and the Indian tribes; to coin money, regulate the value thereof and of foreign coin; to provide for the punishment of counterfeiting the current coin, and securities of the United States; to fix the standard of weights and measures; to establish an uniform rule of naturalization, and uniform laws of bankruptcy; to prescribe the manner in which the public acts, records and judicial proceedings of each State shall be proved, and the effect they shall have in other States; and to establish post-offices, and post-roads.

The defect of power in the existing confederacy, to regulate the commerce between its several members, is in the number of those which have been clearly pointed out by experience. To the proofs and remarks which former papers have brought into view on this subject, it may be added, that without this supplemental provision, the great and essential power of regulating foreign commerce, would have been incompleat, and ineffectual. A very material object of this power was the relief of the States which import and export through other States, from the improper contributions levied on them by the latter. Were these at liberty to regulate the trade between State and State, it must be foreseen that ways would be found out, to load the articles of import and export, during the passage through their jurisdiction, with duties which would fall on the makers of the latter, and the consumers of the former. We may be assured by past experience, that such a practice would be introduced by future contrivances; and both by that and a common knowledge of human affairs, that it would nourish unceasing animosities, and not improbably terminate in serious interruptions of the public tranquility. To those who do not view the question through the medium of passion or of interest, the desire of the commercial States to collect in any form, an indirect revenue from their uncommercial neighbours, must appear not less impolitic than it is unfair; since it would stimulate the injured party, by resentment as well as interest, to resort to less convenient channels for their foreign trade. But the mild voice of reason, pleading the cause of an enlarged and permanent interest, is but too often drowned before public bodies as well as individuals, by the clamours of an impatient avidity for immediate and immoderate gain.

The necessity of a superintending authority over the reciprocal trade of confederated States has been illustrated by other examples as well as our own. In Switzerland, where the Union is so very slight, each Canton is obliged to allow to merchandizes, a passage through its jurisdiction into other Cantons, without an augmentation of the tolls. In Germany, it is a law of the empire, that the Princes and States shall not lay tolls or customs on bridges, rivers, or passages, without the consent of the Emperor and Diet; though it appears from a quotation in an antecedent paper, that the practice in this as in many other instances in that confederacy, has not followed the law, and has produced there the mischiefs which have been foreseen here. Among the restraints imposed by the Union of the Netherlands, on its members, one is, that they shall not establish imposts disadvantageous to their neighbors, without the general permission.

The regulation of commerce with the Indian tribes is very properly unfettered from two limitations in the articles of confederation, which render the provision obscure and contradictory. The power is there restrained to Indians, not members of any of the States, and is not to violate or infringe the legislative right of any State within its own limits. What description of Indians are to be deemed members of a State, is not yet settled; and has been a question of frequent perplexity and contention in the Fœderal Councils. And how the trade with Indians, though not members of a State, yet residing within its legislative jurisdiction, can be regulated by an external authority, without so far intruding on the internal rights of legislation, is absolutely incomprehensible. This is not the only case in which the articles of confederation have inconsiderately endeavored to accomplish impossibilities; to reconcile a partial sovereignty in the Union, with compleat sovereignty in the States; to subvert a mathematical axiom, by taking away a part, and letting the whole remain.

All that need be remarked on the power to coin money, regulate the value thereof, and of foreign coin, is that by providing for this last case, the Constitution has supplied a material omission in the articles of confederation. The authority of the existing Congress is restrained to the regulation of coin *struck* by their own authority, or that of the respective States. It must be seen at once, that the proposed uniformity in the *value* of the current coin might be destroyed by subjecting that of foreign coin to the different regulations of the different States.

The punishment of counterfeiting the public securities as well as of the current coin, is submitted of course to that authority, which is to secure the value of both.

The regulation of weights and measures is transferred from the articles of confederation, and is founded on like considerations with the preceding power of regulating coin.

The dissimilarity in the rules of naturalization, has long been remarked as a fault in our system, and as laying a foundation for intricate and delicate questions. In the 4th article of the confederation, it is declared "that the *free inhabitants* of each of these States, paupers, vagabonds, and fugitives from justice excepted, shall be entitled to all privileges and immunities of *free citizens*, in the several States, and *the people* of each State, shall in every other, enjoy all the privileges of trade and commerce, &c." There is a confusion of language here, which is remarkable. Why the terms *free inhabitants*, are used in one part of the article; *free citizens* in another, and *people* in another, or what was meant by superadding "to all privileges and immunities of free citizens,"—"all the privileges of trade and commerce," cannot easily be determined. It seems to be a construction scarcely avoidable, however, that those who come under the denomination of *free inhabitants* of a State, although not citizens of such State, are entitled in every other State to all the privileges of *free citizens* of the latter; that is, to greater privileges than they may be entitled to in their own State; so that it may be in the power of a particular State, or rather every State is laid under a necessity, not only to confer the rights of citizenship in other States upon any whom it may admit to such rights within itself; but upon any whom it may allow to become inhabitants within its jurisdiction. But were an exposition of the term "inhabitants" to be admitted, which would confine the stipulated privileges to citizens alone, the difficulty is diminished only, not removed. The very improper power would still be retained by each State, of naturalizing aliens in every other State. In one State residence for a short term confers all the rights of citizenship. In another qualifications of greater importance are required. An alien therefore legally incapacitated for certain rights in the latter, may by previous residence only in the former, elude his incapacity; and thus the law of one State, be preposterously rendered paramount to the law of another, within the jurisdiction of the other. We owe it to mere casualty, that very serious embarrassments on this subject, have been hitherto escaped. By the laws of several States, certain descriptions of aliens who had rendered themselves obnoxious, were laid under interdicts inconsistent, not only with the rights of citizenship, but with the privilege of residence. What would have been the consequence, if such persons, by residence or otherwise, had acquired the character of citizens under the laws of another State, and then asserted their rights as such, both to residence and citizenship within the State proscribing them? Whatever the legal consequences might have been, other consequences would probably have resulted of too serious a nature, not to be provided against. The new Constitution has accordingly with great propriety made provision against them, and all others proceeding from the defect of the confederation, on this head, by authorising the general government to establish an uniform rule of naturalization throughout the United States.

The power of establishing uniform laws of bankruptcy, is so intimately connected with the regulation of commerce, and will prevent so many frauds where the parties or their property may lie or be removed into different States, that the expediency of it seems not likely to be drawn into question.

The power of prescribing by general laws the manner in which the public acts, records and judicial proceedings of each State shall be proved, and the effect they shall have in other States, is an evident and valuable improvement on the clause relating to this subject in the articles of confederation. The meaning of the latter is extremely indeterminate; and can be of little importance under any interpretation which it will bear. The power here established, may be rendered a very convenient instrument of justice, and be particularly beneficial on the borders of contiguous States, where the effects liable to justice, may be suddenly and secretly translated in any stage of the process, within a foreign jurisdiction.

The power of establishing post-roads, must in every view be a harmless power; and may perhaps, by judicious management, become productive of great public conveniency. Nothing which tends to facilitate the intercourse between the States, can be deemed unworthy of the public care.

Publius.

No. 43

JAMES MADISON

Explains other aspects of the Constitution and provisions for amendment.

No. 44

JAMES MADISON

January 25, 1788

To the People of the State of New York.

A *Fifth* class of provisions in favor of the fœderal authority, consists of the following restrictions on the authority of the several States:

1. "No State shall enter into any treaty, alliance or confederation, grant letters of marque and reprisal, coin money, emit bills of credit, make any thing but gold and silver a legal tender in payment of debts; pass any bill of attainder, ex post facto law, or law impairing the obligation of contracts, or grant any title of nobility."

The prohibition against treaties, alliances and confederations, makes a part of the existing articles of Union; and for reasons which need no explanation, is copied into the new Constitution. The prohibition of letters of marque is another part of the old system, but is somewhat extended in the new. According to the former, letters of marque could be granted by the States after a declaration of war. According to the latter, these licences must be obtained as well during war as previous to its declaration, from the government of the United States. This alteration is fully justified by the advantage of uniformity in all points which relate to foreign powers; and of immediate responsibility to the nation in all those, for whose conduct the nation itself is to be responsible.

The right of coining money, which is here taken from the States, was left in their hands by the confederation as a concurrent right with that of Congress, under an exception in favor of the exclusive right of Congress to regulate the alloy and value. In this instance also the new provision is an improvement on the old. Whilst the

From *The New-York Packet,* January 25, 1788. This essay appeared on January 26 in *The Independent Journal* and on January 29 in *The Daily Advertiser.*

alloy and value depended on the general authority, a right of coinage in the particular States could have no other effect than to multiply expensive mints, and diversify the forms and weights of the circulating pieces. The latter inconveniency defeats one purpose for which the power was originally submitted to the fœderal head. And as far as the former might prevent an inconvenient remittance of gold and silver to the central mint for recoinage, the end can be as well attained, by local mints established under the general authority.

The extension of the prohibition to bills of credit must give pleasure to every citizen in proportion to his love of justice, and his knowledge of the true springs of public prosperity. The loss which America has sustained since the peace, from the pestilent effects of paper money, on the necessary confidence between man and man; on the necessary confidence in the public councils; on the industry and morals of the people, and on the character of Republican Government, constitutes an enormous debt against the States chargeable with this unadvised measure, which must long remain unsatisfied; or rather an accumulation of guilt, which can be expiated no otherwise than by a voluntary sacrifice on the altar of justice, of the power which has been the instrument of it. In addition to these persuasive considerations, it may be observed that the same reasons which shew the necessity of denying to the States the power of regulating coin, prove with equal force that they ought not to be at liberty to substitute a paper medium in the place of coin. Had every State a right to regulate the value of its coin, there might be as many different currencies as States; and thus the intercourse among them would be impeded; retrospective alterations in its value might be made, and thus the citizens of other States be injured; and animosities be kindled among the States themselves. The subjects of foreign powers might suffer from the same cause, and hence the Union be discredited and embroiled by the indiscretion of a single member. No one of these mischiefs is less incident to a power in the States to emit paper money than to coin gold or silver. The power to make any thing but gold and silver a tender in payment of debts, is withdrawn from the States, on the same principle with that of striking of paper currency.

Bills of attainder, ex post facto laws, and laws impairing the obligation of contracts, are contrary to the first principles of the social compact, and to every principle of sound legislation.

The two former are expressly prohibited by the declarations prefixed to some of the State Constitutions, and all of them are prohibited by the spirit and scope of these fundamental charters. Our own experience has taught us nevertheless, that additional fences against these dangers ought not to be omitted. Very properly therefore have the Convention added this constitutional bulwark in favor of personal security and private rights; and I am much deceived if they have not in so doing as faithfully consulted the genuine sentiments, as the undoubted interests of their constituents. The sober people of America are weary of the fluctuating policy which has directed the public councils. They have seen with regret and with indignation, that sudden changes and legislative interferences in cases affecting personal rights, become jobs in the hands of enterpizing and influential speculators; and snares to the more industrious and less informed part of the community. They have seen, too, that legislative interference, is but the first link of a long chain of repetitions; every subsequent interference being naturally produced by the effects of the preceding. They very rightly infer, therefore, that some thorough reform is wanting which will banish speculations on public measures, inspire a general prudence and industry, and give a regular course to the business of society. The prohibition with respect to titles of nobility, is copied from the articles of confederation, and needs no comment.

2. "No State shall, without the consent of the Congress, lay any imposts or duties on imports or exports, except what may be absolutely necessary for executing its inspection laws, and the neat produce of all duties and imposts laid by any State on imports or exports, shall be for the use of the Treasury of the United States; and all such laws shall be subject to the revision and controul of the Congress. No State shall, without the consent of Congress, lay any duty on tonnage, keep troops or ships of war in time of peace; enter into any agreement or compact with another State, or with a foreign power, or engage in war unless actually invaded, or in such imminent danger as will not admit of delay."

The restraint of the power of the States over imports and exports is enforced by all the arguments which prove the necessity of submitting the regulation of trade to the fœderal councils. It is needless therefore to remark further on this head, than that the manner in which the restraint is qualified, seems well calculated at once to secure to the States a reasonable discretion in providing for the conveniency of their imports and exports; and to the United States a reasonable check against the abuse of this discretion. The remaining particulars of this clause, fall within reasonings which are either so obvious, or have been so fully developed, that they may be passed over without remark.

The sixth and last class consists of the several powers and provisions by which efficacy is given to all the rest.

1. "Of these the first is the power to make all laws which shall be necessary and proper for carrying into execution the foregoing powers, and all other powers vested by this Constitution in the government of the United States."

Few parts of the Constitution have been assailed with more intemperance than this; yet on a fair investigation of it, no part can appear more compleatly invulnerable. Without the *substance* of this power, the whole Constitution would be a dead letter. Those who object to the article therefore as a part of the Constitution, can only mean that the *form* of the provision is improper. But have they considered whether a better form could have been substituted?

There are four other possible methods which the Convention might have taken on this subject. They might have copied the second article of the existing confederation which would have prohibited the exercise of any power not *expressly* delegated; they might have attempted a positive enumeration of the powers comprehended under the general terms "necessary and proper"; they might have attempted a negative enumeration of them, by specifying the powers excepted from the general definition: They might have been altogether silent on the subject; leaving these necessary and proper powers, to construction and inference.

Had the Convention taken the first method of adopting the second article of confederation; it is evident that the new Congress would be continually exposed as their predecessors have been, to the alternative of construing the term *"expressly"* with so much rigour as to disarm the government of all real authority whatever, or with so much latitude as to destroy altogether the force of the restriction. It would be easy to shew if it were necessary, that no important power, delegated by the articles of confederation, has been or can be executed by Congress, without recurring more or less to the doctrine of *construction* or *implication.* As the powers delegated under the new system are more extensive, the government which is to administer it would find itself still more distressed with the alternative of betraying the public interest by doing nothing; or of violating the Constitution by exercising powers, indispensably necessary and proper; but at the same time, not *expressly* granted.

Had the Convention attempted a positive enumeration of the powers necessary and proper for carrying their other powers into effect; the attempt would have involved a complete digest of laws on every subject to which the Constitution relates; accommodated too not only to the existing state of things, but to all the possible changes which futurity may produce: For in every new application of a general power, the *particular powers*, which are the means of attaining the *object* of the general power, must always necessarily vary with that object; and be often properly varied whilst the object remains the same.

Had they attempted to enumerate the particular powers or means, not necessary or proper for carrying the general powers into execution, the task would have been no less chimerical; and would have been liable to this further objection; that every defect in the enumeration, would have been equivalent to a positive grant of authority. If to avoid this consequence they had attempted a partial enumeration of the exceptions, and described the residue by the general terms, *not necessary or proper:* It must have happened that the enumeration would comprehend a few of the excepted powers only; that these would be such as would be least likely to be assumed or tolerated, because the enumeration would of course select such as would be least necessary or proper, and that the unnecessary and improper powers included in the residuum, would be less forceably excepted, than if no partial enumeration had been made.

Had the Constitution been silent on this head, there can be no doubt that all the particular powers, requisite as means of executing the general powers, would have resulted to the government, by unavoidable implication. No axiom is more clearly established in law, or in reason, than that wherever the end is required, the means are authorised; wherever a general power to do a thing is given, every particular power necessary for doing it, is included. Had this last method therefore been pursued by the Convention, every objection now urged against their plan, would remain in all its plausibility; and the real inconveniency would be incurred, of not removing a pretext which may be seized on critical occasions for drawing into question the essential powers of the Union.

If it be asked, what is to be the consequence, in case the Congress shall misconstrue this part of the Constitution, and exercise powers not warranted by its true meaning? I answer the same as if they should misconstrue or enlarge any other power vested in them, as if the general power had been reduced to particulars, and any one of these were to be violated; the same in short, as if the State Legislatures should violate their respective constitutional authorities. In the first instance, the success of the usurpation will depend on the executive and judiciary departments, which are to expound and give effect to the legislative acts; and in the last resort, a remedy must be obtained from the people, who can by the election of more faithful representatives, annul the acts of the usurpers. The truth is, that this ultimate redress may be more confided in against unconstitutional acts of the fœderal than of the State Legislatures, for this plain reason, that as every such act of the former, will be an invasion of the rights of the latter, these will be ever ready to mark the innovation, to sound the alarm to the people, and to exert their local influence in effecting a change of fœderal representatives. There being no such intermediate body between the State Legislatures and the people, interested in watching the conduct of the former, violations of the State Constitutions are more likely to remain unnoticed and unredressed.

2. "This Constitution and the laws of the United States which shall be made in pursuance thereof, and all treaties made, or which shall be made, under the authority of the United States, shall be the supreme law of the land, and the Judges in every State shall be bound thereby, any thing in the Constitution or laws of any State to the contrary notwithstanding."

The indiscreet zeal of the adversaries to the Constitution, has betrayed them into an attack on this part of it also, without which it would have been evidently and radically defective. To be fully sensible of this we need only suppose for a moment, that the supremacy of the State Constitutions had been left compleat by a saving clause in their favor.

In the first place, as these Constitutions invest the State Legislatures with absolute sovereignty, in all cases not excepted by the existing articles of confederation, all the authorities contained in the proposed Constitution, so far as they exceed those enumerated in the confederation, would have been annulled, and the new Congress would have been reduced to the same impotent condition with their predecessors.

In the next place, as the Constitutions of some of the States do not even expressly and fully recognize the existing powers of the confederacy, an express saving of the supremacy of the former, would in such States have brought into question, every power contained in the proposed Constitution.

In the third place, as the Constitutions of the States differ much from each other, it might happen that a treaty or national law of great and equal importance to the States, would interfere with some and not with other Constitutions, and would consequently be valid in some of the States at the same time that it would have no effect in others.

In fine, the world would have seen for the first time, a system of government founded on an inversion of the fundamental principles of all government; it would have seen the authority of the whole society every where subordinate to the authority of the parts; it would have seen a monster in which the head was under the direction of the members.

3. "The Senators and Representatives, and the members of the several State Legislatures; and all executive and judicial officers, both of the United States, and the several States shall be bound by oath or affirmation, to support this Constitution."

It has been asked, why it was thought necessary, that the State magistracy should be bound to support the Fœderal Constitution, and unnecessary, that a like oath should be imposed on the officers of the United States in favor of the State Constitutions?

Several reasons might be assigned for the distinction. I content myself with one which is obvious & conclusive. The members of the Fœderal Government will have no agency in carrying the State Constitutions into effect. The members and officers of the State Governments, on the contrary, will have an essential agency in giving effect to the Fœderal Constitution. The election of the President and Senate, will depend in all cases, on the Legislatures of the several States. And the election of the House of Representatives, will equally depend on the same authority in the first instance; and will probably, for ever be conducted by the officers and according to the laws of the States.

4. Among the provisions for giving efficacy to the fœderal powers, might be added, those which belong to the executive and judiciary departments: But as these are reserved for particular examination in another place, I pass them over in this.

We have now reviewed in detail all the articles composing the sum or quantity of power delegated by the proposed Constitution to the Fœderal Government; and are brought to this undeniable conclusion, that no part of the power is unnecessary or improper for accomplishing the necessary objects of the Union. The question therefore, whether this amount of power shall be granted or not, resolves itself into another question, therefore, whether or not a government commensurate [to the] exigencies of the Union, shall be established, or in other [words] whether the Union itself shall be preserved.

Publius.

No. 45

JAMES MADISON

On general relation of states to federal government.

No. 46

JAMES MADISON

Ultimate authority is in the people. Claims doctrine of popular sovereignty for the Federalists.

No. 47

JAMES MADISON

January 30, 1788

To the People of the State of New York.

Having reviewed the general form of the proposed government, and the general mass of power allotted to it: I proceed to examine the particular structure of this government, and the distribution of this mass of power among its constituent parts.

One of the principal objections inculcated by the more respectable adversaries to the constitution, is its supposed violation of

---

From *The Independent Journal,* January 30, 1788. This essay appeared on February 1 in both *The New-York Packet* and *The Daily Advertiser.*

the political maxim, that the legislative, executive and judiciary departments ought to be separate and distinct. In the structure of the federal government, no regard, it is said, seems to have been paid to this essential precaution in favor of liberty. The several departments of power are distributed and blended in such a manner, as at once to destroy all symmetry and beauty of form; and to expose some of the essential parts of the edifice to the danger of being crushed by the disproportionate weight of other parts.

No political truth is certainly of greater intrinsic value or is stamped with the authority of more enlightened patrons of liberty than that on which the objection is founded. The accumulation of all powers legislative, executive and judiciary in the same hands, whether of one, a few or many, and whether hereditary, self appointed, or elective, may justly be pronounced the very definition of tyranny. Were the federal constitution therefore really chargeable with this accumulation of power or with a mixture of powers having a dangerous tendency to such an accumulation, no further arguments would be necessary to inspire a universal reprobation of the system. I persuade myself however, that it will be made apparent to every one, that the charge cannot be supported, and that the maxim on which it relies, has been totally misconceived and misapplied. In order to form correct ideas on this important subject, it will be proper to investigate the sense, in which the preservation of liberty requires, that the three great departments of power should be separate and distinct.

The oracle who is always consulted and cited on this subject, is the celebrated Montesquieu. If he be not the author of this invaluable precept in the science of politics, he has the merit at least of displaying, and recommending it most effectually to the attention of mankind. Let us endeavour in the first place to ascertain his meaning on this point.

The British constitution was to Montesquieu, what Homer has been to the didactic writers on epic poetry. As the latter have considered the work of the immortal Bard, as the perfect model from which the principles and rules of the epic art were to be drawn, and by which all similar works were to be judged; so this great political critic appears to have viewed the constitution of England, as the standard, or to use his own expression, as the mirrour of political liberty; and to have delivered in the form of elementary truths, the several characteristic principles of that particular system. That we may be sure then not to mistake his meaning in this case, let us recur to the source from which the maxim was drawn.

On the slightest view of the British constitution we must perceive, that the legislative, executive and judiciary departments are by no means totally separate and distinct from each other. The executive magistrate forms an integral part of the legislative authority. He alone has the prerogative of making treaties with foreign sovereigns, which when made have, under certain limitations, the force of legislative acts. All the members of the judiciary department are appointed by him; can be removed by him on the address of the two Houses of Parliament, and form, when he pleases to consult them, one of his constitutional councils. One branch of the legislative department forms also, a great constitutional council to the executive chief; as on another hand, it is the sole depositary of judicial power in cases of impeachment, and is invested with the supreme appellate jurisdiction, in all other cases. The judges again are so far connected with the legislative department, as often to attend and participate in its deliberations, though not admitted to a legislative vote.

From these facts by which Montesquieu was guided it may clearly be inferred, that in saying "there can be no liberty where the legislative and executive powers are united in the same person, or body of magistrates," or "if the power of judging be not separated from the legislative and executive powers," he did not mean that these departments ought to have no *partial agency*, in, or no *controul* over the acts of each other. His meaning, as his own words import, and still more conclusively as illustrated by the example in his eye, can amount to no more than this, that where the *whole* power of one department is exercised by the same hands which possess the *whole* power of another department, the fundamental principles of a free constitution, are subverted. This would have been the case in the constitution examined by him, if the King who is the sole executive magistrate, had possessed also the compleat legislative power, or the supreme administration of justice; or if the entire legislative body, had possessed the supreme judiciary, or the supreme executive authority. This however is not among the vices of that constitution. The magistrate in whom the whole executive power resides cannot of himself make a law, though he can put a negative on every law, nor administer justice in person, though he has the appointment of those who do administer it. The judges can exercise no executive prerogative, though they are shoots from the executive stock, nor any legislative function, though they may be advised with by the legislative councils. The entire legislature, can perform no judiciary act, though by the joint act of two of its branches, the judges may be removed from their offices; and though one of its branches is possessed of the judicial power in the last resort. The entire legislature again can exercise no executive prerogative, though one of its branches constitutes the supreme executive magistracy; and another, on the empeachment of a third, can try and condemn all the subordinate officers in the executive department.

The reasons on which Montesquieu grounds his maxim are a further demonstration of his meaning. "When the legislative and executive powers are united in the same person or body" says he, "there can be no liberty, because apprehensions may arise lest *the same* monarch or senate should *enact* tyrannical laws, to *execute* them in a tyrannical manner." Again "Were the power of judging joined with the legislative, the life and liberty of the subject would be exposed to arbitrary controul, for *the judge* would then be *the legislator.* Were it joined to the executive power, *the judge* might behave with all the violence of *an oppressor.*" Some of these reasons are more fully explained in other passages; but briefly stated as they are here, they sufficiently establish the meaning which we have put on this celebrated maxim of this celebrated author.

If we look into the constitutions of the several states we find that notwithstanding the emphatical, and in some instances, the unqualified terms in which this axiom has been laid down, there is not a single instance in which the several departments of power have been kept absolutely separate and distinct. New-Hampshire, whose constitution was the last formed, seems to have been fully aware of the impossibility and inexpediency of avoiding any mixture whatever of these departments; and has qualified the doctrine by declaring "that the legislative, executive and judiciary powers ought to be kept as separate from, and independent of each other *as the nature of a free government will admit; or as is consistent with that chain of connection, that binds the whole fabric of the constitution in one indissoluble bond of unity and amity.*" Her constitution accordingly mixes these departments in several respects. The senate which is a branch of the legislative department is also a judicial tribunal for the trial of empeachments. The president who is the head of the executive department, is the presiding member also of the senate;

and besides an equal vote in all cases, has a casting vote in case of a tie. The executive head is himself eventually elective every year by the legislative department; and his council is every year chosen by and from the members of the same department. Several of the officers of state are also appointed by the legislature. And the members of the judiciary department are appointed by the executive department.

The constitution of Massachusetts has observed a sufficient though less pointed caution in expressing this fundamental article of liberty. It declares "that the legislative department shall never exercise the executive and judicial powers, or either of them: The executive shall never exercise the legislative and judicial powers, or either of them: The judicial shall never exercise the legislative and executive powers, or either of them." This declaration corresponds precisely with the doctrine of Montesquieu as it has been explained, and is not in a single point violated by the plan of the Convention. It goes no farther than to prohibit any one of the entire departments from exercising the powers of another department. In the very constitution to which it is prefixed, a partial mixture of powers has been admitted. The Executive Magistrate has a qualified negative on the Legislative body; and the Senate, which is a part of the Legislature, is a court of impeachment for members both of the executive and judiciary departments. The members of the judiciary department again are appointable by the executive department, and removeable by the same authority, on the address of the two legislative branches. Lastly, a number of the officers of government are annually appointed by the legislative department. As the appointment to offices, particularly executive offices, is in its nature an executive function, the compilers of the Constitution have in this last point at least, violated the rule established by themselves.

I pass over the constitutions of Rhode-Island and Connecticut, because they were formed prior to the revolution; and even before the principle under examination had become an object of political attention.

The constitution of New-York contains no declaration on this subject; but appears very clearly to have been framed with an eye to the danger of improperly blending the different departments. It gives nevertheless to the executive magistrate a partial controul over the legislative department; and what is more, gives a like controul to the judiciary department, and even blends the executive and judiciary departments in the exercise of this controul. In its council of appointment, members of the legislative are associated with the executive authority in the appointment of officers both executive and judiciary. And its court for the trial of impeachments and correction of errors, is to consist of one branch of the legislature and the principal members of the judiciary department.

The constitution of New-Jersey has blended the different powers of government more than any of the preceding. The governor, who is the executive magistrate, is appointed by the legislature; is chancellor and ordinary or surrogate of the state; is a member of the supreme court of appeals, and president with a casting vote, of one of the legislative branches. The same legislative branch acts again as executive council to the governor, and with him constitutes the court of appeals. The members of the judiciary department are appointed by the legislative department, and removeable by one branch of it, on the impeachment of the other.

According to the constitution of Pennsylvania, the president, who is head of the executive department, is annually elected by a vote in which the legislative department predominates. In conjunction with an executive council, he appoints the members of the judiciary department, and forms a court of impeachments for trial of all officers, judiciary as well as executive. The judges of the supreme court, and justices of the peace, seem also to be removeable by the legislature; and the executive power of pardoning in certain cases to be referred to the same department. The members of the executive council are made EX OFFICIO justices of peace throughout the state.

In Delaware, the chief executive magistrate is annually elected by the legislative department. The speakers of the two legislative branches are vice-presidents in the executive department. The executive chief, with six others, appointed three by each of the legislative branches, constitute the supreme court of appeals: He is joined with the legislative department in the appointment of the other judges. Throughout the states it appears that the members of the legislature may at the same time be justices of the peace. In this state, the members of one branch of it are EX OFFICIO justices of peace; as are also the members of the executive council. The principal officers of the executive department are appointed by the legislative; and one branch of the latter forms a court of impeachments. All officers may be removed on address of the legislature.

Maryland has adopted the maxim in the most unqualified terms;

declaring that the legislative, executive and judicial powers of government, ought to be forever separate and distinct from each other. Her constitution, notwithstanding makes the executive magistrate appointable by the legislative department; and the members of the judiciary, by the executive department.

The language of Virginia is still more pointed on this subject. Her constitution declares, "that the legislative, executive and judiciary departments, shall be separate and distinct; so that neither exercise the powers properly belonging to the other; nor shall any person exercise the powers of more than one of them at the same time; except that the justices of the county courts shall be eligible to either house of assembly." Yet we find not only this express exception, with respect to the members of the inferior courts; but that the chief magistrate with his executive council are appointable by the legislature; that two members of the latter are triennially displaced at the pleasure of the legislature; and that all the principal offices, both executive and judiciary, are filled by the same department. The executive prerogative of pardon, also is in one case vested in the legislative department.

The constitution of North-Carolina, which declares, "that the legislative, executive and supreme judicial powers of government, ought to be forever separate and distinct from each other," refers at the same time to the legislative department, the appointment not only of the executive chief, but all the principal officers within both that and the judiciary department.

In South-Carolina, the constitution makes the executive magistracy eligible by the legislative department. It gives to the latter also the appointment of the members of the judiciary department, including even justices of the peace and sheriffs; and the appointment of officers in the executive department, down to captains in the army and navy of the state.

In the constitution of Georgia, where it is declared, "that the legislative, executive and judiciary departments shall be separate and distinct, so that neither exercise the powers properly belonging to the other." We find that the executive department is to be filled by appointments of the legislature; and the executive prerogative of pardon, to be finally exercised by the same authority. Even justices of the peace are to be appointed by the legislature.

In citing these cases in which the legislative, executive and judiciary departments, have not been kept totally separate and distinct, I wish not to be regarded as an advocate for the particular organizations of the several state governments. I am fully aware that among the many excellent principles which they exemplify, they carry strong marks of the haste, and still stronger of the inexperience, under which they were framed. It is but too obvious that in some instances, the fundamental principle under consideration has been violated by too great a mixture, and even an actual consolidation of the different powers; and that in no instance has a competent provision been made for maintaining in practice the separation delineated on paper. What I have wished to evince is, that the change brought against the proposed constitution, of violating a sacred maxim of free government, is warranted neither by the real meaning annexed to that maxim by its author; nor by the sense in which it has hitherto been understood in America. This interesting subject will be resumed in the ensuing paper.

Publius.

No. 48

JAMES MADISON

On separation of powers and supremacy of legislative power.

No. 49

JAMES MADISON

On preventing legislative tyranny.

No. 50

JAMES MADISON

On preventing violations of the Constitution. Danger of legislators judging themselves.

No. 51

JAMES MADISON

February 6, 1788

To the People of the State of New York.

To what expedient then shall we finally resort for maintaining in practice the necessary partition of power among the several departments, as laid down in the constitution? The only answer that can be given is, that as all these exterior provisions are found to be inadequate, the defect must be supplied, by so contriving the interior structure of the government, as that its several constituent parts may, by their mutual relations, be the means of keeping each other in their proper places. Without presuming to undertake a full development of this important idea, I will hazard a few general observations, which may perhaps place it in a clearer light, and enable us to form a more correct judgment of the principles and structure of the government planned by the convention.

In order to lay a due foundation for that separate and distinct exercise of the different powers of government, which to a certain extent, is admitted on all hands to be essential to the preservation of liberty, it is evident that each department should have a will of its own; and consequently should be so constituted, that the members of each should have as little agency as possible in the appointment of the members of the others. Were this principle rigorously adhered to, it would require that all the appointments for the supreme executive, legislative, and judiciary magistracies, should be drawn from the same fountain of authority, the people, through channels, having no communication whatever with one another. Perhaps such a plan of constructing the several departments would be less difficult in practice than it may in contemplation appear. Some difficulties however, and some additional expence, would attend the execution of it. Some deviations therefore from the principle must be admitted. In the constitution of the judiciary department in particular, it might be inexpedient to insist rigorously on the principle; first, because peculiar qualifications being essential in the members, the primary consideration ought to be to select that mode of choice, which best secures these

---

From *The Independent Journal*, February 6, 1788. This essay appeared on February 8 in *The New-York Packet* and on February 11 in *The Daily Advertiser*.

qualifications; secondly, because the permanent tenure by which the appointments are held in that department, must soon destroy all sense of dependence on the authority conferring them.

It is equally evident that the members of each department should be as little dependent as possible on those of the others, for the emoluments annexed to their offices. Were the executive magistrate, or the judges, not independent of the legislature in this particular, their independence in every other would be merely nominal.

But the great security against a gradual concentration of the several powers in the same department, consists in giving to those who administer each department, the necessary constitutional means, and personal motives, to resist encroachments of the others. The provision for defence must in this, as in all other cases, be made commensurate to the danger of attack. Ambition must be made to counteract ambition. The interest of the man must be connected with the constitutional rights of the place. It may be a reflection on human nature, that such devices should be necessary to controul the abuses of government. But what is government itself but the greatest of all reflections on human nature? If men were angels, no government would be necessary. If angels were to govern men, neither external nor internal controuls on government would be necessary. In framing a government which is to be administered by men over men, the great difficulty lies in this: You must first enable the government to controul the governed; and in the next place, oblige it to controul itself. A dependence on the people is no doubt the primary controul on the government; but experience has taught mankind the necessity of auxiliary precautions.

This policy of supplying by opposite and rival interests, the defect of better motives, might be traced through the whole system of human affairs, private as well as public. We see it particularly displayed in all the subordinate distributions of power; where the constant aim is to divide and arrange the several offices in such a manner as that each may be a check on the other; that the private interest of every individual, may be a centinel over the public rights. These inventions of prudence cannot be less requisite in the distribution of the supreme powers of the state.

But it is not possible to give to each department an equal power of self defence. In republican government the legislative authority, necessarily, predominates. The remedy for this inconveniency is, to divide the legislature into different branches; and to render them by different modes of election, and different principles of action, as little connected with each other, as the nature of their common functions, and their common dependence on the society, will admit. It may even be necessary to guard against dangerous encroachments by still further precautions. As the weight of the legislative authority requires that it should be thus divided, the weakness of the executive may require, on the other hand, that it should be fortified. An absolute negative, on the legislature, appears at first view to be the natural defence with which the executive magistrate should be armed. But perhaps it would be neither altogether safe, nor alone sufficient. On ordinary occasions, it might not be exerted with the requisite firmness; and on extraordinary occasions, it might be perfidiously abused. May not this defect of an absolute negative be supplied, by some qualified connection between this weaker department, and the weaker branch of the stronger department, by which the latter may be led to support the constitutional rights of the former, without being too much detached from the rights of its own department?

If the principles on which these observations are founded be just, as I persuade myself they are, and they be applied as a criterion, to the several state constitutions, and to the federal constitution, it will be found, that if the latter does not perfectly correspond with them, the former are infinitely less able to bear such a test.

There are moreover two considerations particularly applicable to the federal system of America, which place that system in a very interesting point of view.

First. In a single republic, all the power surrendered by the people, is submitted to the administration of a single government; and usurpations are guarded against by a division of the government into distinct and separate departments. In the compound republic of America, the power surrendered by the people, is first divided between two distinct governments, and then the portion allotted to each, subdivided among distinct and separate departments. Hence a double security arises to the rights of the people. The different governments will controul each other; at the same time that each will be controuled by itself.

Second. It is of great importance in a republic, not only to guard the society against the oppression of its rulers; but to guard one part of the society against the injustice of the other part. Different interests necessarily exist in different classes of citizens. If a majority be united by a common interest, the rights of the minority will be insecure. There are but two methods of providing against this evil: The one by creating a will in the community independent of the majority, that is, of the society itself; the other by comprehending in the society so many separate descriptions of citizens, as will render an unjust combination of a majority of the whole, very improbable, if not impracticable. The first method prevails in all governments possessing an hereditary or self appointed authority. This at best is but a precarious security; because a power independent of the society may as well espouse the unjust views of the major, as the rightful interests, of the minor party, and may possibly be turned against both parties. The second method will be exemplified in the federal republic of the United States. Whilst all authority in it will be derived from and dependent on the society, the society itself will be broken into so many parts, interests and classes of citizens, that the rights of individuals or of the minority, will be in little danger from interested combinations of the majority. In a free government, the security for civil rights must be the same as for religious rights. It consists in the one case in the multiplicity of interests, and in the other, in the multiplicity of sects. The degree of security in both cases will depend on the number of interests and sects; and this may be presumed to depend on the extent of country and number of people comprehended under the same government. This view of the subject must particularly recommend a proper federal system to all the sincere and considerate friends of republican government: Since it shews that in exact proportion as the territory of the union may be formed into more circumscribed confederacies or states, oppressive combinations of a majority will be facilitated, the best security under the republican form, for the rights of every class of citizens, will be diminished; and consequently, the stability and independence of some member of the government, the only other security, must be proportionally increased. Justice is the end of government. It is the end of civil society. It ever has been, and ever will be pursued, until it be obtained, or until liberty be lost in the pursuit. In a society under the forms of which the stronger faction can readily unite and oppress the weaker, anarchy may as truly be said to reign, as in a state of nature where the weaker individual is not secured against the violence of the stronger: And as in the latter state even the stronger individuals are prompted by the uncertainty of their condition, to submit to a government which may protect the weak as well as themselves: So in the former state, will the more powerful factions or parties be gradually induced by a like motive, to wish for a government which will protect all parties, the weaker as well as the more powerful. It can be little doubted, that if the state of Rhode Island was separated from the confederacy, and left to itself, the insecurity of rights under the popular form of government within such narrow limits, would be displayed by such reiterated oppressions of factious majorities, that some power altogether independent of the people would soon be called for by the voice of the very factions whose misrule had proved the necessity of it. In the extended republic of the United States, and among the great variety of interests, parties and sects which it embraces, a coalition of a majority of the whole society could seldom take place on any other principles than those of justice and the general good; and there being thus less danger to a minor from the will of the major party, there must be less pretext also, to provide for the security of the former, by introducing into the government a will not dependent on the latter; or in other words, a will independent of the society itself. It is no less certain than it is important, notwithstanding the contrary opinions which have been entertained, that the larger the society, provided it lie within a practicable sphere, the more duly capable it will be of self government. And happily for the *republican cause*, the practicable sphere may be carried to a very great extent, by a judicious modification and mixture of the *federal principle*.

Publius.

No. 52

JAMES MADISON

On legislatures.

No. 53

JAMES MADISON

Discusses legislative terms.

No. 54

JAMES MADISON

February 12, 1788

To the People of the State of New York.

The next view which I shall take of the House of Representatives, relates to the apportionment of its members to the several States, which is to be determined by the same rule with that of direct taxes.

It is not contended that the number of people in each State ought not to be the standard for regulating the proportion of those who are to represent the people of each State. The establishment of the same rule for the apportionment of taxes, will probably be as little contested; though the rule itself in this case, is by no means founded on the same principle. In the former case, the rule is understood to refer to the personal rights of the people, with which it has a natural and universal connection. In the latter, it has reference to the proportion of wealth, of which it is in no case a precise measure, and in ordinary cases a very unfit one. But notwithstanding the imperfection of the rule as applied to the relative wealth and contributions of the States, it is evidently the least exceptionable among the practicable rules; and had too recently obtained the general sanction of America, not to have found a ready preference with the Convention.

All this is admitted, it will perhaps be said: But does it follow from an admission of numbers for the measure of representation, or of slaves combined with free citizens, as a ratio of taxation, that slaves ought to be included in the numerical rule of representation? Slaves are considered as property, not as persons. They ought therefore to be comprehended in estimates of taxation which are founded on property, and to be excluded from representation which is regulated by a census of persons. This is the objection, as I understand it, stated in its full force. I shall be equally candid in stating the reasoning which may be offered on the opposite side.

We subscribe to the doctrine, might one of our southern brethren observe, that representation relates more immediately to persons, and taxation more immediately to property, and we join in

From *The New-York Packet,* February 12, 1788. This essay appeared on February 13 in *The Independent Journal.*

the application of this distinction to the case of our slaves. But we must deny the fact that slaves are considered merely as property, and in no respect whatever as persons. The true state of the case is, that they partake of both these qualities; being considered by our laws, in some respects, as persons, and in other respects, as property. In being compelled to labor not for himself, but for a master; in being vendible by one master to another master; and in being subject at all times to be restrained in his liberty, and chastised in his body, by the capricious will of another, the slave may appear to be degraded from the human rank, and classed with those irrational animals, which fall under the legal denomination of property. In being protected on the other hand in his life & in his limbs, against the violence of all others, even the master of his labor and his liberty; and in being punishable himself for all violence committed against others; the slave is no less evidently regarded by the law as a member of the society; not as a part of the irrational creation; as a moral person, not as a mere article of property. The Fœderal Constitution therefore, decides with great propriety on the case of our slaves, when it views them in the mixt character of persons and of property. This is in fact their true character. It is the character bestowed on them by the laws under which they live; and it will not be denied that these are the proper criterion; because it is only under the pretext that the laws have transformed the negroes into subjects of property, that a place is disputed them in the computation of numbers; and it is admitted that if the laws were to restore the rights which have been taken away, the negroes could no longer be refused an equal share of representation with the other inhabitants.

This question may be placed in another light. It is agreed on all sides, that numbers are the best scale of wealth and taxation, as they are the only proper scale of representation. Would the Convention have been impartial or consistent, if they had rejected the slaves from the list of inhabitants when the shares of representation were to be calculated; and inserted them on the lists when the tariff of contributions were to be adjusted? Could it be reasonably expected that the southern States would concur in a system which considered their slaves in some degree as men, when burdens were to be imposed, but refused to consider them in the same light when advantages were to be conferred? Might not some surprize also be expressed that those who reproach the southern States with the barbarous policy of considering as property a part of their human brethren, should themselves contend that the government to which all the States are to be parties, ought to consider this unfortunate race more compleatly in the unnatural light of property, than the very laws of which they complain!

It may be replied perhaps that slaves are not included in the estimate of representatives in any of the States possessing them. They neither vote themselves, nor increase the votes of their masters. Upon what principle then ought they to be taken into the fœderal estimate of representation? In rejecting them altogether, the Constitution would in this respect have followed the very laws which have been appealed to, as the proper guide.

This objection is repelled by a single observation. It is a fundamental principle of the proposed Constitution, that as the aggregate number of representatives allotted to the several States, is to be determined by a fœderal rule founded on the aggregate number of inhabitants, so the right of choosing this allotted number in each State is to be exercised by such part of the inhabitants, as the State itself may designate. The qualifications on which the right of suffrage depend, are not perhaps the same in any two States. In some of the States the difference is very material. In every State, a certain proportion of inhabitants are deprived of this right by the Constitution of the State, who will be included in the census by which the Fœderal Constitution apportions the representatives. In this point of view, the southern States might retort the complaint, by insisting, that the principle laid down by the Convention required that no regard should be had to the policy of particular States towards their own inhabitants; and consequently, that the slaves as inhabitants should have been admitted into the census according to their full number, in like manner with other inhabitants, who by the policy of other States, are not admitted to all the rights of citizens. A rigorous adherence however to this principle is waved by those who would be gainers by it. All that they ask is, that equal moderation be shewn on the other side. Let the case of the slaves be considered as it is in truth a peculiar one. Let the compromising expedient of the Constitution be mutually adopted, which regards them as inhabitants, but as debased by servitude below the equal level of free inhabitants, which regards the *slave* as divested of two fifth of the *man*.

After all may not another ground be taken on which this article of the Constitution, will admit of a still more ready defence? We have hitherto proceeded on the idea that representation related to persons only, and not at all to property. But is it a just idea? Government is instituted no less for protection of the property, than of the persons of individuals. The one as well as the other, therefore may be considered as represented by those who are charged with the government. Upon this principle it is, that in several of the States, and particularly in the State of New-York, one branch of the government is intended more especially to be the guardian of property, and is accordingly elected by that part of the society which is most interested in this object of government.* In the Fœderal Constitution, this policy does not prevail. The rights of property are committed into the same hands with the personal rights. Some attention ought therefore to be paid to property in the choice of those hands.

For another reason the votes allowed in the Fœderal Legislature to the people of each State, ought to bear some proportion to the comparative wealth of the States. States have not like individuals, an influence over each other arising from superior advantages of fortune. If the law allows an opulent citizen but a single vote in the choice of his representative, the respect and consequence which he derives from his fortunate situation, very frequently guide the votes of others to the objects of his choice; and through this imperceptible channel the rights of property are conveyed into the public representation. A State possesses no such influence over other States. It is not probable that the richest State in the confederacy will ever influence the choice of a single representative in any other State. Nor will the representatives of the larger and richer States possess any other advantage in the Fœderal Legislature over the representatives of other States, than what may result from their superior number alone; as far therefore as their superior wealth and weight may justly entitle them to any advantage, it ought to be secured to them by a superior share of representation. The new Constitution is in this respect materially different from the existing confederation, as well as from that of the United Netherlands, and other similar confederacies. In each of the latter the efficacy of the fœderal resolutions depends on the subsequent and voluntary resolutions of the States composing the Union. Hence the States, though possessing an equal vote in the public councils, have an

* The suffrage for the senate of New York was confined by law to resident freeholders whose freeholds were valued at £100 clear of debt. (Editor)

unequal influence, corresponding with the unequal importance of these subsequent and voluntary resolutions. Under the proposed Constitution, the fœderal acts will take effect without the necessary intervention of the individual States. They will depend merely on the majority of votes in the Fœderal Legislature, and consequently each vote whether proceeding from a larger or a smaller State, or a State more or less wealthy or powerful, will have an equal weight and efficacy; in the same manner as the votes individually given in a State Legislature, by the representatives of unequal counties or other districts, have each a precise equality of value and effect; or if there be any difference in the case, it proceeds from the difference in the personal character of the individual representative, rather than from any regard to the extent of the district from which he comes.

Such is the reasoning which an advocate for the southern interests might employ on this subject: And although it may appear to be a little strained in some points, yet on the whole, I must confess, that it fully reconciles me to the scale of representation, which the Convention have established.

In one respect the establishment of a common measure for representation and taxation will have a very salutary effect. As the accuracy of the census to be obtained by the Congress, will necessarily depend in a considerable degree on the disposition, if not the cooperation of the States, it is of great importance that the States should feel as little bias as possible to swell or to reduce the amount of their numbers. Were their share of representation alone to be governed by this rule they would have an interest in exaggerating their inhabitants. Were the rule to decide their share of taxation alone, a contrary temptation would prevail. By extending the rule to both objects, the States will have opposite interests, which will controul and ballance each other; and produce the requisite impartiality.

Publius.

Nos. 55, 56

JAMES MADISON

Discuss proportions and adequacy of a moderate number of representatives.

No. 57

JAMES MADISON

February 19, 1788

To the People of the State of New York.

The *third* charge against the House of Representatives is, that it will be taken from that class of citizens which will have least sympathy with the mass of the people, and be most likely to aim at an ambitious sacrifice of the many to the aggrandizement of the few.

Of all the objections which have been framed against the Fœderal Constitution, this is perhaps the most extraordinary. Whilst the objection itself is levelled against a pretended oligarchy, the principle of it strikes at the very root of republican government.

The aim of every political Constitution is or ought to be first to obtain for rulers, men who possess most wisdom to discern, and most virtue to pursue the common good of the society; and in the next place, to take the most effectual precautions for keeping them virtuous, whilst they continue to hold their public trust. The elective mode of obtaining rulers is the characteristic policy of republican government. The means relied on in this form of government for preventing their degeneracy are numerous and various. The most effectual one is such a limitation of the term of appointments, as will maintain a proper responsibility to the people.

Let me now ask what circumstance there is in the Constitution of the House of Representatives, that violates the principles of republican government; or favors the elevation of the few on the ruins of the many? Let me ask whether every circumstance is not, on the contrary, strictly conformable to these principles; and scrupulously impartial to the rights and pretensions of every class and description of citizens?

Who are to be the electors of the Fœderal Representatives? Not the rich more than the poor; not the learned more than the ignorant; not the haughty heirs of distinguished names, more than the humble sons of obscure and unpropitious fortune. The electors are to be the great body of the people of the United States. They

---

From *The New-York Packet,* February 19, 1788. This essay appeared on February 20 in *The Independent Journal.*

are to be the same who exercise the right in every State of electing the correspondent branch of the Legislature of the State.

Who are to be the objects of popular choice? Every citizen whose merit may recommend him to the esteem and confidence of his country. No qualification of wealth, of birth, of religious faith, or of civil profession, is permitted to fetter the judgment or disappoint the inclination of the people.

If we consider the situation of the men on whom the free suffrages of their fellow citizens may confer the representative trust, we shall find it involving every security which can be devised or desired for their fidelity to their constituents.

In the first place, as they will have been distinguished by the preference of their fellow citizens, we are to presume, that in general, they will be somewhat distinguished also, by those qualities which entitle them to it, and which promise a sincere and scrupulous regard to the nature of their engagements.

In the second place, they will enter into the public service under circumstances which cannot fail to produce a temporary affection at least to their constituents. There is in every breast a sensibility to marks of honor, of favor, of esteem, and of confidence, which, apart from all considerations of interest, is some pledge for grateful and benevolent returns. Ingratitude is a common topic of declamation against human nature; and it must be confessed, that instances of it are but too frequent and flagrant both in public and in private life. But the universal and extreme indignation which it inspires, is itself a proof of the energy and prevalence of the contrary sentiment.

In the third place, these ties which bind the representative to his constituents are strengthened by motives of a more selfish nature. His pride and vanity attach him to a form of government which favors his pretensions, and gives him a share in its honors and distinctions. Whatever hopes or projects might be entertained by a few aspiring characters, it must generally happen that a great proportion of the men deriving their advancement from their influence with the people, would have more to hope from a preservation of the favor, than from innovations in the government subversive of the authority of the people.

All these securities however would be found very insufficient without the restraint of frequent elections. Hence, in the fourth place, the House of Representatives is so constituted as to support in the members an habitual recollection of their dependence on the people. Before the sentiments impressed on their minds by the mode of their elevation, can be effaced by the exercise of power, they will be compelled to anticipate the moment when their power is to cease, when their exercise of it is to be reviewed, and when they must descend to the level from which they were raised; there for ever to remain, unless a faithful discharge of their trust shall have established their title to a renewal of it.

I will add as a fifth circumstance in the situation of the House of Representatives, restraining them from oppressive measures, that they can make no law which will not have its full operation on themselves and their friends, as well as on the great mass of the society. This has always been deemed one of the strongest bonds by which human policy can connect the rulers and the people together. It creates between them that communion of interests and sympathy of sentiments of which few governments have furnished examples; but without which every government degenerates into tyranny. If it be asked what is to restrain the House of Representatives from making legal discriminations in favor of themselves and a particular class of the society? I answer, the genius of the whole system, the nature of just and constitutional laws, and above all the vigilant and manly spirit which actuates the people of America, a spirit which nourishes freedom, and in return is nourished by it.

If this spirit shall ever be so far debased as to tolerate a law not obligatory on the Legislature as well as on the people, the people will be prepared to tolerate anything but liberty.

Such will be the relation between the House of Representatives and their constituents. Duty, gratitude, interest, ambition itself, are the chords by which they will be bound to fidelity and sympathy with the great mass of the people. It is possible that these may all be insufficient to control the caprice and wickedness of man. But are they not all that government will admit, and that human prudence can devise? Are they not the genuine and the characteristic means by which Republican Government provides for the liberty and happiness of the people? Are they not the identical means on which every State Government in the Union, relies for the attainment of these important ends? What then are we to understand by the objection which this paper has combated? What are we to say to the men who profess the most flaming zeal for Republican Government, yet boldly impeach the fundamental principle of it; who pretend to be champions for the right and the capacity of the people to chuse their own rulers, yet maintain that they will prefer those only who will immediately and infallibly betray the trust committed to them?

Were the objection to be read by one who had not seen the mode prescribed by the Constitution for the choice of representatives, he could suppose nothing less than that some unreasonable qualification of property was annexed to the right of suffrage; or that the right of eligibility was limited to persons of particular families or fortunes; or at least that the mode prescribed by the State Constitutions was in some respect or other very grossly departed from. We have seen how far such a supposition would err as to the two first points. Nor would it in fact be less erroneous as to the last. The only difference discoverable between the two cases, is, that each representative of the United States will be elected by five or six thousand citizens; whilst in the individual States the election of a representative is left to about as many hundred. Will it be pretended that this difference is sufficient to justify an attachment to the State Governments and an abhorrence to the Fœderal Government? If this be the point on which the objection turns, it deserves to be examined.

Is it supported by *reason*? This cannot be said, without maintaining that five or six thousand citizens are less capable of chusing a fit representative, or more liable to be corrupted by an unfit one, than five or six hundred. Reason, on the contrary assures us, that as in so great a number, a fit representative would be most likely to be found, so the choice would be less likely to be diverted from him, by the intrigues of the ambitious, or the bribes of the rich.

Is the *consequence* from this doctrine admissible? If we say that five or six hundred citizens are as many as can jointly exercise their right of suffrage, must we not deprive the people of the immediate choice of their public servants in every instance where the administration of the government does not require as many of them as will amount to one for that number of citizens?

Is the doctrine warranted by *facts*? It was shewn in the last paper, that the real representation in the British House of Commons very little exceeds the proportion of one for every thirty thousand inhabitants. Besides a variety of powerful causes, not existing here, and which favor in that country, the pretensions of rank and wealth, no person is eligible as a representative of a county, unless he possess real estate of the clear value of six hundred pounds sterling per year; nor of a city or borough, unless he possess a like estate of half that annual value. To this qualification on the part of the county representatives, is added another on the part of the county electors, which restrains the right of suffrage to persons having a freehold estate of the annual value of more than twenty pounds sterling according to the present rate of money. Notwithstanding these unfavorable circumstances, and notwithstanding some very unequal laws in the British code, it cannot be said that the representatives of the nation have elevated the few on the ruins of the many.

But we need not resort to foreign experience on this subject. Our own is explicit and decisive. The districts in New-Hampshire in which the Senators are chosen immediately by the people are nearly as large as will be necessary for her representatives in the Congress. Those of Massachusetts are larger, than will be necessary for that purpose. And those of New-York still more so. In the last State the members of Assembly, for the cities and counties of New-York and Albany, are elected by very nearly as many voters, as will be entitled to a representative in the Congress, calculating on the number of sixty-five representatives only. It makes no difference that in these senatorial districts and counties, a number of representatives are voted for by each elector at the same time. If the same electors, at the same time are capable of choosing four or five representatives, they cannot be incapable of choosing one. Pennsylvania is an additional example. Some of her counties which elect her State representatives, are almost as large as her districts will be by which her Fœderal Representatives will be elected. The city of Philadelphia is supposed to contain between fifty and sixty thousand souls. It will therefore form nearly two districts for the choice of Fœderal Representatives. It forms however but one county, in which every elector votes for each of its representatives in the State Legislature. And what may appear to be still more directly to our purpose, the whole city actually elects a *single member* for the executive council. This is the case in all the other counties of the State.

Are not these facts the most satisfactory proofs of the fallacy which has been employed against the branch of the Fœderal Government under consideration: Has it appeared on trial that the Senators of New-Hampshire, Massachusetts, and New-York; or the Executive Council of Pennsylvania; or the members of the Assembly in the two last States, have betrayed any peculiar disposition to sacrifice the many to the few; or are in any respect less worthy of their places than the representatives and magistrates appointed in other States, by very small divisions of the people?

But there are cases of a stronger complexion than any which I have yet quoted. One branch of the Legislature of Connecticut is so constituted that each member of it is elected by the whole State. So is the Governor of that State, of Massachusetts, and of this State, and the President of New-Hampshire. I leave every man to decide whether the result of any one of these experiments can be said to countenance a suspicion that a diffusive mode of chusing representatives of the people tends to elevate traitors, and to undermine the public liberty.

Publius.

No. 58
JAMES MADISON
February 20, 1788

To the People of the State of New York.

The remaining charge against the House of Representatives which I am to examine, is grounded on a supposition that the number of members will not be augmented from time to time, as the progress of population may demand.

It has been admitted that this objection, if well supported, would have great weight. The following observations will shew that like most other objections against the constitution, it can only proceed from a partial view of the subject; or from a jealousy which discolours and disfigures every object which is beheld.

1. Those who urge the objection seem not to have recollected that the federal constitution will not suffer by a comparison with the state constitutions, in the security provided for a gradual augmentation of the number of representatives. The number which is to prevail in the first instance is declared to be temporary. Its duration is limited to the short term of three years.

Within every successive term of ten years, a census of inhabitants is to be repeated. The unequivocal objects of these regulations are, first, to readjust from time to time the apportionment of repre-

---

From *The Independent Journal,* February 20, 1788. This essay appeared on February 22 in *The New-York Packet.*

sentatives to the number of inhabitants; under the single exception that each state shall have one representative at least; Secondly, to augment the number of representatives at the same periods; under the sole limitation, that the whole number shall not exceed one for every thirty thousand inhabitants. If we review the constitutions of the several states, we shall find that some of them contain no determinate regulations on this subject; that others correspond pretty much on this point with the federal constitution; and that the most effectual security in any of them is resolvable into a mere directory provision.

2. As far as experience has taken place on this subject, a gradual increase of representatives under the state constitutions, has at least kept pace with that of the constituents; and it appears that the former have been as ready to concur in such measures, as the latter have been to call for them.

3. There is a peculiarity in the federal constitution which ensures a watchful attention in a majority both of the people and of their representatives, to a constitutional augmentation of the latter. The peculiarity lies in this, that one branch of the legislature is a representation of citizens; the other of the states: in the former consequently the larger states will have most weight; in the latter, the advantage will be in favour of the smaller states. From this circumstance it may with certainty be inferred, that the larger states will be strenuous advocates for increasing the number and weight of that part of the legislature in which their influence predominates. And it so happens that four only of the largest, will have a majority of the whole votes in the house of representatives. Should the representatives or people therefore of the smaller states oppose at any time a reasonable addition of members, a coalition of a very few states will be sufficient to overrule the opposition; a coalition, which notwithstanding the rivalship and local prejudices which might prevent it on ordinary occasions, would not fail to take place, when not merely prompted by common interest, but justified by equity and the principles of the constitution.

It may be alledged, perhaps, that the senate would be prompted by like motives to an adverse coalition; and as their concurrence would be indispensable, the just and constitutional views of the other branch might be defeated. This is the difficulty which has probably created the most serious apprehensions in the zealous friends of a numerous representation. Fortunately it is among the difficulties which, existing only in appearance, vanish on a close and accurate inspection. The following reflections will, if I mistake not, be admitted to be conclusive and satisfactory on this point.

Notwithstanding the equal authority which will subsist between the two houses on all legislative subjects, except the originating of money bills, it cannot be doubted that the house composed of the greater number of members, when supported by the more powerful states, and speaking the known and determined sense of a majority of the people, will have no small advantage in a question depending on the comparative firmness of the two houses.

This advantage must be increased by the consciousness felt by the same side, of being supported in its demands, by right, by reason, and by the constitution; and the consciousness on the opposite side, of contending against the force of all these solemn considerations.

It is farther to be considered that in the graduation between the smallest and largest states, there are several which, though most likely in general to arrange themselves among the former, are too little removed in extent and population from the latter, to second an opposition to their just and legitimate pretensions. Hence it is by no means certain that a majority of votes, even in the senate, would be unfriendly to proper augmentations in the number of representatives.

It will not be looking too far to add, that the senators from all the new states may be gained over to the just views of the house of representatives, by an expedient too obvious to be overlooked. As these states will for a great length of time advance in population with peculiar rapidity, they will be interested in frequent reapportionments of the representatives to the number of inhabitants. The large states therefore, who will prevail in the house of representatives, will have nothing to do, but to make reapportionments and augmentations mutually conditions of each other; and the senators from all the most growing states will be bound to contend for the latter, by the interest which their states will feel in the former.

These considerations seem to afford ample security on this subject; and ought alone to satisfy all the doubts and fears which have been indulged with regard to it. Admitting however that, they should all be insufficient to subdue the unjust policy of the smaller states, or their predominant influence in the councils of the senate; a constitutional and infallible resource, still remains with the larger states, by which they will be able at all times to accomplish their just purposes. The house of representatives can not only refuse, but they alone can propose the supplies requisite for the support of government. They in a word hold the purse; that powerful instrument by which we behold in the history of the British constitution, an infant and humble representation of the people, gradually enlarging the sphere of its activity and importance, and finally reducing, as far as it seems to have wished, all the overgrown prerogatives of the other branches of the government. This power over the purse, may in fact be regarded as the most compleat and effectual weapon with which any constitution can arm the immediate representatives of the people, for obtaining a redress of every grievance, and for carrying into effect every just and salutary measure.

But will not the house of representatives be as much interested as the senate in maintaining the government in its proper functions, and will they not therefore be unwilling to stake its existence or its reputation on the pliancy of the senate? Or if such a trial of firmness between the two branches were hazarded, would not the one be as likely first to yield as the other? These questions will create no difficulty with those who reflect, that in all cases the smaller the number and the more permanent and conspicuous the station of men in power, the stronger must be the interest which they will individually feel in whatever concerns the government. Those who represent the dignity of their country in the eyes of other nations, will be particularly sensible to every prospect of public danger, or of a dishonorable stagnation in public affairs. To those causes we are to ascribe the continual triumph of the British house of commons over the other branches of the government, whenever the engine of a money bill has been employed. An absolute inflexibility on the side of the latter, although it could not have failed to involve every department of the state in the general confusion, has neither been apprehended nor experienced. The utmost degree of firmness that can be displayed by the federal senate or president will not be more than equal to a resistance in which they will be supported by constitutional and patriotic principles.

In this review of the constitution of the house of representatives, I have passed over the circumstance of economy which in the present state of affairs might have had some effect in lessening the temporary number of representatives; and a disregard of which would probably have been as rich a theme of declamation against the constitution as has been furnished by the smallness of the number proposed. I omit also any remarks on the difficulty which might be found, under present circumstances, in engaging in the federal service, a large number of such characters as the people will probably elect. One observation however I must be permitted, to add, on this subject, as claiming in my judgment a very serious attention. It is, that in all legislative assemblies, the greater the number composing them may be, the fewer will be the men who will in fact direct their proceedings. In the first place, the more numerous any assembly may be, of whatever characters composed, the greater is known to be the ascendancy of passion over reason. In the next place, the larger the number, the greater will be the proportion of members of limited information and of weak capacities. Now it is precisely on characters of this description that the eloquence and address of the few are known to act with all their force. In the antient republics, where the whole body of the people assembled in person, a single orator, or an artful statesman, was generally seen to rule with as compleat a sway, as if a sceptre had been placed in his single hands. On the same principle the more multitudinous a representative assembly may be rendered, the more it will partake of the infirmities incident to collective meetings of the people. Ignorance will be the dupe of cunning; and passion the slave of sophistry and declamation. The people can never err more than in supposing that by multiplying their representatives, beyond a certain limit, they strengthen the barrier against the government of a few. Experience will forever admonish them that on the contrary, *after securing a sufficient number for the purposes of safety, of local information, and of diffusive sympathy with the whole society,* they will counteract their own views by every addition to their representatives. The countenance of the government may become more democratic; but the soul that animates it will be more oligarchic. The machine will be enlarged, but the fewer and often, the more secret will be the springs by which its motions are directed.

As connected with the objection against the number of representatives, may properly be here noticed, that which has been suggested against the number made competent for legislative business. It has been said that more than a majority ought to have been required for a quorum, and in particular cases, if not in all, more than a majority of a quorum for a decision. That some advantages might have resulted from such a precaution, cannot be denied. It might have been an additional shield to some particular interests, and another obstacle generally to hasty and partial measures. But these considerations are outweighed by the inconveniencies in the opposite scale. In all cases where justice or the general good might require new laws to be passed, or active measures to be pursued, the fundamental principle of free government would be reversed. It would be no longer the majority that would rule; the power would be transferred to the minority. Were the defensive privilege limited to particular cases, an interested minority might take advantage of it to screen themselves from equitable sacrifices to the general weal, or in particular emergencies to extort unreasonable indulgences. Lastly, it would facilitate and foster the baneful practice of secessions; a practice which has shewn itself even in states where a majority only is required; a practice subversive of all the principles of order and regular government; a practice which leads more directly to public convulsions, and the ruin of popular governments, than any other which has yet been displayed among us.

Publius.

No. 59

ALEXANDER HAMILTON

Defends provisions for congressional power to control state laws governing time, place, manner of elections.

No. 60

ALEXANDER HAMILTON

February 23, 1788

To the People of the State of New York.

We have seen that an incontroulable power over the elections for the federal government could not without hazard be committed to the state legislatures. Let us now see what would be the dangers on the other side; that is, from confiding the ultimate right of

---

From *The Independent Journal*, February 23, 1788. This essay appeared on February 26 in *The New-York Packet*.

regulating its own elections to the union itself. It is not pretended, that this right would ever be used for the exclusion of any state from its share in the representation. The interest of all would in this respect at least be the security of all. But it is alledged that it might be employed in such a manner as to promote the election of some favourite class of men in exclusion of others; by confining the places of election to particular districts, and rendering it impracticable to the citizens at large to partake in the choice. Of all chimerical suppositions, this seems to be the most chimerical. On the one hand no rational calculation of probabilities would lead us to imagine, that the disposition, which a conduct so violent and extraordinary would imply, could ever find its way into the national councils; and on the other, it may be concluded with certainty, that if so improper a spirit should ever gain admittance into them, it would display itself in a form altogether different and far more decisive.

The improbability of the attempt may be satisfactorily inferred from this single reflection, that it could never be made without causing an immediate revolt of the great body of the people,—headed and directed by the state governments. It is not difficult to conceive that this characteristic right of freedom may, in certain turbulent and factious seasons, be violated in respect to a particular class of citizens by a victorious and overbearing majority; but that so fundamental a privilege, in a country so situated and so enlightened, should be invaded to the prejudice of the great mass of the people, by the deliberate policy of the government; without occasioning a popular revolution, is altogether inconceivable and incredible.

In addition to this general reflection, there are considerations of a more precise nature, which forbid all apprehension on the subject. The dissimilarity in the ingredients, which will compose the national government; and still more in the manner in which they will be brought into action in its various branches must form a powerful obstacle to a concert of views, in any partial scheme of elections. There is sufficient diversity in the state of property, in the genius, manners, and habits of the people of the different parts of the union to occasion a material diversity of disposition in their representatives towards the different ranks and conditions in society. And though an intimate intercourse under the same government will promote a gradual assimilation, of temper and sentiment, yet there are causes as well physical as moral, which may in a greater or less degree permanently nourish different propensities and inclinations in this particular. But the circumstance, which will be likely to have the greatest influence in the matter, will be the dissimilar modes of constituting the several component parts of the government. The house of representatives being to be elected immediately by the people; the senate by the state legislatures; the president by electors chosen for that purpose by the people; there would be little probability of a common interest to cement these different branches in a predilection for any particular class of electors.

As to the senate it is impossible that any regulation of "time and manner," which is all that is proposed to be submitted to the national government in respect to that body, can affect the spirit which will direct the choice of its members. The collective sense of the state legislatures can never be influenced by extraneous circumstances of that sort: A consideration, which alone ought to satisfy us that the discrimination apprehended would never be attempted. For what inducement could the senate have to concur in a preference, in which itself would not be included? Or to what purpose would it be established in reference to one branch of the legislature; if it could not be extended to the other? The composition of the one would in this case counteract that of the other. And we can never suppose that it would embrace the appointments to the senate, unless we can at the same time suppose the voluntary co-operation of the state legislatures. If we make the latter supposition, it then becomes immaterial where the power in question is placed; whether in their hands or in those of the union.

But what is to be the object of this capricious partiality in the national councils? Is it to be exercised in a discrimination between the different departments of industry, or between the different kinds of property, or between the different degrees of property? Will it lean in favor of the landed interest, or the monied interest, or the mercantile interest, or the manufacturing interest? Or to speak in the fashionable language of the adversaries of the Constitution; will it court the elevation of the "wealthy and the well born" to the exclusion and debasement of all the rest of the society?

If this partiality is to be exerted in favor of those who are concerned in any particular description of industry or property, I presume it will readily be admitted that the competition for it will lie between landed men and merchants. And I scruple not to affirm, that it is infinitely less likely, that either of them should gain an ascendant in the national councils, than that the one or the other of them should predominate in all the local councils. The inference will be, that a conduct tending to give an undue preference to either is much less to be dreaded from the former than from the latter.

The several states are in various degrees addicted to agriculture and commerce. In most, if not all of them, agriculture is predominant. In a few of them, however, commerce nearly divides its empire, and in most of them has a considerable share of influence. In proportion as either prevails, it will be conveyed into the national representation, and for the very reason that this will be an emanation from a greater variety of interests, and in much more various proportions, than are to be found in any single state, it will be much less apt to espouse either of them, with a decided partiality, than the representation of any single state.

In a country consisting chiefly of the cultivators of land where the rules of an equal representation obtain the landed interest must upon the whole preponderate in the government. As long as this interest prevails in most of the state legislatures, so long it must maintain a correspondent superiority in the national senate, which will generally be a faithful copy of the majorities of those assemblies. It cannot therefore be presumed that a sacrifice of the landed to the mercantile class will ever be a favorite object of this branch of the federal legislature. In applying thus particularly to the senate a general observation suggested by the situation of the country, I am governed by the consideration, that the credulous votaries of state power, cannot upon their own principles suspect that the state legislatures would be warped from their duty by any external influence. But as in reality the same situation must have the same effect in the primitive composition at least of the federal house of representatives; an improper byass towards the mercantile class is as little to be expected from this quarter as from the other.

In order perhaps to give countenance to the objection at any rate, it may be asked, is there not danger of an opposite byass in the national government, which may dispose it to endeavour to secure a monopoly of the federal administration to the landed class? As there is little likelihood that the supposition of such a byass will have any terrors for those who would be immediately injured by it, a laboured answer to this question will be dispensed with.

It will be sufficient to remark, first, that for the reasons elsewhere assigned,* it is less likely that any decided partiality should prevail in the councils of the union than in those of any of its members. Secondly that there would be no temptation to violate the constitution in favor of the landed class, because that class would in the natural course of things enjoy as great a preponderancy as itself could desire. And thirdly that men accustomed to investigate the sources of public prosperity, upon a large scale, must be too well convinced of the utility of commerce, to be inclined to inflict upon it so deep a wound as would result from the entire exclusion of those who would best understand its interest from a share in the management of them. The importance of commerce in the view of revenue alone must effectually guard it against the enmity of a body which would be continually importuned in its favour by the urgent calls of public necessity. I the rather consult brevity in discussing the probability of a preference founded upon a discrimination between the different kinds of industry and property; because, as far as I understand the meaning of the objectors, they contemplate a discrimination of another kind. They appear to have in view, as the objects of the preference with which they endeavour to alarm us, those whom they designate by the description of the "wealthy and the well born." These, it seems, are to be exalted to an odious pre-eminence over the rest of their fellow citizens. At one time however their elevation is to be a necessary consequence of the smallness of the representative body; at another time it is to be effected by depriving the people at large of the opportunity of exercising their right of suffrage in the choice of that body.

But upon what principle is the discrimination of the places of election to be made in order to answer the purpose of the meditated preference? Are the wealthy and the well born, as they are called, confined to particular spots in the several states? Have they by some miraculous instinct or foresight set apart in each of them a common place of residence? Are they only to be met with in the towns or cities? Or are they, on the contrary, scattered over the face of the country as avarice or chance may have happened to cast their own lot, or that of their predecessors? If the latter is the case, (as every intelligent man knows it to be†) is it not evident

---

* See Essay 35.

† Particularly in the Southern States and in this State. (Publius)

that the policy of confining the places of elections to particular districts would be as subversive of its own aim as it would be exceptionable on every other account? The truth is that there is no method of securing to the rich the preference apprehended, but by prescribing qualifications of property either for those who may elect, or be elected. But this forms no part of the power to be conferred upon the national government. Its authority would be expressly restricted to the regulation of the *times*, the *places*, and the *manner* of elections. The qualifications of the persons who may choose or be chosen, as has been remarked upon another occasion,* are defined and fixed in the constitution; and are unalterable by the legislature.

Let it however be admitted, for argument sake, that the expedient suggested might be successful; and let it at the same time be equally taken for granted that all the scruples which a sense of duty or an apprehension of the danger of the experiment might inspire, were overcome in the breasts of the national rulers; still, I imagine, it will hardly be pretended, that they could ever hope to carry such an enterprise into execution, without the aid of a military force sufficient to subdue, the resistance of the great body of the people. The improbability of the existence of a force equal to that object, has been discussed and demonstrated in different parts of these papers;† but that the futility of the objection under consideration may appear in the strongest light, it shall be conceded for a moment that such a force might exist; and the national government shall be supposed to be in the actual possession of it. What will be the conclusion? With a disposition to invade the essential rights of the community, and with the means of gratifying that disposition, is it presumable that the persons who were actuated by it would amuse themselves in the ridiculous task of fabricating election laws for securing a preference to a favourite class of men? Would they not be likely to prefer a conduct better adapted to their own immediate aggrandisement? Would they not rather boldly resolve to perpetuate themselves in office by one decisive act of usurpation, than to trust to precarious expedients, which in spite of all the precautions that might accompany them, might terminate in the dismission, disgrace and ruin of their authors? Would they not fear that citizens not less tenacious than conscious of their

---

* See Essay 59.

† See especially Essays 24–29.

rights would flock from the remotest extremes of their respective states to the places of election, to overthrow their tyrants, and to substitute men who would be disposed to avenge the violated majesty of the people?

Publius.

No. 61

ALEXANDER HAMILTON

On location and times of elections.

No. 62

JAMES MADISON

February 27, 1788

To the People of the State of New York.

Having examined the constitution of the house of representatives, and answered such of the objections against it as seemed to merit notice, I enter next on the examination of the senate. The heads into which this member of the government may be considered, are I. the qualifications of senators. II. the appointment of them by the state legislatures. III. the equality of representation in the senate. IV. the number of senators, and the term for which they are to be elected. V. the powers vested in the senate.

I. The qualifications proposed for senators, as distinguished from those of representatives, consist in a more advanced age, and a longer period of citizenship. A senator must be thirty years of age at least; as a representative, must be twenty-five. And the former must have been a citizen nine years; as seven years are required for the latter. The propriety of these distinctions is explained by the nature of the senatorial trust; which requiring greater extent of information and stability of character, requires at the same time that the senator should have reached a period of life most likely to supply these advantages; and which participating immediately in transactions with foreign nations, ought to be exercised by none

---

From *The Independent Journal,* February 27, 1788. This essay appeared on February 29 in *The New-York Packet.*

who are not thoroughly weaned from the prepossessions and habits incident to foreign birth and education. The term of nine years appears to be a prudent mediocrity between a total exclusion of adopted citizens, whose merit and talents may claim a share in the public confidence; and an indiscriminate and hasty admission of them, which might create a channel for foreign influence on the national councils.

II. It is equally unnecessary to dilate on the appointment of senators by the state legislatures. Among the various modes which might have been devised for constituting this branch of the government, that which has been proposed by the convention is probably the most congenial with the public opinion. It is recommended by the double advantage of favouring a select appointment, and of giving to the state governments such an agency in the formation of the federal government, as must secure the authority of the former; and may form a convenient link between the two systems.

III. The equality of representation in the senate is another point, which, being evidently the result of compromise between the opposite pretensions of the large and the small states, does not call for much discussion. If indeed it be right that among a people thoroughly incorporated into one nation, every district ought to have a *proportional* share in the government; and that among independent and sovereign states bound together by a simple league, the parties however unequal in size, ought to have an *equal* share in the common councils, it does not appear to be without some reason, that in a compound republic partaking both of the national and federal character, the government ought to be founded on a mixture of the principles of proportional and equal representation. But it is superfluous to try by the standards of theory, a part of the constitution which is allowed on all hands to be the result not of theory, but "of a spirit of amity, and that mutual deference and concession which the peculiarity of our political situation rendered indispensable." A common government with powers equal to its objects, is called for by the voice, and still more loudly by the political situation of America. A government founded on principles more consonant to the wishes of the larger states, is not likely to be obtained from the smaller states. The only option then for the former lies between the proposed government and a government still more objectionable. Under this alternative the advice of prudence must be, to embrace the lesser evil; and instead of indulging a fruitless anticipation of the possible mischiefs which may ensue, to contemplate rather the advantageous consequences which may qualify the sacrifice.

In this spirit it may be remarked, that the equal vote allowed to each state, is at once a constitutional recognition of the portion of sovereignty remaining in the individual states, and an instrument for preserving that residuary sovereignty. So far the equality ought to be no less acceptable to the large than to the small states; since they are not less solicitous to guard by every possible expedient against an improper consolidation of the states into one simple republic.

Another advantage accruing from this ingredient in the constitution of the senate, is the additional impediment it must prove against improper acts of legislation. No law or resolution can now be passed without the concurrence first of a majority of the people, and then of a majority of the states. It must be acknowledged that this complicated check on legislation may in some instances be injurious as well as beneficial; and that the peculiar defence which it involves in favour of the smaller states would be more rational, if any interests common to them, and distinct from those of the other states, would otherwise be exposed to peculiar danger. But as the larger states will always be able by their power over the supplies to defeat unreasonable exertions of this prerogative of the lesser states; and as the facility and excess of law-making seem to be the diseases to which our governments are most liable, it is not impossible that this part of the constitution may be more convenient in practice than it appears to many in contemplation.

IV. The number of senators and the duration of their appointment come next to be considered. In order to form an accurate judgment on both these points, it will be proper to enquire into the purposes which are to be answered by a senate; and in order to ascertain these it will be necessary to review the inconveniencies which a republic must suffer from the want of such an institution.

First. It is a misfortune incident to republican government, though in a less degree than to other governments, that those who administer it, may forget their obligations to their constituents, and prove unfaithful to their important trust. In this point of view, a senate, as a second branch of the legislative assembly, distinct from, and dividing the power with, a first, must be in all cases a salutary check on the government. It doubles the security to the people, by requiring the concurrence of two distinct bodies in schemes of usurpation or perfidy, where the ambition or corruption of one, would otherwise be sufficient. This is a precaution founded on such clear principles, and now so well understood in the United States, that it would be more than superfluous to enlarge on it. I will barely remark that as the improbability of sinister combinations will be in proportion to the dissimilarity in the genius of the two bodies; it must be politic to distinguish them from each other by every circumstance which will consist with a due harmony in all proper measures, and with the genuine principles of republican government.

Secondly. The necessity of a senate is not less indicated by the propensity of all single and numerous assemblies, to yield to the impulse of sudden and violent passions, and to be seduced by factious leaders, into intemperate and pernicious resolutions. Examples on this subject might be cited without number; and from proceedings within the United States, as well as from the history of other nations. But a position that will not be contradicted need not be proved. All that need be remarked is that a body which is to correct this infirmity ought itself be free from it, and consequently ought to be less numerous. It ought moreover to possess great firmness, and consequently ought to hold its authority by a tenure of considerable duration.

Thirdly. Another defect to be supplied by a senate lies in a want of due acquaintance with the objects and principles of legislation. It is not possible that an assembly of men called for the most part from pursuits of a private nature, continued in appointment for a short time, and led by no permanent motive to devote the intervals of public occupation to a study of the laws, the affairs and the comprehensive interests of their country, should, if left wholly to themselves, escape a variety of important errors in the exercise of their legislative trust. It may be affirmed, on the best grounds, that no small share of the present embarrassments of America is to be charged on the blunders of our governments; and that these have proceeded from the heads rather than the hearts of most of the authors of them. What indeed are all the repealing, explaining and amending laws, which fill and disgrace our voluminous codes, but so many monuments of deficient wisdom; so many impeachments exhibited by each succeeding, against each preceding session; so many admonitions to the people of the value of those aids which may be expected from a well constituted senate?

A good government implies two things; first, *fidelity* to the object of government, which is the happiness of the people; secondly, a *knowledge* of the means by which that object can be best attained. Some governments are deficient in both these qualities: Most governments are deficient in the first. I scruple not to assert that in the American governments, too little attention has been paid to the last. The federal constitution avoids this error; and what merits particular notice, it provides for the last in a mode which increases the security for the first.

Fourthly. The mutability in the public councils, arising from a rapid succession of new members, however qualified they may be, points out in the strongest manner, the necessity of some stable institution in the government. Every new election in the states, is found to change one half of the representatives. From this change of men must proceed a change of opinions; and from a change of opinions, a change of measures. But a continual change even of good measures is inconsistent with every rule of prudence, and every prospect of success. The remark is verified in private life, and becomes more just as well as more important, in national transactions.

To trace the mischievous effects of a mutable government would fill a volume. I will hint a few only, each of which will be perceived to be a source of innumerable others.

In the first place it forfeits the respect and confidence of other nations, and all the advantages connected with national character. An individual who is observed to be inconstant to his plans, or perhaps to carry on his affairs without any plan at all, is marked at once by all prudent people as a speedy victim to his own unsteadiness and folly. His more friendly neighbours may pity him; but all will decline to connect their fortunes with his; and not a few will seize the opportunity of making their fortunes out of his. One nation is to another what one individual is to another; with this melancholy distinction perhaps, that the former with fewer of the benevolent emotions than the latter, are under fewer restraints also from taking undue advantage of the indiscretions of each other. Every nation consequently whose affairs betray a want of wisdom and stability, may calculate on every loss which can be sustained from the more systematic policy of its wiser neighbours. But the best instruction on this subject is unhappily conveyed to America by the example of her own situation. She finds that she is held in no respect by her friends; that she is the derision of her enemies; and that she is a prey to every nation which has an interest in speculating on her fluctuating councils and embarrassed affairs.

The internal effects of a mutable policy are still more calamitous. It poisons the blessings of liberty itself. It will be of little avail to the people that the laws are made by men of their own choice, if the laws be so voluminous that they cannot be read, or so incoherent that they cannot be understood; if they be repealed or revised before they are promulged, or undergo such incessant changes that no man who knows what the law is to-day can guess what it will be to-morrow. Law is defined to be a rule of action; but how can that be a rule, which is little known and less fixed?

Another effect of public instability is the unreasonable advantage it gives to the sagacious, the enterprising and the moneyed few, over the industrious and uninformed mass of the people. Every new regulation concerning commerce or revenue, or in any manner affecting the value of the different species of property, presents a new harvest to those who watch the change, and can trace its consequences; a harvest reared not by themselves but by the toils and cares of the great body of their fellow citizens. This is a state of things in which it may be said with some truth that laws are made for the *few* not for the *many*.

In another point of view great injury results from an unstable government. The want of confidence in the public councils damps every useful undertaking; the success and profit of which may depend on a continuance of existing arrangements. What prudent merchant will hazard his fortunes in any new branch of commerce, when he knows not but that his plans may be rendered unlawful before they can be executed? What farmer or manufacturer will lay himself out for the encouragement given to any particular cultivation or establishment, when he can have no assurance that his preparatory labors and advances will not render him a victim to an inconstant government? In a word no great improvement or laudable enterprise, can go forward, which requires the auspices of a steady system of national policy.

But the most deplorable effect of all is that diminution of attachment and reverence which steals into the hearts of the people, towards a political system which betrays so many marks of infirmity, and disappoints so many of their flattering hopes. No government any more than an individual will long be respected, without being truly respectable, nor be truly respectable without possessing a certain portion of order and stability.

Publius.

No. 63

JAMES MADISON

March 1, 1788

To the People of the State of New York.

A fifth desideratum illustrating the utility of a Senate, is the want of a due sense of national character. Without a select and stable member of the government, the esteem of foreign powers will not only be forfeited by an unenlightened and variable policy, proceeding from the causes already mentioned; but the national councils will not possess that sensibility to the opinion of the world, which is perhaps not less necessary in order to merit, than it is to obtain, its respect and confidence.

An attention to the judgment of other nations is important to every government for two reasons: The one is, that independently of the merits of any particular plan or measure, it is desireable on various accounts, that it should appear to other nations as the offspring of a wise and honorable policy: The second is, that in doubtful cases, particularly where the national councils may be warped by some strong passion, or momentary interest, the presumed or known opinion of the impartial world, may be the best guide that can be followed. What has not America lost by her want of character with foreign nations? And how many errors and follies would she not have avoided, if the justice and propriety of her measures had in every instance been previously tried by the light in which they would probably appear to the unbiassed part of mankind?

Yet however requisite a sense of national character may be, it is evident that it can never be sufficiently possessed by a numerous and changeable body. It can only be found in a number so small, that a sensible degree of the praise and blame of public measures may be the portion of each individual; or in an assembly so durably

---

From *The Independent Journal,* March 1, 1788. This essay appeared on March 4 in *The New-York Packet.*

invested with public trust, that the pride and consequence of its members may be sensibly incorporated with the reputation and prosperity of the community. The half-yearly representatives of Rhode-Island, would probably have been little affected in their deliberations on the iniquitous measures of that state, by arguments drawn from the light in which such measures would be viewed by foreign nations, or even by the sister states; whilst it can scarcely be doubted, that if the concurrence of a select and stable body had been necessary, a regard to national character alone, would have prevented the calamities under which that misguided people is now labouring.

I add as a *sixth* defect, the want in some important cases of a due responsibility in the government to the people, arising from that frequency of elections, which in other cases produces this responsibility. This remark will perhaps appear not only new but paradoxical. It must nevertheless be acknowledged, when explained, to be as undeniable as it is important.

Responsibility in order to be reasonable must be limited to objects within the power of the responsible party; and in order to be effectual, must relate to operations of that power, of which a ready and proper judgment can be formed by the constituents. The objects of government may be divided into two general classes; the one depending on measures which have singly an immediate and sensible operation; the other depending on a succession of well chosen and well connected measures, which have a gradual and perhaps unobserved operation. The importance of the latter description to the collective and permanent welfare of every country needs no explanation. And yet it is evident, that an assembly elected for so short a term as to be unable to provide more than one or two links in a chain of measures, on which the general welfare may essentially depend, ought not to be answerable for the final result, any more than a steward or tenant, engaged for one year, could be justly made to answer for places or improvements, which could not be accomplished in less than half a dozen years. Nor is it possible for the people to estimate the *share* of influence which their annual assemblies may respectively have on events resulting from the mixed transactions of several years. It is sufficiently difficult at any rate to preserve a personal responsibility in the members of a *numerous* body, for such acts of the body as have an immediate, detached and palpable operation on its constituents.

The proper remedy for this defect must be an additional body in the legislative department, which, having sufficient permanency to provide for such objects as require a continued attention, and a train of measures, may be justly and effectually answerable for the attainment of those objects.

Thus far I have considered the circumstances which point out the necessity of a well constructed senate, only as they relate to the representatives of the people. To a people as little blinded by prejudice, or corrupted by flattery, as those whom I address, I shall not scruple to add, that such an institution may be sometimes necessary, as a defence to the people against their own temporary errors and delusions. As the cool and deliberate sense of the community ought in all governments, and actually will in all free governments ultimately prevail over the views of its rulers; so there are particular moments in public affairs, when the people stimulated by some irregular passion, or some illicit advantage, or misled by the artful misrepresentations of interested men, may call for measures which they themselves will afterwards be the most ready to lament and condemn. In these critical moments, how salutary will be the interference of some temperate and respectable body of citizens, in order to check the misguided career, and to suspend the blow meditated by the people against themselves, until reason, justice and truth, can regain their authority over the public mind? What bitter anguish would not the people of Athens have often escaped, if their government had contained so provident a safeguard against the tyranny of their own passions? Popular liberty might then have escaped the indelible reproach of decreeing to the same citizens, the hemlock on one day, and statues on the next.

It may be suggested that a people spread over an extensive region, cannot like the crouded inhabitants of a small district, be subject to the infection of violent passions; or to the danger of combining in the pursuit of unjust measures. I am far from denying that this is a distinction of peculiar importance. I have on the contrary endeavoured in a former paper, to shew that it is one of the principal recommendations of a confederated republic. At the same time this advantage ought not to be considered as superseding the use of auxiliary precautions. It may even be remarked that the same extended situation which will exempt the people of America from some of the dangers incident to lesser republics, will expose them to the inconveniency of remaining for a longer time, under the influence of those misrepresentations which the combined industry of interested men may succeed in distributing among them.

It adds no small weight to all these considerations, to recollect, that history informs us of no long lived republic which had not a senate. Sparta, Rome and Carthage are in fact the only states to whom that character can be applied, In each of the two first there was a senate for life. The constitution of the senate in the last, is less known. Circumstantial evidence makes it probable that it was not different in this particular from the two others. It is at least certain that it had some quality or other which rendered it an anchor against popular fluctuations; and that a smaller council drawn out of the senate was appointed not only for life; but filled up vacancies itself. These examples, though as unfit for the imitation, as they are repugnant to the genius of America, are notwithstanding, when compared with the fugitive and turbulent existence of other antient republics, very instructive proofs of the necessity of some institution that will blend stability with liberty. I am not unaware of the circumstances which distinguish the American from other popular governments, as well antient as modern; and which render extreme circumspection necessary in reasoning from the one case to the other. But after allowing due weight to this consideration, it may still be maintained that there are many points of similitude which render these examples not unworthy of our attention. Many of the defects as we have seen, which can only be supplied by a senatorial institution, are common to a numerous assembly frequently elected by the people, and to the people themselves. There are others peculiar to the former, which require the controul of such an institution. The people can never wilfully betray their own interests: But they may possibly be betrayed by the representatives of the people; and the danger will be evidently greater where the whole legislative trust is lodged in the hands of one body of men, than where the concurrence of separate and dissimilar bodies is required in every public act.

The difference most relied on between the American and other republics, consists in the principle of representation, which is the pivot on which the former move, and which is supposed to have been unknown to the latter, or at least to the antient part of them. The use which has been made of this difference, in reasonings contained in former papers, will have shewn that I am disposed neither to deny its existence nor to undervalue its importance. I feel the less restraint therefore in observing that the position concerning the ignorance of the antient government on the subject of representation is by no means precisely true in the latitude commonly given to it. Without entering into a disquisition which here would be misplaced, I will refer to a few known facts in support of what I advance.

In the most pure democracies of Greece, many of the executive functions were performed not by the people themselves, but by officers elected by the people, and *representing* the people in their *executive* capacity.

Prior to the reform of Solon, Athens was governed by nine Archons, annually *elected by the people at large.* The degree of power delegated to them seems to be left in great obscurity. Subsequent to that period, we find an assembly first of four and afterwards of six hundred members, annually *elected by the people;* and *partially* representing them in their *legislative* capacity; since they were not only associated with the people in the function of making laws; but had the exclusive right of originating legislative propositions to the people. The senate of Carthage also, whatever might be its power or the duration of its appointment, appears to have been *elective* by the suffrages of the people. Similar instances might be traced in most if not all the popular governments of antiquity.

Lastly in Sparta, we meet with the Ephori, and in Rome with the Tribunes; two bodies, small indeed in number, but annually *elected by the whole body of the people,* and considered as the *representatives* of the people, almost in their *plenipotentiary* capacity. The Cosmi of Crete were also annually *elected by the people;* and have been considered by some authors as an institution analogous to those of Sparta and Rome; with this difference only that in the election of that representative body, the right of suffrage was communicated to a part only of the people.

From these facts, to which many others might be added, it is clear that the principle of representation was neither unknown to the antients, nor wholly overlooked in their political constitutions. The true distinction between these and the American Governments lies *in the total exclusion of the people in their collective capacity* from any share in the *latter,* and not in the *total exclusion of representatives of the people,* from the administration of the *former.* The distinction however thus qualified must be admitted to leave a most advantageous superiority in favor of the United States. But to ensure to this advantage its full effect, we must be careful not to separate it from the other advantage, of an extensive territory. For it cannot be believed that any form of representative government, could have succeeded within the narrow limits occupied by the democracies of Greece.

In answer to all these arguments, suggested by reason, illustrated by examples, and enforced by our own experience, the jealous adversary of the constitution will probably content himself with repeating, that a senate appointed not immediately by the people, and for the term of six years, must gradually acquire a dangerous preeminence in the government, and finally transform it into a tyrannical aristocracy.

To this general answer the general reply ought to be sufficient; that liberty may be endangered by the abuses of liberty, as well as by the abuses of power; that there are numerous instances of the former as well as of the latter; and that the former rather than the latter is apparently most to be apprehended by the United States. But a more particular reply may be given.

Before such a revolution can be effected, the senate, it is to be observed, must in the first place corrupt itself; must next corrupt the state legislatures, must then corrupt the house of representatives, and must finally corrupt the people at large. It is evident that the senate must be first corrupted, before it can attempt an establishment of tyranny. Without corrupting the state legislatures, it cannot prosecute the attempt, because the periodical change of members would otherwise regenerate the whole body. Without exerting the means of corruption with equal success on the house of representatives, the opposition of that co-equal branch of the government would inevitably defeat the attempt; and without corrupting the people themselves, a succession of new representatives would speedily restore all things to their pristine order. Is there any man who can seriously persuade himself, that the proposed senate can, by any possible means within the compass of human address, arrive at the object of a lawless ambition, through all these obstructions?

If reason condemns the suspicion, the same sentence is pronounced by experience. The constitution of Maryland furnishes the most apposite example. The senate of that state is elected, as the federal senate will be, indirectly by the people; and for a term less by one year only, than the federal senate. It is distinguished also by the remarkable prerogative of filling up its own vacancies within the term of its appointment: and at the same time, is not under the controul of any such rotation, as is provided for the federal senate. There are some other lesser distinctions, which would expose the former to colorable objections that do not lie against the latter. If the federal senate therefore really contained the danger which has been so loudly proclaimed, some symptoms at least of a like danger ought by this time to have been betrayed by the senate of Maryland; but no such symptoms have appeared. On the contrary the jealousies at first entertained by men of the same description with those who view with terror the correspondent part of the federal constitution, have been gradually extinguished by the progress of the experiment; and the Maryland constitution is daily deriving from the salutary operations of this part of it, a reputation in which it will probably not be rivalled by that of any state in the union.

But if any thing could silence the jealousies on this subject, it ought to be the British example. The senate there, instead of being elected for a term of six years, and of being unconfined to particular families or fortunes, is an hereditary assembly of opulent nobles. The house of representatives, instead of being elected for two years and by the whole body of people, is elected for seven years; and in very great proportion, by a very small proportion of the people. Here unquestionably ought to be seen in full display, the aristocratic usurpations and tyranny, which are at some future period to be exemplified in the United States. Unfortunately however for the antifederal argument the British history informs us, that this hereditary assembly has not even been able to defend itself against the continual encroachments of the house of representatives; and that it no sooner lost the support of the monarch, than it was actually crushed by the weight of the popular branch.

As far as antiquity can instruct us on this subject, its examples support the reasoning which we have employed. In Sparta the Ephori, the annual representatives of the people, were found an overmatch for the senate for life, continually gained on its authority, and finally drew all power into their own hands. The tribunes of Rome, who were the representatives of the people, prevailed, it is well known, in almost every contest with the senate for life, and in the end gained the most complete triumph over it. This fact is the more remarkable, as unanimity was required in every act of the tribunes, even after their number was augmented to ten. It proves the irresistable force possessed by that branch of a free government, which has the people on its side. To these examples might be added that of Carthage, whose senate, according to the testimony of Polybius, instead of drawing all power into its vortex, had at the commencement of the second punic war, lost almost the whole of its original portion.

Besides the conclusive evidence resulting from this assemblage of facts, that the federal senate will never be able to transform itself, by gradual usurpations, into an independent and aristocratic body; we are warranted in believing that if such a revolution should ever happen from causes which the foresight of man cannot guard against, the house of representatives with the people on their side will at all times be able to bring back the constitution to its primitive form and principles. Against the force of the immediate representatives of the people, nothing will be able to maintain even the constitutional authority of the senate, but such a display of enlightened policy, and attachment to the public good, as will divide with that branch of the legislature, the affections and support of the entire body of the people themselves.

Publius.

No. 64

JOHN JAY

Senate's powers on treaties: importance of secrecy and speed.

No. 65

ALEXANDER HAMILTON

On the Senate as committee of impeachment.

No. 66

ALEXANDER HAMILTON

On the Senate's powers and limits.

No. 67

ALEXANDER HAMILTON

March 11, 1788

To the People of the State of New York.

The Constitution of the executive department of the proposed government claims next our attention.

There is hardly any part of the system which could have been attended with greater difficulty in the arrangement of it than this; and there is perhaps none, which has been inveighed against with less candor, or criticised with less judgment.

Here the writers against the Constitution seem to have taken pains to signalize their talent of misrepresentation, calculating upon the aversion of the people to monarchy, they have endeavoured to inlist all their jealousies and apprehensions in opposition to the intended President of the United States; not merely as the embryo but as the full grown progeny of that detested parent. To establish the pretended affinity they have not scrupled to draw resources even from the regions of fiction. The authorities of a magistrate, in few instances greater, and in some instances less, than those of a Governor of New-York, have been magnified into more than royal prerogatives. He has been decorated with attributes superior in dignity and splendor to those of a King of Great-Britain. He has been shown to us with the diadem sparkling on his brow, and the imperial purple flowing in his train. He has been seated on a throne surrounded with minions and mistresses; giving audience to the envoys of foreign potentates, in all the supercilious pomp of majesty. The images of Asiatic despotism and voluptuousness have scarcely been wanting to crown the exaggerated scene. We have been almost taught to tremble at the terrific visages of murdering janizaries; and to blush at the unveiled mysteries of a future seraglio.

Attempts so extravagant as these to disfigure, or it might rather be said, to metamorphose the object, render it necessary to take an accurate view of its real nature and form; in order as well to ascertain its true aspect and genuine appearance, as to unmask the disingenuity and expose the fallacy of the counterfeit resemblances

---

From *The New-York Packet*, March 11, 1788. This essay appeared on March 12 in *The Independent Journal*.

which have been so insidiously as well as industriously propagated.

In the execution of this task there is no man, who would not find it an arduous effort, either to behold with moderation or to treat with seriousness the devices, not less weak than wicked, which have been contrived to pervert the public opinion in relation to the subject. They so far exceed the usual, though unjustifiable, licenses of party-artifice, that even in a disposition the most candid and tolerant they must force the sentiments which favor an indulgent construction of the conduct of political adversaries to give place to a voluntary and unreserved indignation. It is impossible not to bestow the imputation of deliberate imposture and deception upon the gross pretence of a similitude between a King of Great-Britain and a magistrate of the character marked out for that of the President of the United States. It is still more impossible to withhold that imputation from the rash and barefaced expedients which have been employed to give success to the attempted imposition.

In one instance, which I cite as a sample of the general spirit, the temerity has proceeded so far as to ascribe to the President of the United States a power, which by the instrument reported is *expressly* allotted to the executives of the individual States. I mean the power of filling casual vacancies in the Senate.

This bold experiment upon the discernment of his countrymen, has been hazarded by a writer who (whatever may be his real merit) has had no inconsiderable share in the applauses of his party;* and who upon this false and unfounded suggestion, has built a series of observations equally false and unfounded. Let him now be confronted with the evidence of the fact; and let him, if he be able, justify or extenuate the shameful outrage he has offered to the dictates of truth and to the rules of fair dealing.

The second clause of the second section of the second article empowers the President of the United States "to nominate, and by and with the advice and consent of the Senate to appoint ambassadors, other public ministers and consuls, judges of the Supreme Court, and all other *officers* of the United States, whose appointments are *not* in the Constitution *otherwise provided for*, and

---

* *See Cato No. 5.* (Publius) Hamilton was referring to the fifth of a series of newspaper articles signed "Cato," presumably written by George Clinton, which appeared November 22, 1787, in *The New-York Journal.* The essay was reprinted in Paul Leicester Ford, ed., *Essays on the Constitution of the United States* (Brooklyn, 1892), 265–269.

which shall be established by law." Immediately after this clause follows another in these words—"The President shall have power to fill up all *vacancies* that may happen *during the recess of the Senate*, by granting commissions which shall *expire at the end of their next session.*" It is from this last provision that the pretended power of the President to fill vacancies in the Senate has been deduced. A slight attention to the connection of the clauses and to the obvious meaning of the terms will satisfy us that the deduction is not even colorable.

The first of these two clauses it is clear only provides a mode for appointing such officers, "whose appointments are *not otherwise provided for* in the Constitution, and which *shall be established by law*"; of course it cannot extend to the appointment of senators; whose appointments are *otherwise provided for* in the Constitution,* and who are *established by the Constitution*, and will not require a future establishment by law. This position will hardly be contested.

The last of these two clauses, it is equally clear, cannot be understood to comprehend the power of filling vacancies in the Senate, for the following reasons—*First.* The relation in which that clause stands to the other, which declares the general mode of appointing officers of the United States, denotes it to be nothing more than a supplement to the other; for the purpose of establishing an auxiliary method of appointment in cases, to which the general method was inadequate. The ordinary power of appointment is confided to the President and Senate *jointly*, and can therefore only be exercised during the session of the Senate; but as it would have been improper to oblige this body to be continually in session for the appointment of officers; and as vacancies might happen *in their recess*, which it might be necessary for the public service to fill without delay, the succeeding clause is evidently intended to authorise the President *singly* to make temporary appointments "during the recess of the Senate, by granting commissions which should expire at the end of their next session." *Secondly*. If this clause is to be considered as supplementary to the one which precedes, the *vacancies* of which it speaks must be construed to relate to the "officers" described in the preceding one; and this we have seen excludes from its description the members of the Senate. *Thirdly*. The time within which the power is to operate "during the recess

* *Article* I.§3. *Clause* I. (Publius)

of the Senate" and the duration of the appointments "to the end of the next session" of that body, conspire to elucidate the sense of the provision; which if it had been intended to comprehend Senators would naturally have referred the temporary power of filling vacancies to the recess of the State Legislatures, who are to make the permanent appointments, and not to the recess of the national Senate, who are to have no concern in those appointments; and would have extended the duration in office of the temporary Senators to the next session of the Legislature of the State, in whose representation the vacancies had happened, instead of making it to expire at the end of the ensuing session of the national Senate. The circumstances of the body authorised to make the permanent appointments, would of course have governed the modification of a power which related to the temporary appointments; and as the national Senate is the body whose situation is alone contemplated in the clause upon which the suggestion under examination has been founded, the vacancies to which it alludes can only be deemed to respect those officers, in whose appointment that body has a concurrent agency with the President. But, *lastly*, the first and second clauses of the third section of the first article, not only obviate the possibility of doubt, but destroy the pretext of misconception. The former provides that "the Senate of the United States shall be composed of two Senators from each State, chosen *by the Legislature thereof* for six years," and the latter directs that "if vacancies in that body should happen by resignation or otherwise *during the recess of the Legislature of* ANY STATE, the Executive THEREOF may make temporary appointments until the *next meeting of the Legislature*, which shall then fill such vacancies." Here is an express power given, in clear and unambiguous terms, to the State executives to fill the casual vacancies in the Senate by temporary appointments; which not only invalidates the supposition, that the clause before considered could have been intended to confer that power upon the President of the United States; but proves that this supposition, destitute as it is even of the merit of plausibility, must have originated in an intention to deceive the people, too palpable to be obscured by sophistry, and too atrocious to be palliated by hypocrisy.

I have taken the pains to select this instance of misrepresentation, and to place it in a clear and strong light, as an unequivocal proof of the unwarrantable arts which are practised to prevent a fair and impartial judgment of the real merits of the constitution submitted to the consideration of the people. Nor have I scrupled in so flagrant a case to allow myself in a severity of animadversion little congenial with the general spirit of these papers. I hesitate not to submit it to the decision of any candid and honest adversary of the proposed government, whether language can furnish epithets of too much asperity for so shameless and so prostitute an attempt to impose on the citizens of America.

Publius.

No. 68
ALEXANDER HAMILTON
March 12, 1788

To the People of the State of New York.

The mode of appointment of the chief magistrate of the United States is almost the only part of the system, of any consequence, which has escaped without severe censure, or which has received the slightest mark of approbation from its opponents. The most plausible of these, who has appeared in print, has even deigned to admit, that the election of the president is pretty well guarded.* I venture somewhat further; and hesitate not to affirm, that if the manner of it be not perfect, it is at least excellent. It unites in an eminent degree all the advantages; the union of which was to be desired.

It was desireable, that the sense of the people should operate in the choice of the person to whom so important a trust was to be confided. This end will be answered by committing the right of making it, not to any pre-established body, but to men, chosen by the people for the special purpose, and at the particular conjuncture.

It was equally desirable, that the immediate election should be made by men most capable of analizing the qualities adapted to the station, and acting under circumstances favourable to delib-

---

From *The Independent Journal*, March 12, 1788. This essay appeared on March 14 in *The New-York Packet*.

* Hamilton referred to Letter III of *Observation leading to a fair examination of the system of government, proposed by the late Convention; and to several essential and necessary alterations in it. In a number of Letters from the Federal Farmer to the Republican* (New York, 1787), reprinted, with discussion of authorship, by Murray Day, ed., *The Anti-Federalist* (Chicago, 1985), pp. 23–101.

eration and to a judicious combination of all the reasons and inducements, which were proper to govern their choice. A small number of persons, selected by their fellow citizens from the general mass, will be most likely to possess the information and discernment requisite to so complicated an investigation.

It was also peculiarly desirable, to afford as little opportunity as possible to tumult and disorder. This evil was not least to be dreaded in the election of a magistrate, who was to have so important an agency in the administration of the government, as the president of the United States. But the precautions which have been so happily concerted in the system under consideration, promise an effectual security against this mischief. The choice of *several* to form an intermediate body of electors, will be much less apt to convulse the community, with any extraordinary or violent movements, than the choice of *one* who was himself to be the final object of the public wishes. And as the electors, chosen in each state, are to assemble and vote in the state, in which they are chosen, this detached and divided situation will expose them much less to heats and ferments, which might be communicated from them to the people, than if they were all to be convened at one time, in one place.

Nothing was more to be desired, than that every practicable obstacle should be opposed to cabal, intrigue and corruption. These most deadly adversaries of republican government might naturally have been expected to make their approaches from more than one quarter, but chiefly from the desire in foreign powers to gain an improper ascendant in our councils. How could they better gratify this, than by raising a creature of their own to the chief magistracy of the union? But the convention have guarded against all danger of this sort with the most provident and judicious attention. They have not made the appointment of the president to depend on any pre-existing bodies of men who might be tampered with before hand to prostitute their votes; but they have referred it in the first instance to an immediate act of the people of America, to be exerted in the choice of persons for the temporary and sole purpose of making the appointment. And they have excluded from eligibility to this trust, all those who from situation might be suspected of too great devotion to the president in office. No senator, representative, or other person holding a place of trust or profit under the United States, can be of the number of the electors. Thus, without corrupting the body of the people, the immediate agents in the election will at least enter upon the task, free from any sinister byass. Their transient existence, and their detached situation, already taken notice of, afford a satisfactory prospect of their continuing so, to the conclusion of it. The business of corruption, when it is to embrace so considerable a number of men, requires time, as well as means. Nor would it be found easy suddenly to embark them, dispersed as they would be over thirteen states, in any combinations, founded upon motives, which though they could not properly be denominated corrupt, might yet be of a nature to mislead them from their duty.

Another and no less important desideratum was, that the executive should be independent for his continuance in office on all, but the people themselves. He might otherwise be tempted to sacrifice his duty to his complaisance for those whose favor was necessary to the duration of his official consequence. This advantage will also be secured, by making his re-election to depend on a special body of representatives, deputed by the society for the single purpose of making the important choice.

All these advantages will be happily combined in the plan devised by the convention; which is, that the people of each state shall choose a number of persons as electors, equal to the number of senators and representatives of such state in the national government, who shall assemble within the state and vote for some fit person as president. Their votes, thus given, are to be transmitted to the seat of the national government, and the person who may happen to have a majority of the whole number of votes will be the president. But as a majority of the votes might not always happen to centre on one man and as it might be unsafe to permit less than a majority to be conclusive, it is provided, that in such a contingency, the house of representatives shall select out of the candidates, who shall have the five highest numbers of votes, the man who in their opinion may be best qualified for the office.

This process of election affords a moral certainty, that the office of president, will seldom fall to the lot of any man, who is not in an eminent degree endowed with the requisite qualifications. Talents for low intrigue and the little arts of popularity may alone suffice to elevate a man to the first honors in a single state; but it will require other talents and a different kind of merit to establish him in the esteem and confidence of the whole union, or of so considerable a portion of it as would be necessary to make him a successful candidate for the distinguished office of president of the United States. It will not be too strong to say, that there will be a constant probability of seeing the station filled by characters pre-eminent for ability and virtue. And this will be thought no inconsiderable recommendation of the constitution, by those, who are able to estimate the share, which the executive in every government must necessarily have in its good or ill administration. Though we cannot acquiesce in the political heresy of the poet who says—

"For forms of government let fools contest—
That which is best administered is best."*

—yet we may safely pronounce, that the true test of a good government is its aptitude and tendency to produce a good administration.

The vice-president is to be chosen in the same manner with the president; with this difference, that the senate is to do, in respect to the former, what is to be done by the house of representatives, in respect to the latter.

The appointment of an extraordinary person, as vice president, has been objected to as superfluous, if not mischievous. It has been alleged, that it would have been preferable to have authorised the senate to elect out of their own body an officer, answering that description. But two considerations seem to justify the ideas of the convention in this respect. One is, that to secure at all times the possibility of a definitive resolution of the body, it is necessary that the president should have only a casting vote. And to take the senator of any state from his seat as senator, to place him in that of president of the senate, would be to exchange, in regard to the state from which he came, a constant for a contingent vote. The other consideration is, that as the vice-president may occasionally become a substitute for the president, in the supreme executive magistracy, all the reasons, which recommend the mode of election prescribed for the one, apply with great, if not with equal, force to the manner of appointing the other. It is remarkable, that in this as in most other instances, the objection, which is made, would be against the constitution of this state. We have a Lieutenant Governor chosen by the people at large, who presides

* Alexander Pope, *Essay on Man,* III. Correctly, "Whate'er is best administer'd is best." (Editor)

in the senate, and is the constitutional substitute for the Governor in casualties similar to those, which would authorise the vice-president to exercise the authorities and discharge the duties of the president.

Publius.

No. 69

ALEXANDER HAMILTON

March 14, 1788

To the People of the State of New York.

I proceed now to trace the real characters of the proposed executive as they are marked out in the plan of the Convention. This will serve to place in a strong light the unfairness of the representations which have been made in regard to it.

The first thing which strikes our attention is that the executive authority, with few exceptions, is to be vested in a single magistrate. This will scarcely however be considered as a point upon which any comparison can be grounded; for if in this particular there be a resemblance to the King of Great-Britain, there is not less a resemblance to the Grand Signior, to the Khan of Tartary, to the man of the seven mountains, or to the Governor of New-York.

That magistrate is to be elected for *four* years; and is to be re-eligible as often as the People of the United States shall think him worthy of their confidence. In these circumstances, there is a total dissimilitude between *him* and a King of Great-Britain; who is an *hereditary* monarch, possessing the crown as a patrimony descendible to his heirs forever; but there is a close analogy between *him* and a Governor of New-York, who is elected for *three* years, and is re-eligible without limitation or intermission. If we consider how much less time would be requisite for establishing a dangerous influence in a single State, than for establishing a like influence throughout the United States, we must conclude that a duration of *four* years for the Chief Magistrate of the Union, is a degree of permanency far less to be dreaded in that office, than a duration of *three* years for a correspondent office in a single State.

From *The New-York Packet*, March 14, 1788. This essay appeared in *The Independent Journal* on March 15.

The President of the United States would be liable to be impeached, tried, and upon conviction of treason, bribery, or other high crimes or misdemeanors, removed from office; and would afterwards be liable to prosecution and punishment in the ordinary course of law. The person of the King of Great-Britain is sacred and inviolable: There is no constitutional tribunal to which he is amenable; no punishment to which he can be subjected without involving the crisis of a national revolution. In this delicate and important circumstance of personal responsibility, the President of confederated America would stand upon no better ground than a Governor of New-York, and upon worse ground than the Governors of Virginia and Delaware.

The President of the United States is to have power to return a bill, which shall have passed the two branches of the Legislature, for re-consideration; but the bill so returned is to become a law, if upon that re-consideration it be approved by two thirds of both houses. The King of Great Britain, on his part, has an absolute negative upon the acts of the two houses of Parliament. The disuse of that power for a considerable time past, does not affect the reality of its existence; and is to be ascribed wholly to the crown's having found the means of substituting influence to authority, or the art of gaining a majority in one or the other of the two houses, to the necessity of exerting a prerogative which could seldom be exerted without hazarding some degree of national agitation. The qualified negative of the President differs widely from this absolute negative of the British sovereign; and tallies exactly with the revisionary authority of the Council of revision of this State, of which the Governor is a constituent part. In this respect, the power of the President would exceed that of the Governor of New-York; because the former would possess singly what the latter shares with the Chancellor and Judges: But it would be precisely the same with that of the Governor of Massachusetts, whose constitution, as to this article, seems to have been the original from which the Convention have copied.

The President is to be the "Commander in Chief of the army and navy of the United States, and of the militia of the several States, when called into the actual service of the United States. He is to have power to grant reprieves and pardons for offences against the United States, *except in cases of impeachment*; to recommend to the consideration of Congress such measures as he shall judge necessary and expedient; to convene on extraordinary occasions both houses of the Legislature, or either of them, and in case of disagreement between them *with respect to the time of adjournment*, to adjourn them to such time as he shall think proper; to take care that the laws be faithfully executed; and to commission all officers of the United States." In most of these particulars the power of the President will resemble equally that of the King of Great-Britain and of the Governor of New-York. The most material points of difference are these—First; the President will have only the occasional command of such part of the militia of the nation, as by legislative provision may be called into the actual service of the Union. The King of Great-Britain and the Governor of New-York have at all times the entire command of all the militia within their several jurisdictions. In this article therefore the power of the President would be inferior to that of either the Monarch or the Governor. Secondly; the President is to be Commander in Chief of the army and navy of the United States. In this respect his authority would be nominally the same with that of the King of Great-Britain, but in substance much inferior to it. It would amount to nothing more than the supreme command and direction of the military and naval forces, as first General and Admiral of the confederacy; while that of the British King extends to the *declaring* of war and to the *raising* and *regulating* of fleets and armies; all which by the Constitution under consideration would appertain to the Legislature.* The Governor of New-York on the other hand, is by the Constitution of the State vested only with the command of its militia and navy. But the Constitutions of several of the States, expressly declare their Governors to be the Commanders in Chief as well of the army as navy; and it may well be a question whether those of New-Hampshire and Massachusetts, in particular, do not in this instance confer larger pow-

---

* A writer in a Pennsylvania paper, under the signature of *Tamony* has asserted that the King of Great-Britain owes his prerogatives as Commander in Chief to an annual mutiny bill. The truth is on the contrary that his prerogative in this respect is immemorial, and was only disputed "contrary to all reason and precedent," as Blackstone, vol. 1, p. 262, expresses it, by the long parliament of Charles the first, but by the statute the 13, of Charles second, ch. 6, it was declared to be in the King alone, for that the sole supreme government and command of the militia within his Majesty's realms and dominions, and of all forces by sea and land, and of all forts and places of strength, ever was and is the undoubted right of his Majesty and his royal predecessors Kings and Queens of England, and that both or either House of Parliament cannot nor ought to pretend to the same. (Publius)

ers upon their respective Governors, than could be claimed by a President of the United States. Thirdly; the power of the President in respect to pardons would extend to all cases, *except those of impeachment*. The Governor of New-York may pardon in all cases, even in those of impeachment, except for treason and murder. Is not the power of the Governor in this article, on a calculation of political consequences, greater than that of the President? All conspiracies and plots against the government, which have not been matured into actual treason, may be screened from punishment of every kind, by the interposition of the prerogative of pardoning. If a Governor of New-York therefore should be at the head of any such conspiracy, until the design had been ripened into actual hostility, he could ensure his accomplices and adherents an entire impunity. A President of the Union on the other hand, though he may even pardon treason, when prosecuted in the ordinary course of law, could shelter no offender in any degree from the effects of impeachment & conviction. Would not the prospect of a total indemnity for all the preliminary steps be a greater temptation to undertake and persevere in an enterprise against the public liberty than the mere prospect of an exemption from death and confiscation, if the final execution of the design, upon an actual appeal to arms, should miscarry? Would this last expectation have any influence at all, when the probability was computed that the person who was to afford that exemption might himself be involved in the consequences of the measure; and might be incapacitated by his agency in it, from affording the desired impunity? The better to judge of this matter, it will be necessary to recollect that by the proposed Constitution the offence of treason is limited "to levying war upon the United States, and adhering to their enemies, giving them aid and comfort," and that by the laws of New-York it is confined within similar bounds. Fourthly; the President can only adjourn the national Legislature in the single case of disagreement about the time of adjournment. The British monarch may prorogue or even dissolve the Parliament. The Governor of New-York may also prorogue the Legislature of this State for a limited time; a power which in certain situations may be employed to very important purposes.

The President is to have power with the advice and consent of the Senate to make treaties; provided two thirds of the Senators present concur. The King of Great-Britain is the sole and absolute representative of the nation in all foreign transactions. He can of his own accord make treaties of peace, commerce, alliance, and of every other description. It has been insinuated, that his authority in this respect is not conclusive, and that his conventions with foreign powers are subject to the revision, and stand in need of the ratification of Parliament. But I believe this doctrine was never heard of 'till it was broached upon the present occasion. Every jurist* of that kingdom, and every other man acquainted with its constitution knows, as an established fact, that the prerogative of making treaties exists in the crown in its utmost plenitude; and that the compacts entered into by the royal authority have the most complete legal validity and perfection, independent of any other sanction. The Parliament, it is true, is sometimes seen employing itself in altering the existing laws to conform them to the stipulations in a new treaty; and this may have possibly given birth to the imagination that its co-operation was necessary to the obligatory efficacy of the treaty. But this parliamentary interposition proceeds from a different cause; from the necessity of adjusting a most artificial and intricate system of revenue and commercial laws to the changes made in them by the operation of the treaty; and of adapting new provisions and precautions to the new state of things, to keep the machine from running into disorder. In this respect therefore, there is no comparison between the intended power of the President, and the actual power of the British sovereign. The one can perform alone, what the other can only do with the concurrence of a branch of the Legislature. It must be admitted that in this instance the power of the fœderal executive would exceed that of any State executive. But this arises naturally from the exclusive possession by the Union of that part of the sovereign power, which relates to treaties. If the confederacy were to be dissolved, it would become a question, whether the executives of the several States were not solely invested with that delicate and important prerogative.

The President is also to be authorised to receive Ambassadors and other public Ministers. This, though it has been a rich theme of declamation, is more a matter of dignity than of authority. It is a circumstance, which will be without consequence in the administration of the government; and it was far more convenient that it should be arranged in this manner, than that there should be a necessity of convening the Legislature, or one of its branches, upon

* Vide Blackstone's *Commentaries*, vol. 1, page 257. (Publius)

every arrival of a foreign minister; though it were merely to take the place of a departed predecessor.

The President is to nominate and *with the advice and consent of the Senate* to appoint Ambassadors and other public Ministers, Judges of the Supreme Court, and in general all officers of the United States established by law and whose appointments are not otherwise provided for by the Constitution. The King of Great-Britain is emphatically and truly stiled the fountain of honor. He not only appoints to all offices, but can create offices. He can confer titles of nobility at pleasure; and has the disposal of an immense number of church preferments. There is evidently a great inferiority, in the power of the President in this particular, to that of the British King; nor is it equal to that of the Governor of New-York, if we are to interpret the meaning of the constitution of the State by the practice which has obtained under it. The power of appointment is with us lodged in a Council composed of the Governor and four members of the Senate chosen by the Assembly. The Governor *claims* and has frequently *exercised* the right of nomination, and is *entitled* to a casting vote in the appointment. If he really has the right of nominating, his authority is in this respect equal to that of the President, and exceeds it in the article of the casting vote. In the national government, if the Senate should be divided, no appointment could be made: In the government of New-York, if the Council should be divided the Governor can turn the scale and confirm his own nomination.* If we compare the publicity which must necessarily attend the mode of appointment by the President and an entire branch of the national Legislature, with the privacy in the mode of appointment by the Governor of New-York, closeted in a secret apartment with at most four, and frequently with only two persons; and if we at the same time consider how much more easy it must be to influence the small number of which a Council of Appointment consist than the considerable number of which the national Senate would consist, we cannot hesitate to pronounce, that the power of the Chief Magistrate of this State in the disposition of offices must in practice

---

* Candor however demands an acknowledgment; that I do not think the claim of the Governor to a right of nomination well founded. Yet it is always justifiable to reason from the practice of a government till its propriety has been constitutionally questioned. And independent of this claim, when we take into view the other considerations and pursue them through all their consequences, we shall be inclined to draw much the same conclusion. (Publius)

be greatly superior to that of the Chief Magistrate of the Union.

Hence it appears, that except as to the concurrent authority of the President in the articles of treaties, it would be difficult to determine whether that Magistrate would in the aggregate, possess more or less power than the Governor of New-York. And it appears yet more unequivocally that there is no pretence for the parallel which has been attempted between him and the King of Great-Britain. But to render the contrast, in this respect, still more striking, it may be of use to throw the principal circumstances of dissimilitude into a closer groupe.

The President of the United States would be an officer elected by the people for *four* years. The King of Great-Britain is a perpetual and *hereditary* prince. The one would be amenable to personal punishment and disgrace: The person of the other is sacred and inviolable. The one would have a *qualified* negative upon the acts of the legislative body: The other has an *absolute* negative. The one would have a right to command the military and naval forces of the nation: The other in addition to this right, possesses that of *declaring* war, and of *raising* and *regulating* fleets and armies by his own authority. The one would have a concurrent power with a branch of the Legislature in the formation of treaties: The other is the *sole possessor* of the power of making treaties. The one would have a like concurrent authority in appointing to offices: The other is the sole author of all appointments. The one can infer no privileges whatever: The other can make denizens of aliens, noblemen of commoners, can erect corporations with all the rights incident to corporate bodies. The one can prescribe no rules concerning the commerce or currency of the nation: The other is in several respects the arbiter of commerce, and in this capacity can establish markets and fairs, can regulate weights and measures, can lay embargoes for a limited time, can coin money, can authorise or prohibit the circulation of foreign coin. The one has no particle of spiritual jurisdiction: The other is the supreme head and Governor of the national church! What answer shall we give to those who would persuade us that things so unlike resemble each other? The same that ought to be given to those who tell us, that a government, the whole power of which would be in the hands of the elective and periodical servants of the people, is an aristocracy, a monarchy, and a despotism.

Publius.

No. 70

ALEXANDER HAMILTON

March 15, 1788

To the People of the State of New York.

There is an idea, which is not without its advocates, that a vigorous executive is inconsistent with the genius of republican government. The enlightened well wishers to this species of government must at least hope that the supposition is destitute of foundation; since they can never admit its truth, without at the same time admitting the condemnation of their own principles. Energy in the executive is a leading character in the definition of good government. It is essential to the protection of the community against foreign attacks: It is not less essential to the steady administration of the laws, to the protection of property against those irregular and high handed combinations, which sometimes interrupt the ordinary course of justice, to the security of liberty against the enterprises and assaults of ambition, of faction and of anarchy. Every man the least conversant in Roman story knows how often that republic was obliged to take refuge in the absolute power of a single man, under the formidable title of dictator, as well against the intrigues of ambitious individuals, who aspired to the tyranny, and the seditions of whole classes of the community, whose conduct threatened the existence of all government, as against the invasions of external enemies, who menaced the conquest and destruction of Rome.

There can be no need however to multiply arguments or examples on this head. A feeble executive implies a feeble execution of the government. A feeble execution is but another phrase for a bad execution: And a government ill executed, whatever it may be in theory, must be in practice a bad government.

Taking it for granted, therefore, that all men of sense will agree in the necessity of an energetic executive; it will only remain to inquire, what are the ingredients which constitute this energy—how far can they be combined with those other ingredients which constitute safety in the republican sense? And how far does this

---

From *The Independent Journal*, March 15, 1788. This essay appeared on March 18 in *The New-York Packet.*

combination characterise the plan, which has been reported by the convention?

The ingredients, which constitute energy in the executive, are first unity, secondly duration, thirdly an adequate provision for its support, fourthly competent powers.

The circumstances which constitute safety in the republican sense are, 1st. a due dependence on the people, secondly a due responsibility.

Those politicians and statesmen, who have been the most celebrated for the soundness of their principles, and for the justness of their views, have declared in favor of a single executive and a numerous legislature. They have with great propriety considered energy as the most necessary qualification of the former, and have regarded this as most applicable to power in a single hand; while they have with equal propriety considered the latter as best adapted to deliberation and wisdom, and best calculated to conciliate the confidence of the people and to secure their privileges and interests.

That unity is conducive to energy will not be disputed. Decision, activity, secrecy, and dispatch will generally characterise the proceedings of one man, in a much more eminent degree, than the proceedings of any greater number; and in proportion as the number is increased, these qualities will be diminished.

This unity may be destroyed in two ways; either by vesting the power in two or more magistrates of equal dignity and authority; or by vesting it ostensibly in one man, subject in whole or in part to the controul and co-operation of others, in the capacity of counsellors to him. Of the first the two consuls of Rome may serve as an example; of the last we shall find examples in the constitutions of several of the states. New-York and New-Jersey, if I recollect right, are the only states, which have entrusted the executive authority wholly to single men. Both these methods of destroying the unity of the executive have their partisans; but the votaries of an executive council are the most numerous. They are both liable, if not to equal, to similar objections; and may in most lights be examined in conjunction. . . .

No. 71

ALEXANDER HAMILTON

March 18, 1788

To the People of the State of New York.

Duration in office has been mentioned as the second requisite to the energy of the executive authority. This has relation to two objects: To the personal firmness of the Executive Magistrate in the employment of his constitutional powers; and to the stability of the system of administration which may have been adopted under his auspices. With regard to the first, it must be evident, that the longer the duration in office, the greater will be the probability of obtaining so important an advantage. It is a general principle of human nature, that a man will be interested in whatever he possesses, in proportion to the firmness or precariousness of the tenure, by which he holds it; will be less attached to what he holds by a momentary or uncertain title, than to what he enjoys by a durable or certain title; and of course will be willing to risk more for the sake of the one, than for the sake of the other. This remark is not less applicable to a political privilege, or honor, or trust, than to any article of ordinary property. The inference from it is, that a man acting in the capacity of Chief Magistrate, under a consciousness, that in a very short time he *must* lay down his office, will be apt to feel himself too little interested in it, to hazard any material censure or perplexity, from the independent exertion of his powers, or from encountering the ill-humors, however transient, which may happen to prevail either in a considerable part of the society itself, or even in a predominant faction in the legislative body. If the case should only be, that he *might* lay it down, unless continued by a new choice; and if he should be desirous of being continued, his wishes conspiring with his fears would tend still more powerfully to corrupt his integrity, or debase his fortitude. In either case feebleness and irresolution must be the characteristics of the station.

There are some, who would be inclined to regard the servile pliancy of the executive to a prevailing current, either in the community, or in the Legislature, as its best recommendation. But

From *The New-York Packet*, March 18, 1788. This essay appeared in *The Independent Journal* on March 19.

such men entertain very crude notions, as well of the purposes for which government was instituted, as of the true means by which the public happiness may be promoted. The republican principle demands, that the deliberate sense of the community should govern the conduct of those to whom they entrust the management of their affairs; but it does not require an unqualified complaisance to every sudden breese of passion, or to every transient impulse which the people may receive from the arts of men, who flatter their prejudices to betray their interests. It is a just observation, that the people commonly *intend* the PUBLIC GOOD. This often applies to their very errors. But their good sense would despise the adulator, who should pretend that they always *reason right* about the *means* of promoting it. They know from experience, that they sometimes err; and the wonder is, that they so seldom err as they do; beset as they continually are by the wiles of parasites and sycophants, by the snares of the ambitious, the avaricious, the desperate; by the artifices of men, who possess their confidence more than they deserve it, and of those who seek to possess, rather than to deserve it. When occasions present themselves in which the interests of the people are at variance with their inclinations, it is the duty of the persons whom they have appointed to be the guardians of those interests, to withstand the temporary delusion, in order to give them time and opportunity for more cool and sedate reflection. Instances might be cited, in which a conduct of this kind has saved the people from very fatal consequences of their own mistakes, and has procured lasting monuments of their gratitude to the men, who had courage and magnanimity enough to serve them at the peril of their displeasure.

But however inclined we might be to insist upon an unbounded complaisance in the executive to the inclinations of the people, we can with no propriety contend for a like complaisance to the humors of the Legislature. The latter may sometimes stand in opposition to the former; and at other times the people may be entirely neutral. In either supposition, it is certainly desirable that the executive should be in a situation to dare to act his own opinion with vigor and decision.

The same rule, which teaches the propriety of a partition between the various branches of power, teaches us likewise that this partition ought to be so contrived as to render the one independent of the other. To what purpose separate the executive, or the judiciary, from the legislative, if both the executive and the judiciary are so constituted as to be at the absolute devotion of the legislative? Such a separation must be merely nominal and incapable of producing the ends for which it was established. It is one thing to be subordinate to the laws, and another to be dependent on the legislative body. The first comports with, the last violates, the fundamental principles of good government; and whatever may be the forms of the Constitution, unites all power in the same hands. The tendency of the legislative authority to absorb every other, has been fully displayed and illustrated by examples, in some preceding numbers. In governments purely republican, this tendency is almost irresistable. The representatives of the people, in a popular assembly, seem sometimes to fancy that they are the people themselves; and betray strong symptoms of impatience and disgust at the least sign of opposition from any other quarter; as if the exercise of its rights by either the executive or judiciary, were a breach of their privilege and an outrage to their dignity. They often appear disposed to exert an imperious controul over the other departments; and as they commonly have the people on their side, they always act with such momentum as to make it very difficult for the other members of the government to maintain the balance of the Constitution.

It may perhaps be asked how the shortness of the duration in office can affect the independence of the executive on the legislature, unless the one were possessed of the power of appointing or displacing the other? One answer to this enquiry may be drawn from the principle already remarked, that is from the slender interest a man is apt to take in a short lived advantage, and the little inducement it affords him to expose himself on account of it to any considerable inconvenience or hazard. Another answer, perhaps more obvious, though not more conclusive, will result from the consideration of the influence of the legislative body over the people, which might be employed to prevent the re-election of a man, who by an upright resistance to any sinister project of that body, should have made himself obnoxious to its resentment.

It may be asked also whether a duration of four years would answer the end proposed, and if it would not, whether a less period which would at least be recommended by greater security against ambitious designs, would not for that reason be preferable to a longer period, which was at the same time too short for the purpose of inspiring the desired firmness and independence of the magistrate?

It cannot be affirmed, that a duration of four years or any other limited duration would completely answer the end proposed; but it would contribute towards it in a degree which would have a material influence upon the spirit and character of the government. Between the commencement and termination of such a period there would always be a considerable interval, in which the prospect of annihilation would be sufficiently remote not to have an improper effect upon the conduct of a man endued with a tolerable portion of fortitude; and in which he might reasonably promise himself, that there would be time enough, before it arrived, to make the community sensible of the propriety of the measures he might incline to pursue. Though it be probable, that as he approached the moment when the public were by a new election to signify their sense of his conduct, his confidence and with it, his firmness would decline; yet both the one and the other would derive support from the opportunities, which his previous continuance in the station had afforded him of establishing himself in the esteem and good will of his constituents. He might then hazard with safety, in proportion to the proofs he had given of his wisdom and integrity, and to the title he had acquired to the respect and attachment of his fellow citizens. As on the one hand, a duration of four years will contribute to the firmness of the executive in a sufficient degree to render it a very valuable ingredient in the composition; so on the other, it is not long enough to justify any alarm for the public liberty. If a British House of Commons, from the most feeble beginnings, *from the mere power of assenting or disagreeing to the imposition of a new tax*, have by rapid strides, reduced the prerogatives of the crown and the privileges of the nobility within the limits they conceived to be compatible with the principles of a free government; while they raised themselves to the rank and consequence of a coequal branch of the Legislature; if they have been able in one instance to abolish both the royalty and the aristocracy, and to overturn all the ancient establishments as well in the church as State; if they have been able on a recent occasion to make the monarch tremble at the prospect of an innovation* attempted by them; what would be to be feared from an elective magistrate of four years duration, with the confined

* This was the case with respect to Mr. Fox's India bill which was carried in the House of Commons, and rejected in the House of Lords, to the entire satisfaction, as it is said, of the people. (Publius)

authorities of a President of the United States? What but that he might be unequal to the task which the Constitution assigns him? I shall only add that if his duration be such as to leave a doubt of his firmness, that doubt is inconsistent with a jealousy of his encroachments.

Publius.

No. 72

ALEXANDER HAMILTON

March 19, 1788

. . . Nothing appears more plausible at first sight, nor more ill founded upon close inspection, than a scheme, which in relation to the present point has had some respectable advocates—I mean that of continuing the chief magistrate in office for a certain time, and then excluding him from it, either for a limited period, or for ever after. This exclusion whether temporary or perpetual would have nearly the same effects; and these effects would be for the most part rather pernicious than salutary.

One ill effect of the exclusion would be a diminution of the inducements to good behaviour. There are few men who would not feel much less zeal in the discharge of a duty, when they were conscious that the advantages of the station, with which it was connected, must be relinquished at a determinate period, than when they were permitted to entertain a hope of *obtaining* by *meriting* a continuance of them. This position will not be disputed, so long as it is admitted that the desire of reward is one of the strongest incentives of human conduct, or that the best security for the fidelity of mankind is to make their interest coincide with their duty. Even the love of fame, the ruling passion of the noblest minds, which would prompt a man to plan and undertake extensive and arduous enterprises for the public benefit, requiring considerable time to mature and perfect them, if he could flatter himself with the prospect of being allowed to finish what he had begun, would on the contrary deter him from the undertaking, when he foresaw that he must quit the scene, before he could accomplish the work, and must commit that, together with his own reputa-

From *The Independent Journal*, March 19, 1788.

tion, to hands which might be unequal or unfriendly to the task. The most to be expected from the generality of men, in such a situation, is the negative merit of not doing harm instead of the positive merit of doing good. . . .

No. 73

ALEXANDER HAMILTON

March 21, 1788

To the People of the State of New York.

The third ingredient towards constituting the vigor of the executive authority is an adequate provision for its support. It is evident that without proper attention to this article, the separation of the executive from the legislative department would be merely nominal and nugatory. The Legislature, with a discretionary power over the salary and emoluments of the Chief Magistrate, could render him as obsequious to their will, as they might think proper to make him. They might in most cases either reduce him by famine, or tempt him by largesses, to surrender at discretion his judgment to their inclinations. These expressions taken in all the latitude of the terms would no doubt convey more than is intended. There are men who could neither be distressed nor won into a sacrifice of their duty; but this stern virtue is the growth of few soils: And in the main it will be found, that a power over a man's support is a power over his will. If it were necessary to confirm so plain a truth by facts, examples would not be wanting, even in this country, of the intimidation or seduction of the executive by the terrors, or allurements, of the pecuniary arrangements of the legislative body.

It is not easy therefore to commend too highly the judicious attention which has been paid to this subject in the proposed Constitution. It is there provided that "The President of the United States shall, at stated times, receive for his services a compensation, *which shall neither be increased nor diminished, during the period for which he shall have been elected*, and he shall *not receive within that period any other emolument* from the United States or any of them."

From *The New-York Packet*, March 21, 1788. This essay appeared on March 22 in *The Independent Journal*.

It is impossible to imagine any provision which would have been more eligible than this. The Legislature on the appointment of a President is once for all to declare what shall be the compensation for his services during the time for which he shall have been elected. This done, they will have no power to alter it either by increase or diminution, till a new period of service by a new election commences. They can neither weaken his fortitude by operating upon his necessities; nor corrupt his integrity, by appealing to his avarice. Neither the Union nor any of its members will be at liberty to give, nor will he be at liberty to receive any other emolument, than that which may have been determined by the first act. He can of course have no pecuniary inducement to renounce or desert the independence intended for him by the Constitution.

The last of the requisites to energy which have been enumerated are competent powers. Let us proceed to consider those which are proposed to be vested in the President of the United States.

The first thing that offers itself to our observation, is the qualified negative of the President upon the acts or resolutions of the two Houses of the Legislature; or in other words his power of returning all bills with objections; to have the effect of preventing their becoming laws, unless they should afterwards be ratified by two thirds of each of the component members of the legislative body.

The propensity of the legislative department to intrude upon the rights and to absorb the powers of the other departments, has been already suggested and repeated; the insufficiency of a mere parchment delineation of the boundaries of each, has also been remarked upon; and the necessity of furnishing each with constitutional arms for its own defence, has been inferred and proved. From these clear and indubitable principles results the propriety of a negative, either absolute or qualified, in the executive, upon the acts of the legislative branches. Without the one or the other the former would be absolutely unable to defend himself against the depredations of the latter. He might gradually be stripped of his authorities by successive resolutions, or annihilated by a single vote. And in the one mode or the other, the legislative and executive powers might speedily come to be blended in the same hands. If even no propensity had ever discovered itself in the legislative body, to invade the rights of the executive, the rules of just reasoning and theoretic propriety would of themselves teach us, that the one ought not to be left at the mercy of the other, but ought to possess a constitutional and effectual power of self defence.

But the power in question has a further use. It not only serves as a shield to the executive, but it furnishes an additional security against the enaction of improper laws. It establishes a salutary check upon the legislative body calculated to guard the community against the effects of faction, precipitancy, or of any impulse unfriendly to the public good, which may happen to influence a majority of that body.

The propriety of a negative, has upon some occasions been combated by an observation, that it was not to be presumed a single man would possess more virtue or wisdom, than a number of men; and that unless this presumption should be entertained, it would be improper to give the executive magistrate any species of controul over the legislative body.

But this observation when examined will appear rather specious than solid. The propriety of the thing does not turn upon the supposition of superior wisdom or virtue in the executive: But upon the supposition that the legislative will not be infallible: That the love of power may sometimes betray it into a disposition to encroach upon the rights of the other members of the government; that a spirit of faction may sometimes pervert its deliberations; that impressions of the moment may sometimes hurry it into measures which itself on maturer reflection would condemn. The primary inducement to conferring the power in question upon the executive, is to enable him to defend himself; the secondary one is to encrease the chances in favor of the community, against the passing of bad laws, through haste, inadvertence, or design. The oftener a measure is brought under examination, the greater the diversity in the situations of those who are to examine it, the less must be the danger of those errors which flow from want of due deliberation, or of those misteps which proceed from the contagion of some common passion or interest. It is far less probable, that culpable views of any kind should infect all the parts of the government, at the same moment and in relation to the same object, than that they should by turns govern and mislead every one of them.

It may perhaps be said, that the power of preventing bad laws includes that of preventing good ones; and may be used to the one purpose as well as to the other. But this objection will have little weight with those who can properly estimate the mischiefs of that inconstancy and mutability in the laws, which form the greatest blemish in the character and genius of our governments. They will consider every institution calculated to restrain the excess of law-making, and to keep things in the same state, in which they may happen to be at any given period, as much more likely to do good than harm; because it is favorable to greater stability in the system of legislation. The injury which may possibly be done by defeating a few good laws will be amply compensated by the advantage of preventing a number of bad ones.

Nor is this all. The superior weight and influence of the legislative body in a free government, and the hazard to the executive in a trial of strength with that body, afford a satisfactory security, that the negative would generally be employed with great caution, and that there would oftener be room for a charge of timidity than of rashness, in the exercise of it. A King of Great-Britain, with all his train of sovereign attributes, and with all the influence he draws from a thousand sources, would at this day hesitate to put a negative upon the joint resolutions of the two houses of Parliament. He would not fail to exert the utmost resources of that influence to strangle a measure disagreeable to him, in its progress to the throne, to avoid being reduced to the dilemma of permitting it to take effect, or of risking the displeasure of the nation, by an opposition to the sense of the legislative body. Nor is it probable that he would ultimately venture to exert his prerogative, but in a case of manifest propriety, or extreme necessity. All well informed men in that kingdom will accede to the justness of this remark. A very considerable period has elapsed since the negative of the crown has been exercised.

If a magistrate, so powerful and so well fortified as a British monarch, would have scruples about the exercise of the power under consideration, how much greater caution may be reasonably expected in a President of the United States, cloathed for the short period of four years with the executive authority of a government wholly and purely republican?

It is evident that there would be greater danger of his not using his power when necessary, than of his using it too often, or too much. An argument indeed against its expediency has been drawn from this very source. It has been represented on this account as a power odious in appearance; useless in practice. But it will not follow, that because it might be rarely exercised, it would never be exercised. In the case for which it is chiefly designed, that of an immediate attack upon the constitutional rights of the executive, or in a case in which the public good was evidently and palpably sacrificed, a man of tolerable firmness would avail himself of his constitutional means of defence, and would listen to the admonitions of duty and responsibility. In the former supposition, his fortitude would be stimulated by his immediate interest in the power of his office; in the latter by the probability of the sanction of his constituents; who though they would naturally incline to the legislative body in a doubtful case, would hardly suffer their partiality to delude them in a very plain case. I speak now with an eye to a magistrate possessing only a common share of firmness. There are men, who under any circumstances will have the courage to do their duty at every hazard.

But the Convention have pursued a mean in this business; which will both facilitate the exercise of the power vested in this respect in the executive magistrate, and make its efficacy to depend on the sense of a considerable part of the legislative body. Instead of an absolute negative, it is proposed to give the executive the qualified negative already described. This is a power, which would be much more readily exercised than the other. A man who might be afraid to defeat a law by his single VETO, might not scruple to return it for re-consideration; subject to being finally rejected only in the event of more than one third of each house concurring in the sufficiency of his objections. He would be encouraged by the reflection, that if his opposition should prevail, it would embark in it a very respectable proportion of the legislative body, whose influence would be united with his in supporting the propriety of his conduct, in the public opinion. A direct and categorical negative has something in the appearance of it more harsh, and more apt to irritate, than the mere suggestion of argumentative objections to be approved or disapproved, by those to whom they are addressed. In proportion as it would be less apt to offend, it would be more apt to be exercised; and for this very reason it may in practice be found more effectual. It is to be hoped that it will not often happen, that improper views will govern so large a proportion as two-thirds of both branches of the Legislature at the same time; and this too in defiance of the counterpoising weight of the executive. It is at any rate far less probable, that this should be the case, than that such views should taint the resolutions and conduct of a bare majority. A power of this nature, in the executive, will often have a silent and unperceived though forcible operation. When men engaged in unjustifiable pursuits are aware, that obstructions may come from a quarter which they cannot controul, they will often be restrained, by the bare apprehension of opposition, from doing what they would with eagerness rush into, if no such external impediments were to be feared.

This qualified negative, as has been elsewhere remarked, is in this State vested in a council, consisting of the Governor, with the Chancellor and Judges of the Supreme Court, or any two of them. It has been freely employed upon a variety of occasions, and frequently with success. And its utility has become so apparent, that persons who in compiling the Constitution were violent opposers of it, have from experience become its declared admirers.*

I have in another place remarked, that the Convention in the formation of this part of their plan, had departed from the model of the Constitution of this State, in favor of that of Massachusetts—two strong reasons may be imagined for this preference. One is that the Judges, who are to be the interpreters of the law, might receive an improper bias from having given a previous opinion in their revisionary capacities. The other is that by being often associated with the executive they might be induced to embark too far in the political views of that magistrate, and thus a dangerous combination might by degrees be cemented between the executive and judiciary departments. It is impossible to keep the Judges too distinct from every other avocation than that of expounding the laws. It is peculiarly dangerous to place them in a situation to be either corrupted or influenced by the executive.

Publius.

No. 74

ALEXANDER HAMILTON

On other Presidential powers.

* Mr. Abraham Yates, a warm opponent of the plan of the Convention, is of this number. (Publius)

No. 75

ALEXANDER HAMILTON

On treaty-making powers.

No. 76

ALEXANDER HAMILTON

On powers of nomination.

No. 77

ALEXANDER HAMILTON

On powers of appointment.

No. 78

ALEXANDER HAMILTON

May 28, 1788

We proceed now to an examination of the judiciary department of the proposed government.

In unfolding the defects of the existing confederation, the utility and necessity of a federal judicature have been clearly pointed out. It is the less necessary to recapitulate the considerations there urged; as the propriety of the institution in the abstract is not disputed: The only questions which have been raised being relative to the manner of constituting it, and to its extent. To these points therefore our observations shall be confined.

The manner of constituting it seems to embrace these several objects—1st. The mode of appointing the judges. 2d. The tenure by which they are to hold their places. 3d. The partition of the

---

From J. and A. McLean, *The Federalist*, II, 290–99, where this essay was first published on May 28, 1788, and numbered 78. It appeared on June 14 in *The Independent Journal*, where it was numbered 77, and was begun on June 17 and concluded on June 20 in *The New-York Packet*, where it was numbered 78.

judiciary authority between different courts, and their relations to each other.

First. As to the mode of appointing the judges: This is the same with that of appointing the officers of the union in general, and has been so fully discussed in the two last numbers, that nothing can be said here which would not be useless repetition.

Second. As to the tenure by which the judges are to hold their places: This chiefly concerns their duration in office; the provisions for their support; and the precautions for their responsibility.

According to the plan of the convention, all the judges who may be appointed by the United States are to hold their offices *during good behaviour*, which is conformable to the most approved of the state constitutions; and among the rest to that of this state. Its propriety having been drawn into question by the adversaries of that plan, is no light symptom of the rage for objection which disorders their imaginations and judgments. The standard of good behaviour for the continuance in office of the judicial magistracy is certainly one of the most valuable of the modern improvements in the practice of government. In a monarchy it is an excellent barrier to the despotism of the prince: In a republic it is a no less excellent barrier to the encroachments and oppressions of the representative body. And it is the best expedient which can be devised in any government, to secure a steady, upright and impartial administration of the laws.

Whoever attentively considers the different departments of power must perceive, that in a government in which they are separated from each other, the judiciary, from the nature of its functions, will always be the least dangerous to the political rights of the constitution; because it will be least in a capacity to annoy or injure them. The executive not only dispenses the honors, but holds the sword of the community. The legislature not only commands the purse, but prescribes the rules by which the duties and rights of every citizen are to be regulated. The judiciary on the contrary has no influence over either the sword or the purse, no direction either of the strength or of the wealth of the society, and can take no active resolution whatever. It may truly be said to have neither Force nor Will, but merely judgment; and must ultimately depend upon the aid of the executive arm even for the efficacy of its judgments.

This simple view of the matter suggests several important consequences. It proves incontestibly that the judiciary is beyond comparison the weakest of the three departments of power;* that it can never attack with success either of the other two; and that all possible care is requisite to enable it to defend itself against their attacks. It equally proves, that though individual oppression may now and then proceed from the courts of justice, the general liberty of the people can never be endangered from that quarter: I mean, so long as the judiciary remains truly distinct from both the legislative and executive. For I agree that "there is no liberty, if the power of judging be not separated from the legislative and executive powers."† And it proves, in the last place, that as liberty can have nothing to fear from the judiciary alone, but would have every thing to fear from its union with either of the other departments; that as all the effects of such an union must ensue from a dependence of the former on the latter, notwithstanding a nominal and apparent separation; that as from the natural feebleness of the judiciary, it is in continual jeopardy of being overpowered, awed or influenced by its coordinate branches; and that as nothing can contribute so much to its firmness and independence, as permanency in office, this quality may therefore be justly regarded as an indispensable ingredient in its constitution; and in a great measure as the citadel of the public justice and the public security.

The complete independence of the courts of justice is peculiarly essential in a limited constitution. By a limited constitution I understand one which contains certain specified exceptions to the legislative authority; such for instance as that it shall pass no bills of attainder, no *ex post facto* laws, and the like. Limitations of this kind can be preserved in practice no other way than through the medium of the courts of justice; whose duty it must be to declare all acts contrary to the manifest tenor of the constitution void. Without this, all the reservations of particular rights or privileges would amount to nothing.

Some perplexity respecting the right of the courts to pronounce legislative acts void, because contrary to the constitution, has arisen from an imagination that the doctrine would imply a superiority of the judiciary to the legislative power. It is urged that the au-

* The celebrated Montesquieu speaking of them says, "of the three powers above mentioned, the judiciary is next to nothing." *Spirit of Laws*, vol. I, page 186. (Publius)

† Idem, page 181. (Publius)

thority which can declare the acts of another void, must necessarily be superior to the one whose acts may be declared void. As this doctrine is of great importance in all the American constitutions, a brief discussion of the grounds on which it rests cannot be unacceptable.

There is no position which depends on clearer principles, than that every act of a delegated authority, contrary to the tenor of the commission under which it is exercised, is void. No legislative act therefore contrary to the constitution can be valid. To deny this would be to affirm that the deputy is greater than his principal; that the servant is above his master; that the representatives of the people are superior to the people themselves; that men acting by virtue of powers may do not only what their powers do not authorise, but what they forbid.

If it be said that the legislative body are themselves the constitutional judges of their own powers, and that the construction they put upon them is conclusive upon the other departments, it may be answered, that this cannot be the natural presumption, where it is not to be collected from any particular provisions in the constitution. It is not otherwise to be supposed that the constitution could intend to enable the representatives of the people to substitute their *will* to that of their constituents. It is far more rational to suppose that the courts were designed to be an intermediate body between the people and the legislature, in order, among other things, to keep the latter within the limits assigned to their authority. The interpretation of the laws is the proper and peculiar province of the courts. A constitution is in fact, and must be, regarded by the judges as a fundamental law. It therefore belongs to them to ascertain its meaning as well as the meaning of any particular act proceeding from the legislative body. If there should happen to be an irreconcileable variance between the two, that which has the superior obligation and validity ought of course to be preferred; or in other words, the constitution ought to be preferred to the statute, the intention of the people to the intention of their agents.

Nor does this conclusion by any means suppose a superiority of the judicial to the legislative power. It only supposes that the power of the people is superior to both; and that where the will of the legislature declared in its statutes, stands in opposition to that of the people declared in the constitution, the judges ought to be governed by the latter, rather than the former. They ought to regulate their decisions by the fundamental laws, rather than by those which are not fundamental.

This exercise of judicial discretion in determining between two contradictory laws, is exemplified in a familiar instance. It not uncommonly happens, that there are two statutes existing at one time, clashing in whole or in part with each other, and neither of them containing any repealing clause or expression. In such a case, it is the province of the courts to liquidate and fix their meaning and operation: So far as they can by any fair construction be reconciled to each other; reason and law conspire to dictate that this should be done. Where this is impracticable, it becomes a matter of necessity to give effect to one, in exclusion of the other. The rule which has obtained in the courts for determining their relative validity is that the last in order of time shall be preferred to the first. But this is mere rule of construction, not derived from any positive law, but from the nature and reason of the thing. It is a rule not enjoined upon the courts by legislative provision, but adopted by themselves, as consonant to truth and propriety, for the direction of their conduct as interpreters of the law. They thought it reasonable, that between the interfering acts of an *equal* authority, that which was the last indication of its will, should have the preference.

But in regard to the interfering acts of a superior and subordinate authority, of an original and derivative power, the nature and reason of the thing indicate the converse of that rule as proper to be followed. They teach us that the prior act of a superior ought to be preferred to the subsequent act of an inferior and subordinate authority; and that, accordingly, whenever a particular statute contravenes the constitution, it will be the duty of the judicial tribunals to adhere to the latter, and disregard the former.

It can be of no weight to say, that the courts on the pretence of a repugnancy, may substitute their own pleasure to the constitutional intentions of the legislature. This might as well happen in the case of two contradictory statutes; or it might as well happen in every adjudication upon any single statute. The courts must declare the sense of the law; and if they should be disposed to exercise WILL instead of JUDGMENT, the consequence would equally be the substitution of their pleasure to that of the legislative body. The observation, if it proved any thing, would prove that there ought to be no judges distinct from that body.

If then the courts of justice are to be considered as the bulwarks of a limited constitution against legislative encroachments, this consideration will afford a strong argument for the permanent tenure of judicial offices, since nothing will contribute so much as this to that independent spirit in the judges, which must be essential to the faithful performance of so arduous a duty.

This independence of the judges is equally requisite to guard the constitution and the rights of individuals from the effects of those ill humours which the arts of designing men, or the influence of particular conjunctures, sometimes disseminate among the people themselves, and which, though they speedily give place to better information and more deliberate reflection, have a tendency in the mean time to occasion dangerous innovations in the government, and serious oppressions of the minor party in the community. Though I trust the friends of the proposed constitution will never concur with its enemies* in questioning that fundamental principle of republican government, which admits the right of the people to alter or abolish the established constitution whenever they find it inconsistent with their happiness; yet it is not to be inferred from this principle, that the representatives of the people, whenever a momentary inclination happens to lay hold of a majority of their constituents incompatible with the provisions in the existing constitution, would on that account be justifiable in a violation of those provisions; or that the courts would be under a greater obligation to connive at infractions in this shape, than when they had proceeded wholly from the cabals of the representative body. Until the people have by some solemn and authoritative act annulled or changed the established form, it is binding upon themselves collectively, as well as individually; and no presumption, or even knowledge of their sentiments, can warrant their representatives in a departure from it, prior to such an act. But it is easy to see that it would require an uncommon portion of fortitude in the judges to do their duty as faithful guardians of the constitution, where legislative invasions of it had been instigated by the major voice of the community.

But it is not with a view to infractions of the constitution only that the independence of the judges may be an essential safeguard against the effects of occasional ill humours in the society. These sometimes extend no farther than to the injury of the private rights

* Vide Protest of the minority of the convention of Pennsylvania, Martin's speech, &c. (Publius)

of particular classes of citizens, by unjust and partial laws. Here also the firmness of the judicial magistracy is of vast importance in mitigating the severity, and confining the operation of such laws. It not only serves to moderate the immediate mischiefs of those which may have been passed, but it operates as a check upon the legislative body in passing them; who, perceiving that obstacles to the success of an iniquitous intention are to be expected from the scruples of the courts, are in a manner compelled by the very motives of the injustice they meditate, to qualify their attempts. This is a circumstance calculated to have more influence upon the character of our governments, than but few may be aware of. The benefits of the integrity and moderation of the judiciary have already been felt in more states than one; and though they may have displeased those whose sinister expectations they may have disappointed, they must have commanded the esteem and applause of all the virtuous and disinterested. Considerate men of every description ought to prize whatever will tend to beget or fortify that temper in the courts; as no man can be sure that he may not be tomorrow the victim of a spirit of injustice, by which he may be a gainer to-day. And every man must now feel that the inevitable tendency of such a spirit is to sap the foundations of public and private confidence, and to introduce in its stead, universal distrust and distress.

That inflexible and uniform adherence to the rights of the constitution and of individuals, which we perceive to be indispensable in the courts of justice, can certainly not be expected from judges who hold their offices by a temporary commission. Periodical appointments, however regulated, or by whomsoever made, would in some way or other be fatal to their necessary independence. If the power of making them was committed either to the executive or legislature, there would be danger of an improper complaisance to the branch which possessed it; if to both, there would be an unwillingness to hazard the displeasure of either; if to the people, or to persons chosen by them for the special purpose, there would be too great a disposition to consult popularity, to justify a reliance that nothing would be consulted but the constitution and the laws.

There is yet a further and a weighty reason for the permanency of the judicial offices; which is deducible from the nature of the qualifications they require. It has been frequently remarked with great propriety, that a voluminous code of laws is one of the inconveniences necessarily connected with the advantages of a free government. To avoid an arbitrary discretion in the courts, it is indispensable that they should be bound down by strict rules and precedents, which serve to define and point out their duty in every particular case that comes before them; and it will readily be conceived from the variety of controversies which grow out of the folly and wickedness of mankind, that the records of those precedents must unavoidably swell to a very considerable bulk, and must demand long and laborious study to acquire a competent knowledge of them. Hence it is that there can be but few men in the society, who will have sufficient skill in the laws to qualify them for the stations of judges. And making the proper deductions for the ordinary depravity of human nature, the number must be still smaller of those who unite the requisite integrity with the requisite knowledge. These considerations apprise us, that the government can have no great option between fit characters; and that a temporary duration in office, which would naturally discourage such characters from quitting a lucrative line of practice to accept a seat on the bench, would have a tendency to throw the administration of justice into hands less able, and less well qualified to conduct it with utility and dignity. In the present circumstances of this country, and in those in which it is likely to be for a long time to come, the disadvantages on this score would be greater than they may at first sight appear; but it must be confessed that they are far inferior to those which present themselves under the other aspects of the subject.

Upon the whole there can be no room to doubt that the convention acted wisely in copying from the models of those constitutions which have established *good behaviour* as the tenure of their judicial offices in point of duration; and that so far from being blameable on this account, their plan would have been inexcuseably defective if it had wanted this important feature of good government. The experience of Great Britain affords an illustrious comment on the excellence of the institution.

Publius.

No. 79

ALEXANDER HAMILTON

On payment of judges.

No. 80

ALEXANDER HAMILTON

Detailed consideration of the judiciary clauses.

No. 81

ALEXANDER HAMILTON

May 28, 1788

. . . That there ought to be one court of supreme and final jurisdiction is a proposition which has not been, and is not likely be contested. The reasons for it have been assigned in another place, and are too obvious to need repetition. The only question that seems to have been raised concerning it, is whether it ought to be a distinct body, or a branch of the legislature. The same contradiction is observable in regard to this matter, which has been remarked in several other cases. The very men who object to the senate as a court of impeachments, on the ground of an improper intermixture of powers, advocate, by implication at least, the propriety of vesting the ultimate decision of all causes in the whole, or in a part of the legislative body.

The arguments or rather suggestions, upon which this charge is founded, are to this effect: "The authority of the proposed supreme court of the United States, which is to be a separate and independent body, will be superior to that of the legislature. The power of construing the laws, according to the *spirit* of the constitution, will enable that court to mould them into whatever shape it may think proper; especially as its decisions will not be in any manner subject to the revision or correction of the legislative body. This is as unprecedented as it is dangerous. In Britain, the judicial power in the last resort, resides in the house of lords, which is a branch of the legislature; and this part of the British government has been imitated in the state constitutions in general. The parliament of Great-Britain, and the legislatures of the several states, can at any time rectify by law, the exceptionable decisions of their

---

From J. and A. McLean, *The Federalist*, II, May 28, 1788. This essay also appeared successively on June 25 and 28 in *The Independent Journal*, where it was numbered 80.

respective courts. But the errors and usurpations of the supreme court of the United States will be uncontrolable and remediless." This, upon examination, will be found to be altogether made up of false reasoning upon misconceived fact.

In the first place, there is not a syllable in the plan under consideration, which *directly* empowers the national courts to construe the laws according to the spirit of the constitution, or which gives them any greater latitude in this respect, than may be claimed by the courts of every state. I admit however, that the constitution ought to be the standard of construction for the laws, and that wherever there is an evident opposition, the laws ought to give place to the constitution. But this doctrine is not deducible from any circumstance peculiar to the plan of the convention; but from the general theory of a limited constitution; and as far as it is true, is equally applicable to most, if not to all the state governments. There can be no objection therefore, on this account, to the federal judicature, which will not lie against the local judicatures in general, and which will not serve to condemn every constitution that attempts to set bounds to the legislative discretion. . . .

No. 82

ALEXANDER HAMILTON

By implication, seems to anticipate the development of national sovereignty.

No. 83

ALEXANDER HAMILTON

On judicial aspects.

No. 84

ALEXANDER HAMILTON

May 28, 1788

In the course of the foregoing review of the constitution I have taken notice of, and endeavoured to answer, most of the objections which have appeared against it. There however remain a few which either did not fall naturally under any particular head, or were forgotten in their proper places. These shall now be discussed; but as the subject has been drawn into great length, I shall so far consult brevity as to comprise all my observations on these miscellaneous points in a single paper.

The most considerable of these remaining objections is, that the plan of the convention contains no bill of rights. Among other answers given to this, it has been upon different occasions remarked, that the constitutions of several of the states are in a similar predicament. I add, that New-York is of this number. And yet the opposers of the new system in this state, who profess an unlimited admiration for its constitution, are among the most intemperate partizans of a bill of rights. To justify their zeal in this matter, they alledge two things; one is, that though the constitution of New-York has no bill of rights prefixed to it, yet it contains in the body of it various provisions in favour of particular privileges and rights, which in substance amount to the same thing; the other is, that the constitution adopts in their full extent the common and statute law of Great-Britain, by which many other rights not expressed in it are equally secured.

To the first I answer, that the constitution proposed by the convention contains, as well as the constitution of this state, a number of such provisions.

Independent of those, which relate to the structure of the government, we find the following: Article I. section 3. clause 7. "Judgment in cases of impeachment shall not extend further than to removal from office, and disqualification to hold and enjoy any office to honour, trust or profit under the United States; but the

---

From J. and A. McLean, *The Federalist*, II, 344–57, where this essay was first published on May 28, 1788, and numbered 84. It was begun on July 16, continued on July 26, and concluded on August 9 in *The Independent Journal*, where it was numbered 83; and begun on July 29, continued on August 8, and concluded on August 12 in *The New-York Packet*, where it was numbered 84.

party convicted shall nevertheless be liable and subject to indictment, trial, judgment and punishment, according to law." Section 9. of the same article, clause 2. "The privilege of the writ of *habeas corpus* shall not be suspended, unless when in cases of rebellion or invasion the public safety may require it." Clause 3. "No bill of attainder or *ex post facto* law shall be passed." Clause 7.* "No title of nobility shall be granted by the United States: And no person holding any office of profit or trust under them, shall, without the consent of the congress, accept of any present, emolument, office or title, of any kind whatever, from any king, prince or foreign state." Article III. section 2. clause 3. "The trial of all crimes, except in cases of impeachment, shall be by jury; and such trial shall be held in the state where the said crimes shall have been committed; but when not committed within any state, the trial shall be at such place or places as the congress may by law have directed." Section 3, of the same article, "Treason against the United States shall consist only in levying war against them, or in adhering to their enemies, giving them aid and comfort. No person shall be convicted of treason unless on the testimony of two witnesses to the same overt act, or on confession in open court." And clause 3,† of the same section. "The congress shall have power to declare the punishment of treason, but no attainder of treason shall work corruption of blood, or forfeiture, except during the life of the person attainted."

It may well be a question whether these are not upon the whole, of equal importance with any which are to be found in the constitution of this state. The establishment of the writ of *habeas corpus*, the prohibition of *ex post facto* laws, and of TITLES OF NOBILITY, *to which we have no corresponding provisions in our constitution,* are perhaps greater securities to liberty and republicanism than any it contains. The creation of crimes after the commission of the fact, or in other words, the subjecting of men to punishment for things which, when they were done, were breaches of no law, and the practice of arbitrary imprisonments have been in all ages the favourite and most formidable instruments of tyranny. The observations of the judicious Blackstone‡ in reference to the latter, are well worthy of recital. "To bereave a man of life (says he) or by

---

* This is Clause 8 in the present-day Constitution.

† This is Clause 2 in the present-day Constitution.

‡ Vide Blackstone's *Commentaries,* vol. 1, page 136. (Publius)

violence to confiscate his estate, without accusation or trial, would be so gross and notorious an act of despotism, as must at once convey the alarm of tyranny throughout the whole nation; but confinement of the person by secretly hurrying him to gaol, where his sufferings are unknown or forgotten, is a less public, a less striking, and therefore *a more dangerous engine* of arbitrary government." And as a remedy for this fatal evil, he is every where peculiarly emphatical in his encomiums on the *habeas corpus* act, which in one place he calls "the BULWARK of the British constitution."*

Nothing need be said to illustrate the importance of the prohibition of titles of nobility. This may truly be denominated the corner stone of republican government; for so long as they are excluded, there can never be serious danger that the government will be any other than that of the people.

To the second, that is, to the pretended establishment of the common and statute law by the constitution, I answer, that they are expressly made subject "to such alterations and provisions as the legislature shall from time to time make concerning the same." They are therefore at any moment liable to repeal by the ordinary legislative power, and of course have no constitutional sanction. The only use of the declaration was to recognize the ancient law, and to remove doubts which might have been occasioned by the revolution. This consequently can be considered as no part of a declaration of rights, which under our constitutions must be intended as limitations of the power of the government itself.

It has been several times truly remarked, that bills of rights are in their origin, stipulations between kings and their subjects, abridgments of prerogative in favor of privilege, reservations of rights not surrendered to the prince. Such was MAGNA CHARTA, obtained by the Barons, sword in hand, from king John. Such were the subsequent confirmations of that charter by subsequent princes. Such was the *petition of right* assented to by Charles the First, in the beginning of his reign.† Such also was the declaration of right presented by the lords and commons to the prince of Orange in 1688, and afterwards thrown into the form of an act

---

* Idem, vol. 4, page 438. (Publius) *Ibid.* The correct page reference is 421 instead of 438. (Cooke)

† Charles I assented to the Petition of Right, but subsequently rejected the interpretation put on it by the House of Commons. (Editor)

of parliament, called the bill of rights. It is evident, therefore, that according to their primitive signification, they have no application to constitutions professedly founded upon the power of the people, and executed by their immediate representatives and servants. Here, in strictness, the people surrender nothing, and as they retain every thing, they have no need of particular reservations. "WE THE PEOPLE of the United States, to secure the blessings of liberty to ourselves and our posterity, do *ordain* and *establish* this constitution for the United States of America." Here is a better recognition of popular rights than volumes of those aphorisms which make the principal figure in several of our state bills of rights, and which would sound much better in a treatise of ethics than in a constitution of government.

But a minute detail of particular rights is certainly far less applicable to a constitution like that under consideration, which is merely intended to regulate the general political interests of the nation, than to a constitution which has the regulation of every species of personal and private concerns. If therefore the loud clamours against the plan of the convention on this score, are well founded, no epithets of reprobation will be too strong for the constitution of this state. But the truth is, that both of them contain all, which in relation to their objects, is reasonably to be desired.

I go further, and affirm that bills of rights, in the sense and in the extent in which they are contended for, are not only unnecessary in the proposed constitution, but would even be dangerous. They would contain various exceptions to powers which are not granted; and on this very account, would afford a colourable pretext to claim more than were granted. For why declare that things shall not be done which there is no power to do? Why for instance, should it be said, that the liberty of the press shall not be restrained, when no power is given by which restrictions may be imposed? I will not contend that such a provision would confer a regulating power; but it is evident that it would furnish, to men disposed to usurp, a plausible pretence for claiming that power. They might urge with a semblance of reason, that the constitution ought not to be charged with the absurdity of providing against the abuse of an authority, which was not given, and that the provision against restraining the liberty of the press afforded a clear implication, that a power to prescribe proper regulations concerning it, was intended to be vested in the national government. This may serve as a specimen of the numerous handles which would be given to the doctrine of constructive powers, by the indulgence of an injudicious zeal for bills of rights.

On the subject of the liberty of the press, as much has been said, I cannot forbear adding a remark or two: In the first place, I observe that there is not a syllable concerning it in the constitution of this state, and in the next, I contend that whatever has been said about it in that of any other state, amounts to nothing. What signifies a declaration that "the liberty of the press shall be inviolably preserved?" What is the liberty of the press? Who can give it any definition which would not leave the utmost latitude for evasion? I hold it to be impracticable; and from this, I infer, that its security, whatever fine declarations may be inserted in any constitution respecting it, must altogether depend on public opinion, and on the general spirit of the people and of the government.* And here, after all, as intimated upon another occasion, must we seek for the only solid basis of all our rights.

There remains but one other view of this matter to conclude the point. The truth is, after all the declamation we have heard, that the constitution is itself in every rational sense, and to every useful purpose, A BILL OF RIGHTS. The several bills of rights, in Great-Britain, form its constitution, and conversely the constitution of each state is its bill of rights. And the proposed constitution, if adopted, will be the bill of rights of the union. Is it one object of a bill of rights to declare and specify the political privileges

* To show that there is a power in the constitution by which the liberty of the press may be affected, recourse has been had to the power of taxation. It is said that duties may be laid upon publications so high as to amount to a prohibition. I know not by what logic it could be maintained that the declarations in the state constitutions, in favour of the freedom of the press, would be a constitutional impediment to the imposition of duties upon publications by the state legislatures. It cannot certainly be pretended that any degree of duties, however low, would be an abrigement of the liberty of the press. We know that newspapers are taxed in Great-Britain, and yet it is notorious that the press no where enjoys greater liberty than in that country. And if duties of any kind may be laid without a violation of that liberty, it is evident that the extent must depend on legislative discretion, regulated by public opinion; so that after all, general declarations respecting the liberty of the press will give it no greater security than it will have without them. The same invasions of it may be effected under the state constitutions which contain those declarations through the means of taxation, as under the proposed constitution which has nothing of the kind. It would be quite as significant to declare that government ought to be free, that taxes ought not to be excessive, &c., as that the liberty of the press ought not to be restrained. (Publius)

of the citizens in the structure and administration of the government? This is done in the most ample and precise manner in the plan of the convention, comprehending various precautions for the public security, which are not to be found in any of the state constitutions. Is another object of a bill of rights to define certain immunities and modes of proceeding, which are relative to personal and private concerns? This we have seen has also been attended to, in a variety of cases, in the same plan. Adverting therefore to the substantial meaning of a bill of rights, it is absurd to allege that it is not to be found in the work of the convention. It may be said that it does not go far enough, though it will not be easy to make this appear; but it can with no propriety be contended that there is no such a thing. It certainly must be immaterial what mode is observed as to the order of declaring the rights of the citizens, if they are to be found in any part of the instrument which establishes the government. And hence it must be apparent that much of what has been said on this subject rests merely on verbal and nominal distinctions, which are entirely foreign from the substance of the thing. . . .

No. 85

ALEXANDER HAMILTON

A Nation without a national Government is, in my view, an awful spectacle.

CONSTITUTION
OF THE
UNITED STATES OF AMERICA

We, the people of the United States, in order to form a more perfect union, establish justice, insure domestic tranquility, provide for the common defence, promote the general welfare, and secure the blessings of liberty to ourselves and our posterity, do ordain and establish this CONSTITUTION for the United States of America.

ARTICLE I

SECT. 1. All legislative powers herein granted shall be vested in a Congress of the United States, which shall consist of a Senate and a House of Representatives.

SECT. 2. The House of Representatives shall be composed of members chosen every second year by the people of the several States, and the electors in each State shall have the qualifications requisite for electors of the most numerous branch of the State Legislature.

No person shall be a Representative who shall not have attained to the age of twenty-five years, and been seven years a citizen of the United States, and who shall not, when elected, be an inhabitant of that State in which he shall be chosen.

Representatives and direct taxes shall be apportioned among the several States which may be included within this Union, according to their respective numbers, which shall be determined by adding to the whole number of free persons, including those bound to service for a term of years, and excluding Indians not taxed, three fifths of all other persons. The actual enumeration shall be made within three years after the first meeting of the Congress of the United States, and within every subsequent term of ten years, in such manner as they shall by law direct. The number of Representatives shall not exceed one for every thirty thousand, but each State shall have at least one representative; and until such enumeration shall be made, the State of New Hampshire shall be entitled to choose three, Massachusetts eight, Rhode Island and Providence Plantations one, Connecticut five, New York six,

New Jersey four, Pennsylvania eight, Delaware one, Maryland six, Virginia ten, North Carolina five, South Carolina five, and Georgia three.

When vacancies happen in the representation from any State, the Executive authority thereof shall issue writs of election to fill such vacancies.

The House of Representatives shall choose their Speaker and other officers; and shall have the sole power of impeachment.

SECT. 3. The Senate of the United States shall be composed of two Senators from each State, chosen by the Legislature thereof, for six years; and each Senator shall have one vote.

Immediately after they shall be assembled in consequence of the first election, they shall be divided as equally as may be into three classes. The seats of the Senators of the first class shall be vacated at the expiration of the second year, of the second class at the expiration of the fourth year, and of the third class at the expiration of the sixth year so that one third may be chosen every second year; and if vacancies happen by resignation, or otherwise, during the recess of the Legislature of any State, the Executive thereof may make temporary appointments until the next meeting of the Legislature, which shall then fill such vacancies.

No person shall be a Senator who shall not have attained to the age of thirty years, and been nine years a citizen of the United States, and who shall not, when elected, be an inhabitant of that State for which he shall be chosen.

The Vice-President of the United States shall be President of the Senate, but shall have no vote, unless they be equally divided.

The Senate shall choose their other officers, and also a president *pro tempore*, in the absence of the Vice-President, or when he shall exercise the office of President of the United States.

The Senate shall have the sole power to try all impeachments. When sitting for that purpose, they shall be on oath or affirmation. When the President of the United States is tried, the Chief Justice shall preside and no person shall be convicted without the concurrence of two thirds of the members present.

Judgment in cases of impeachment shall not extend further than to removal from office, and disqualification to hold and enjoy any office of honor, trust, or profit under the United States: but the party convicted shall nevertheless be liable and subject to indictment, trial, judgment, and punishment, according to law.

SECT. 4. The times, places, and manner of holding elections for Senators and Representatives shall be prescribed in each State by the Legislature thereof; but the Congress may at any time by law make or alter such regulations, except as to the places of choosing Senators.

The Congress shall assemble at least once in every year, and such meeting shall be on the first Monday in December, unless they shall by law appoint a different day.

SECT. 5. Each House shall be the judge of the elections, returns, and qualifications of its own members, and a majority of each shall constitute a quorum to do business; but a smaller number may adjourn from day to day, and may be authorized to compel the attendance of absent members in such manner, and under such penalties, as each House may provide.

Each House may determine the rules of its proceedings, punish its members for disorderly behavior, and, with the concurrence of two thirds, expel a member.

Each House shall keep a journal of its proceedings, and from time to time publish the same, excepting such parts as may in their judgment require secrecy; and the yeas and nays of the members of either House on any question shall, at the desire of one fifth of those present, be entered on the journal.

Neither House, during the session of Congress, shall, without the consent of the other, adjourn for more than three days, nor to any other place than that in which the two Houses shall be sitting.

SECT. 6. The Senators and Representatives shall receive a compensation for their services, to be ascertained by law, and paid out of the Treasury of the United States. They shall in all cases, except treason, felony, and breach of the peace, be privileged from arrest during their attendance at the session of their respective Houses, and in going to and returning from the same; and for any speech or debate in either House they shall not be questioned in any other place.

No Senator or Representative shall, during the time for which he was elected, be appointed to any civil office under the authority of the United States, which shall have been created, or the emoluments whereof shall have been increased, during such time; and no person holding any office under the United States shall be a member of either House during his continuance in office.

SECT. 7. All bills for raising revenue shall originate in the House of Representatives; but the Senate may propose or concur with amendments as on other bills.

Every bill which shall have passed the House of Representatives and the Senate shall, before it becomes a law, be presented to the President of the United States; if he approve he shall sign it, but if not he shall return it with his objections to that House in which it shall have originated, who shall enter the objections at large on their journal, and proceed to reconsider it. If after such reconsideration two thirds of that House shall agree to pass the bill, it shall be sent, together with the objections, to the other House, by which it shall likewise be reconsidered, and, if approved by two thirds of that House, it shall become a law. But in all such cases the votes of both Houses shall be determined by yeas and nays and the names of the persons voting for and against the bill shall be entered on the journal of each House respectively. If any bill shall not be returned by the President within ten days (Sundays excepted) after it shall have been presented to him, the same shall be a law, in like manner as if he had signed it, unless the Congress by their adjournment prevent its return, in which case it shall not be a law.

Every order, resolution, or vote to which the concurrence of the Senate and House of Representatives may be necessary (except on a question of adjournment) shall be presented to the President of the United States; and, before the same shall take effect, shall be approved by him, or, being disapproved by him, shall be repassed by two thirds of the Senate and House of Representatives, according to the rules and limitations prescribed in the case of a bill.

SECT. 8. The Congress shall have power,—

To lay and collect taxes, duties, imposts, and excises to pay the debts and provide for the common defence and general welfare of the United States; but all duties, imposts, and excises shall be uniform throughout the United States;

To borrow money on the credit of the United States;

To regulate commerce with foreign nations, and among the several States, and with the Indian tribes;

To establish an uniform rule of naturalization, and uniform laws on the subject of bankruptcies throughout the United States;

To coin money, regulate the value thereof, and of foreign coin, and fix the standard of weights and measures;

To provide for the punishment of counterfeiting the securities and current coin of the United States;

To establish post-offices and post-roads;

To promote the progress of science and useful arts, by securing for limited times to authors and inventors the exclusive right to their respective writings and discoveries;

To constitute tribunals inferior to the Supreme Court;

To define and punish piracies and felonies committed on the high seas, and offences against the law of nations;

To declare war, grant letters of marque and reprisal, and make rules concerning captures on land and water;

To raise and support armies, but no appropriation of money to that use shall be for a longer term than two years;

To provide and maintain a navy;

To make rules for the government and regulation of the land and naval forces;

To provide for calling forth the militia to execute the laws of the Union, suppress insurrections, and repel invasions;

To provide for organizing, arming, and disciplining the militia, and for governing such part of them as may be employed in the service of the United States, reserving to the States respectively, the appointment of the officers, and the authority of training the militia according to the discipline prescribed by Congress;

To exercise exclusive legislation, in all cases whatsoever, over such district (not exceeding ten miles square) as may, by cession of particular States, and the acceptance of Congress, become the seat of the government of the United States; and to exercise like authority over all places purchased by the consent of the Legislature of the State in which the same shall be, for the erection of forts, magazines, arsenals, dockyards, and other needful buildings;—and

To make all laws which shall be necessary and proper for carrying into execution the foregoing powers, and all other powers vested by this Constitution in the government of the United States, or in any department or officer thereof.

SECT. 9. The migration or importation of such persons as any of the States now existing shall think proper to admit, shall not be prohibited by the Congress prior to the year one thousand eight hundred and eight, but a tax or duty may be imposed on such importation, not exceeding ten dollars for each person.

The privilege of the writ of *habeas corpus* shall not be suspended, unless when in cases of rebellion or invasion the public safety may require it.

No bill of attainder or *ex post facto* law shall be passed.

No capitation or other direct tax shall be laid, unless in proportion to the census or enumeration herein before directed to be taken.

No tax or duty shall be laid on articles exported from any State.

No preference shall be given by any regulation of commerce or revenue to the ports of one State over those of another; nor shall vessels bound to, or from, one State, be obliged to enter, clear, or pay duties in another.

No money shall be drawn from the treasury, but in consequence of appropriations made by law; and a regular statement and account of the receipts and expenditures of all public money shall be published from time to time.

No title of nobility shall be granted by the United States; and no person holding any office of profit or trust under them shall, without the consent of the Congress, accept of any present, emolument, office, or title, of any kind whatever, from any king, prince, or foreign state.

SECT. 10. No State shall enter into any treaty, alliance, or confederation; grant letters of marque and reprisal; coin money; emit bills of credit; make anything but gold and silver coin a tender in payment of debts; pass any bill of attainder, *ex post facto* law, or law impairing the obligation of contracts, or grant any title of nobility.

No State shall, without the consent of the Congress, lay any imposts or duties on imports or exports, except what may be absolutely necessary for executing its inspection laws; and the net produce of all duties and imposts, laid by any State on imports or exports, shall be for the use of the treasury of the United States; and all such laws shall be subject to the revision and control of the Congress.

No State shall, without the consent of Congress, lay any duty of tonnage, keep troops or ships of war in time of peace, enter into any agreement or compact with another State, or with a foreign power, or engage in war, unless actually invaded, or in such imminent danger as will not admit of delay.

ARTICLE II

SECT. 1. The executive power shall be vested in a President of the United States of America. He shall hold his office during the term of four years, and, together with the Vice-President, chosen for the same term, be elected as follows:—

Each State shall appoint, in such manner as the Legislature thereof may direct, a number of Electors equal to the whole number of Senators and Representatives to which the State may be entitled in the Congress: but no Senator or Representative, or person holding an office of trust or profit under the United States, shall be appointed an Elector.

[The Electors shall meet in their respective States, and vote by ballot for two persons, of whom one at least shall not be an inhabitant of the same State with themselves. And they shall make a list of all the persons voted for, and of the number of votes for each; which list they shall sign and certify, and transmit sealed to the seat of the government of the United States, directed to the President of the Senate. The President of the Senate shall, in the presence of the Senate and House of Representatives, open all the certificates, and the votes shall then be counted. The person having the greatest number of votes shall be the President, if such number be a majority of the whole number of Electors appointed; and if there be more than one who have such majority, and have an equal number of votes, then the House of Representatives shall immediately choose by ballot one of them for President; and if no person have a majority, then from the five highest on the list the said House shall in like manner choose the President. But in choosing the President, the votes shall be taken by States, the representation from each State having one vote; a quorum for this purpose shall consist of a member or members from two thirds of the States, and a majority of all the States shall be necessary to a choice. In every case, after the choice of the President, the person having the greatest number of votes of the Electors shall be the Vice-President. But if there should remain two or more who have equal votes, the Senate shall choose from them by ballot the Vice-President.—*Repealed by Amendment* XII.]

Congress may determine the time of choosing the Electors, and the day on which they shall give their votes; which day shall be the same throughout the United States.

No person except a natural-born citizen, or a citizen of the United States at the time of the adoption of this Constitution, shall be eligible to the office of President; neither shall any person be eligible to that office who shall not have attained to the age of thirty-five years, and been fourteen years a resident within the United States.

In case of the removal of the President from office, or of his death, resignation, or inability to discharge the powers and duties of the said office, the same shall devolve on the Vice-President, and the Congress may by law provide for the case of removal, death, resignation, or inability, both of the President and Vice-President, declaring what officer shall then act as President, and such officer shall act accordingly, until the disability be removed, or a President shall be elected.

The President shall, at stated times, receive for his services a compensation, which shall neither be increased nor diminished during the period for which he shall have been elected, and he shall not receive within that period any other emolument from the United States, or any of them.

Before he enter on the execution of his office, he shall take the following oath or affirmation:—"I do solemnly swear (or affirm) that I will faithfully execute the office of President of the United States, and will, to the best of my ability, preserve, protect, and defend the Constitution of the United States."

SECT. 2. The President shall be commander-in-chief of the army and navy of the United States, and of the militia of the several States, when called into the actual service of the United States; he may require the opinion, in writing, of the principal officer in each of the executive departments, upon any subject relating to the duties of their respective offices, and he shall have power to grant reprieves and pardons for offences against the United States, except in cases of impeachment.

He shall have power, by and with the advice and consent of the Senate, to make treaties, provided two thirds of the Senators present concur; and he shall nominate, and, by and with the advice and consent of the Senate, shall appoint ambassadors, other public ministers, and consuls, judges of the Supreme Court, and all other officers of the United States, whose appointments are not herein otherwise provided for, and which shall be established by law; but the Congress may by law vest the appointment of such inferior officers, as they think proper, in the President alone, in the courts of law, or in the heads of departments.

The President shall have power to fill up all vacancies that may happen during the recess of the Senate, by granting commissions which shall expire at the end of their next session.

SECT. 3. He shall from time to time give to the Congress information of the state of the Union, and recommend to their consideration such measures as he shall judge necessary and expedient; he may, on extraordinary occasions, convene both Houses, or either of them, and in case of disagreement between them, with respect to the time of adjournment, he may adjourn them to such time as he shall think proper; he shall receive ambassadors and other public ministers; he shall take care that the laws be faithfully executed, and shall commission all the officers of the United States.

SECT. 4. The President, Vice-President, and all civil officers of the United States, shall be removed from office on impeachment for, and conviction of, treason, bribery, or other high crimes and misdemeanors.

ARTICLE III

SECT. 1. The judicial power of the United States shall be vested in one Supreme Court, and in such inferior courts as the Congress may from time to time ordain and establish. The judges, both of the Supreme and inferior courts, shall hold their offices during good behavior, and shall at stated times, receive for their services a compensation, which shall not be diminished during their continuance in office.

SECT. 2. The judicial power shall extend to all cases, in law and equity, arising under this Constitution, the laws of the United States, and treaties made, or which shall be made, under their authority; to all cases affecting ambassadors, other public ministers, and consuls; to all cases of admiralty and maritime jurisdiction; to controversies to which the United States shall be a party; to controversies between two or more States, between a State and citizens of another State, between citizens of different States, between citizens of the same State claiming lands under grants of different States, and between a State, or the citizens thereof, and foreign states, citizens, or subjects.

In all cases affecting ambassadors, other public ministers, and consuls, and those in which a State shall be party, the Supreme Court shall have original jurisdiction. In all the other cases before mentioned, the Supreme Court shall have appellate jurisdiction, both as to law and fact, with such exceptions, and under such regulations, as the Congress shall make.

The trial of all crimes, except in cases of impeachment, shall be by jury; and such trial shall be held in the State where the said crimes shall have been committed; but when not committed within any State, the trial shall be at such placc or places as the Congress may by law have directed.

SECT. 3. Treason against the United States shall consist only in levying war against them, or in adhering to their enemies, giving them aid and comfort. No person shall be convicted of treason unless on the testimony of two witnesses to the same overt act, or on confession in open court.

The Congress shall have power to declare the punishment of treason, but no attainder of treason shall work corruption of blood, or forfeiture except during the life of the person attainted.

ARTICLE IV

SECT. 1. Full faith and credit shall be given in each State to the public acts, records, and judicial proceedings of every other State. And the Congress may by general laws prescribe the manner in which such acts, records, and proceedings shall be proved, and the effect thereof.

SECT. 2. The citizens of each State shall be entitled to all privileges and immunities of citizens in the several States.

A person charged in any State with treason, felony, or other crime, who shall flee from justice, and be found in another State, shall, on demand of the executive authority of the State from which he fled, be delivered up, to be removed to the State having jurisdiction of the crime.

No person held to service or labor in one State, under the laws thereof, escaping into another, shall, in consequence of any law or regulation therein, be discharged from such service or labor, but shall be delivered up on claim of the party to whom such service or labor may be due.

SECT. 3. New States may be admitted by the Congress into this Union; but no new State shall be formed or erected within the jurisdiction of any other State; nor any State be formed by the junction of two or more States, or parts of States, without the consent of the Legislatures of the States concerned, as well as of the Congress.

The Congress shall have power to dispose of and make all needful rules and regulations respecting the territory or other property belonging to the United States; and nothing in this Constitution shall be so construed as to prejudice any claims of the United States, or of any particular State.

SECT. 4. The United States shall guarantee to every State in this Union a republican form of government, and shall protect each of them against invasion; and on application of the Legislature, or of the Executive (when the Legislature can not be convened), against domestic violence.

ARTICLE V

The Congress, whenever two thirds of both houses shall deem it necessary, shall propose amendments to this Constitution, or, on the application of the Legislatures of two thirds of the several States, shall call a convention for proposing amendments, which, in either case, shall be valid to all intents and purposes, as part of this Constitution, when ratified by the Legislatures of three fourths of the several States, or by conventions in three fourths thereof, as the one or the other mode of ratification may be proposed by the Congress; provided that no amendment which may be made prior to the year one thousand eight hundred and eight shall in any manner affect the first and fourth clauses in the ninth section of the first article; and that no State, without its consent, shall be deprived of its equal suffrage in the Senate.

ARTICLE VI

All debts contracted and engagements entered into, before the adoption of this Constitution, shall be as valid against the United States under this Constitution as under the Confederation.

This Constitution, and the laws of the United States which shall be made in pursuance thereof, and all treaties made, or which shall be made, under the authority of the United States, shall be the supreme law of the land; and the judges in every State shall be bound thereby, anything in the constitution or laws of any State to the contrary notwithstanding.

The Senators and Representatives before mentioned, and the members of the several State Legislatures, and all executive and judicial officers, both of the United States and of the several States, shall be bound by oath or affirmation to support this Constitution; but no religious test shall ever be required as a qualification to any office or public trust under the United States.

ARTICLE VII

The ratification of the conventions of nine States shall be sufficient for the establishment of this Constitution between the States so ratifying the same.

Done in Convention, by the unanimous consent of the States present, the seventeenth day of September, in the year of our Lord one thousand seven hundred and eighty-seven, and of the Independence of the United States of America the twelfth.

In Witness whereof we have hereunto subscribed our names.

AMENDMENTS

ARTICLE I

Congress shall make no law respecting an establishment of religion, or prohibiting the free exercise thereof; or abridging the freedom of speech, or of the press, or the right of the people peaceably to assemble, and to petition the government for a redress of grievances.

ARTICLE II

A well regulated militia being necessary to the security of a free state, the right of the people to keep and bear arms shall not be infringed.

ARTICLE III

No soldier shall, in time of peace, be quartered in any house, without the consent of the owner, nor in time of war, but in a manner to be prescribed by law.

ARTICLE IV

The right of the people to be secure in their persons, houses, papers, and effects, against unreasonable searches and seizures, shall not be violated, and no warrants shall issue but upon probable cause, supported by oath or affirmation, and particularly describing the place to be searched, and the persons or things to be seized.

ARTICLE V

No person shall be held to answer for a capital, or otherwise infamous crime, unless on a presentment or indictment of a grand jury, except in cases arising in the land or naval forces, or in the militia, when in actual service in time of war or public danger; nor shall any person be subject for the same offence to be twice put in jeopardy of life and limb; nor shall be compelled in any criminal case to be a witness against himself, nor be deprived of life, liberty, or property, without due process of law; nor shall private property be taken for public use without just compensation.

ARTICLE VI

In all criminal prosecutions, the accused shall enjoy the right to a speedy and public trial, by an impartial jury of the State and district wherein the crime shall have been committed, which district shall have been previously ascertained by law, and to be informed of the nature and cause of the accusation; to be confronted with the witnesses against him; to have compulsory process for obtaining witnesses in his favor, and to have the assistance of counsel for his defence.

ARTICLE VII

In suits at common law, where the value in controversy shall exceed twenty dollars, the right of trial by jury shall be preserved, and no fact tried by a jury shall be otherwise re-examined in any court of the United States, than according to the rules of the common law.

ARTICLE VIII

Excessive bail shall not be required, nor excessive fines imposed, nor cruel and unusual punishments inflicted.

ARTICLE IX

The enumeration in the Constitution, of certain rights, shall not be construed to deny or disparage others retained by the people.

ARTICLE X

The powers not delegated to the United States by the Constitution, nor prohibited by it to the States, are reserved to the States respectively, or to the people.

SUGGESTED FURTHER READINGS

DOCUMENTS

Max Farrand, ed., *The Records of the Federal Convention of 1787* (New Haven, Conn., 1911–37).

Jonathan Elliot, ed., *Debates of the State Conventions on the Adoption of the Federal Constitution . . .* (Philadelphia, 1866).

SECONDARY WORKS

Douglass Adair, "The Authorship of the Disputed Federalist Papers"; "The Tenth Federalist Revisited"; "A Note on Certain of Hamilton's Pseudonyms," in *Fame and the Founding Fathers*, ed. Trevor Colbourn (Williamsburg, Va., 1974).

Max Beloff, Introduction to his edition of *The Federalist* (Oxford, 1948).

Martin Diamond, "Democracy and *The Federalist*: a Reconsideration of the Framers' Intent," *American Political Science Review* 53, 1959.

Gottfried Dietze, *The Federalist—A Classic on Federalism and Free Government* (Baltimore, Md., 1960).

David F. Epstein, *The Political Theory of The Federalist* (Chicago, 1984).

Jackson Turner Main, *The Antifederalists, 1781–1788* (Chicago, 1961).

Alpheus Thomas Mason, "The Federalist—A Split Personality," *American Historical Review* LVII, 1952.

J. R. Pole, *Political Representation in England and the Origins of the American Republic* (London and New York, 1966; Berkeley, 1971).

Robert Rutland, *The Ordeal of the Constitution: The Anti-Federalists and the Ratification Struggle of 1787–1788* (Norman, Okla., 1960).

Herbert J. Storing, *What the Anti-Federalists Were For*, being vol. I of *The Complete Anti-Federalist* (Chicago, 1981).

Gordon S. Wood, *The Creation of the American Republic, 1776–1787* (Chapel Hill, N.C., 1969).

Index